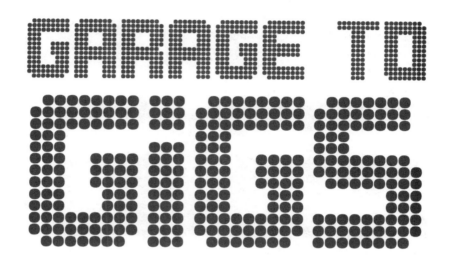

GARAGE TO GIGS

A MUSICIAN'S GUIDE

Andrew S. Thomas

Billboard Books
an imprint of Watson-Guptill Publications/New York

Project Editor: Ross Plotkin
Production Manager: Salvatore Destro
Interior Designer: Timothy Hsu

First published in 2008 by Billboard Books,
an imprint of Watson-Guptill Publications,
Crown Publishing Group,
A division of Random House, Inc., New York
www.crownpublishing.com
www.watsonguptill.com

Library of Congress Control Number: 2007942908
ISBN-13: 978-0-8230-8274-2
ISBN-10: 0-8230-8274-1

Printed in the United States
First printing, 2008
1 2 3 4 5 6 7 8 9 / 15 14 13 12 11 10 09 08

CONTENTS

ACKNOWLEDGMENTS   **7**

INTRODUCTION   **9**

CHAPTER 1: PREPARING YOURSELF TO PLAY IN A BAND   **13**

- UNDERSTANDING YOUR LOCAL MUSIC SCENE   13

  Identifying What Kinds of Music Are Popular in Your Area   14

  Learning What Kinds of Bands Are Gigging Where   15

  Networking to Learn More About Your Local Music Scene   16

- MEETING THE BASIC CRITERIA FOR BEING A MUSICIAN IN A BAND   18

  Committing Yourself to Being an Active Member of a Team   18

  Providing Yourself with the Right Equipment to Meet Your Needs   20

  Ensuring You Have Transportation to Get to Where You Need to Be   23

CHAPTER 2: CONSIDERING WHAT KIND OF BAND TO FORM OR JOIN   **25**

- DEFINING YOURSELF AS A MUSICIAN AND ESTABLISHING WITH WHOM
  YOU WANT TO PLAY   26

  Identifying Your Priorities   26

  Understanding that Personality Counts as Much as Talent   30

- IDENTIFYING WHAT TYPE OF BAND YOU WANT TO FORM OR JOIN   32

  Deciding Whether You Want to Be a Leader or a Member of a Team   32

  Deciding Whether You Want to Play Cover Music or Original Music   36

CHAPTER 3: FINDING MUSICIANS OR A BAND   **41**

- CREATING, CIRCULATING, AND FINDING ADS   41

  Creating Your Ad   42

  Circulating and Finding Ads   48

- RESPONDING TO ADS   54

  Preparing and Anticipating Questions   54

  Determining How to Respond to an Ad and Deciding Whether to Audition   60

CHAPTER 4: AUDITIONING MUSICIANS FOR YOUR BAND OR AUDITIONING

TO JOIN A BAND   **68**

- PREPARING FOR THE AUDITION   69

  Establishing Audition Parameters   69

  Preparing Your Band for the Audition   78

  Preparing Yourself for the Audition   80

- PERFORMING AT THE AUDITION   87
- FOLLOWING UP THE AUDITION   95

Following Up with the Band   95

Following Up with the Musician   97

CHAPTER 5: PULLING YOUR BAND TOGETHER   **100**

- ESTABLISHING A REHEARSAL STRATEGY   100

Finding a Rehearsal Space   101

Determining What Needs to Be Accomplished at Rehearsals   107

Deciding How Often to Rehearse and Creating a Rehearsal Schedule   108

Establishing the Rules of Rehearsals   115

- PREPARING YOUR SONG LIST   117

Writing Original Material   118

Selecting Songs Written by Others   121

- REHEARSING YOUR MATERIAL   123

CHAPTER 6: RECORDING A DEMO TO GET GIGS AND MARKET YOUR BAND   **126**

- KNOWING YOUR RECORDING OPTIONS AND ESTABLISHING A BUDGET   127

Understanding Your Recording Options and Their Costs   127

Creating a Recording Budget   130

- PREPARING TO RECORD YOUR DEMO   133

Recording Your Practice Sessions   133

Recording Your Band in Preproduction   135

- SELECTING A RECORDING STUDIO   135

Finding Recording Studios in Your Area   136

Interviewing Studios   137

Touring Studios and Deciding Where to Record   146

- RECORDING YOUR DEMO   149

Setting Up at the Studio   149

Tracking Your Demo   153

Mixing Your Demo   154

Mastering Your Demo   160

CHAPTER 7: CREATING YOUR BAND'S PROMOTIONAL MATERIALS   **162**

- CREATING YOUR DEMO PACKAGE   162

Compiling Information for the Package   163

Taking or Contracting for a Band Photo 164

Creating or Acquiring Artwork 167

Designing the Demo Package 169

Duplicating the Package 170

• CREATING YOUR PRESS KIT 172

Writing a Band Bio 172

Getting Press 175

Assembling Your Press Kit 177

• BUILDING YOUR WEB SITE 179

CHAPTER 8: FINDING GIGS FOR YOUR BAND **182**

• DECIDING HOW MUCH TO CHARGE FOR PERFORMING 182

Understanding How Bands Are Paid 182

Determining Your Band's Overhead and Profit 188

Playing for Free 193

• GETTING GIGS 195

Preparing to Contact Bookers and Special-Event Planners 196

Contacting Bookers and Planners, and Landing Gigs 200

CHAPTER 9: PROMOTING YOUR GIGS **220**

• CREATING YOUR PROMOTIONAL MATERIALS 220

Organizing Your Information 220

Creating Flyers, Posters, and Press Releases 221

• DISTRIBUTING YOUR PROMOTIONAL MATERIALS 225

Distributing Your Materials by Personal Contact 225

Distributing Your Materials by Mass Marketing 227

CHAPTER 10: PREPARING FOR YOUR GIG **232**

• PREPARING YOUR SONGS FOR THE GIG 233

Creating Your Set List 233

Rehearsing Your Show 241

• PREPARING FOR THE GIG ON THE DAY OF THE SHOW 246

Warming Up 246

Packing Your Gear 247

Getting to the Show 249

CHAPTER 11: PLAYING THE GIG   **251**

• PREPARING TO PLAY   251

   Loading In and Setting Up   252

   Sound Checking   252

   Taking Care of Everything Else   257

• PLAYING THE GIG   259

   Getting Ready to Play   259

   Performing   260

   Leaving the Gig   262

CHAPTER 12: BUILDING AND MAINTAINING MOMENTUM   **266**

• BUILDING A FAN BASE   266

   Understanding Your Fans   267

   Earning the Support of Your Fans   269

• CREATING A BUZZ   270

   Understanding the Importance of Your Reputation   270

   Recognizing Why It's Important to Be Friendly with Other Bands 271

   Working Hard and Staying Positive   272

INDEX   **275**

ACKNOWLEDGMENTS

I would like to thank Victoria Craven, Ross Plotkin, Helen Chin, Amy Vinchesi, Brian Phair, and everyone at Billboard Books for their trust, guidance, and support. I also would like to thank Bob Nirkind and Maria Fotopoulos, without whom this book would not be.

To everyone I interviewed, my everlasting gratitude. Your words are the true binding to these pages.

Finally, love to my wife, Karen, and my children, Stephan and Elizabeth. You bless me not only with your support for me as a writer, but as a musician who will never, ever give up.

INTRODUCTION

"How far do you plan to take this music thing?" It's a question most musicians hear at some point in their lives.

I first heard the question from my family after telling them I was applying to music school. I later heard it from an employer who insisted I wait tables during a night shift and blow off my gig. I also heard it from friends who wanted to know why I was spending time and the little money I had promoting the CD my unsigned band had just released.

The implication behind the question is clear: Music is not a traditional or "serious" career.

There's truth in the implication. Musicians don't work behind a desk from nine to five. There are no sick days, health benefits, or direct deposit of regular earnings. And typical workers aren't asked to spend thousands of dollars on equipment before earning their first paycheck. Yet despite all of this, the consistent response to "How far do you plan to take this music thing?" is, "As far as I can take it."

So, why do musicians pursue their artistic passions? Every musician who picks up an instrument dreams of playing a great show, of recording the perfect album, and of succeeding beyond his or her wildest imaginings.

This passion makes it intensely frustrating to hear the "music thing" question. It's condescending, and it both belittles the enormous effort musicians invest in their craft and diminishes the sacrifice involved. Yet for some reason, many people think it's acceptable to challenge someone who is pursuing creative endeavors in music, art, or theater. You never hear someone ask, "Where do you plan on taking this nuclear physics thing?" even though that is no more difficult an undertaking than music.

I would argue that succeeding in a musical group is more difficult than succeeding in a traditional career. While specific training, education, and a direct path to success may be available for conventional vocations, musicians in bands involving multiple people with multiple personalities—sometimes literally—must succeed usually without any guidance or formal training.

There are plenty of books written about how to secure a record deal or how to get your song played on the radio, but few explore what it takes to grow from never having played in a band to becoming a gigging musician. Why is this? Perhaps it's because there is a more visceral appeal to dreaming about signing a record deal or being played on the radio than doing the hard work of figuring out how to land an audition or how to find a place to rehearse. Maybe it's because our society would rather skip over challenges and go straight to a get-rich-quick scheme. Whatever the reasons, a musician will never have the opportunity to review a record contract or to drink champagne while listening to his or her band on the radio without having had to learn how to take the band from the garage to the gig.

Garage to Gigs: A Musician's Guide provides a substantive road map for any musician seeking the guidance and direction to propel him or her to the stage. If you are a musician, the information in this book will be relevant to you, regardless of whether you plan to cover other artists' music or write and perform your own, and whether you intend to manage your band collaboratively or run your own show. It will take you through steps like determining what kind of band to start or join, managing auditions, holding effective rehearsals, recording, marketing a group, and, finally, gigging. This book differs from any other of its kind because it delves into the precise methodology that a musician and band need in order to excel in their career.

In writing *Garage to Gigs* I've drawn from more than twenty years of industry knowledge. In addition, I've interviewed people working in the music industry, mostly musicians with varying levels of experience, but also recording engineers, rehearsal studio owners, and others. You'll find no lofty superstars here who may have forgotten what it's like to audition for a gig or to struggle to create a recording budget—just working musicians who understand exactly what it takes to launch a band.

So, in response to those who question commitment to this "music thing," we musicians should be immensely proud of our aspirations and achievements. In bands we make lifelong friends and share extraordinary experiences that forever color our lives. Music shapes opinion, transforms thinking, and drives change. Every day a new musician begins a journey familiar to thousands of preceding artists, many of whom have changed our world. Think of the Beatles, the Rolling Stones, Elvis, Madonna, Nirvana, and U2.

Somewhere along the way to legendary status, they learned exactly how far they could take this music thing.

September 2008
Los Angeles

CHAPTER 1

PREPARING YOURSELF TO PLAY IN A BAND

There's more to being a musician in a band than having great chops. Aside from musical ability, you've got to be committed to your musical goals, be tuned in to your local music scene, have the right equipment, and have transportation to be able to travel to and from where you need to go, be it to gigs, rehearsals, or auditions.

Opportunities to jam with friends, try out for a band, or perform onstage may arise in seemingly random ways—by way of an e-mail notice weeks in advance, a phone call from a bandleader just days before a show, or at a music club with little notice when you're invited to sit in with a group. If you've spent enough time getting ready for these sometimes-serendipitous events, you can take advantage of such situations. If not, you may blow a good opportunity that might not come again.

UNDERSTANDING YOUR LOCAL MUSIC SCENE

As a musician, you need to prepare properly for performance opportunities. Preparation means you spend countless hours honing your musical craft and investing hundreds, if not thousands, of dollars on reliable and professional equipment. It also means you have to understand your local music scene. Each town's music scene is different, each having its own personality. To become part of the scene as a working musician, you need to be aware of what kinds of music are popular in your area. You also need to familiarize yourself with the local clubs and to understand the types of music and musicians they book. And finally, you need to start networking with musicians, club-goers, and those working on the business side of the music scene, from bookers to club owners to event planners.

Identifying What Kinds of Music Are Popular in Your Area

In some areas it's easy to figure out what kinds of music are popular because these scenes have an inherent character and musical history that influence and dominate the musical landscape. These prevailing genres are evident and sometimes even clichéd. For example, New Orleans is traditionally a great market for funk and Dixieland jazz, Chicago has a legendary blues scene, and Detroit—as the birthplace of Motown—is known for its soul and R&B.

Having a dominant type of music in an area doesn't mean these scenes are exclusive to that genre but simply that it is the prevailing music in that town. Musicians living in areas with clearly defined musical genres have a greater chance of finding bands to play with by embracing the character of the scene due to the higher volume of opportunities available. Musicians who play types of music that are less common to an area may still be able to find bands and shows, but not at the same level of opportunity. If you're a drummer in Nashville, a community with a historically strong country music scene, you probably won't have any problem finding or starting a band to play with if you want to play country music. However, if you're a hip-hop drummer in Nashville, finding a band may be a little trickier, because you're looking for opportunities in a market that doesn't favor your style of music.

Not every community has a music scene as clearly defined as Nashville or New Orleans. Los Angeles, for example, has no dominant musical style. The L.A. scene is so diverse that every style is being played every night of the week. Musicians from all over the world come to Los Angeles for the opportunity to play in such a musical hotbed. On the opposite side of the spectrum, some smaller towns might not have a primary musical style either, but this is more likely because they have little support for live music, so no genre is able to emerge.

Some music scenes are created due to their locations and attractions rather than their character or history. Las Vegas, for example, is paradise for working musicians banging out disco and dance hits, since the town's many casinos book this kind of music for their patrons every night of the week, often on multiple stages. Special-event bands that cater to weddings and private parties find an equally advantageous scene working in the resort communities in Southern California and New England that host weddings every weekend of the season.

Learning What Kinds of Bands Are Gigging Where

If your area doesn't have a dominant genre, you need to dig a little deeper to learn which types of music are popular, or at least sustainable. To discover this, you need to identify the locations where music is performed and find out what kinds of bands are consistently gigging.

Every scene has venues where people go to see bands perform. In most cases, these venues are music clubs that book bands they feel fit the vibe of the club and will bring in revenue. In some instances, these venues are private facilities, like reception halls, large restaurants, and hotel ballrooms that are available for rent by a client, who in turn hires the band to play there.

To determine how active a private special-event scene is in your community, you should call potential venues listed in the Yellow Pages or go online to find out if they host events with live music. (Don't visit these venues and try to crash a private event—especially if you're hoping to play there in the future!) For example, if you're looking for special-event opportunities in Laguna Niguel, California, a good starting point would be the Ritz Carlton, a high-end, large hotel. Their event coordinator might tell you that the hotel hosts several weddings per weekend, typically two on Friday, four on Saturday, and four more on Sunday. She might also note that the neighboring St. Regis and Montage resorts host a similar number of weddings and special events. This information is a great indicator of the special-event scene in Laguna Niguel.

To find where music clubs are and what kinds of music they book you can skim local entertainment publications that post calendar listings, a schedule of events in your scene. Music clubs in cities typically advertise in these weekly or biweekly publications. Weekly newspapers like the San Francisco *Bay Guardian*, Los Angeles' *LA Weekly*, New Orleans' *Gambit Weekly*, and many daily newspapers are great resources for musicians because they feature popular venues, contact information, and the names of the bands playing that week. If the calendar section shows multiple rock clubs with shows most nights of the week, then you're living in a great town for rock 'n' roll. If the publication lists numerous jazz clubs, then it's safe to assume there's a successful jazz scene in town. Conversely, if certain styles of music aren't represented, then this is probably not a good scene for those genres.

Some club listings leave the reader without a clue as to what kind of bands they book. This may be because the name of the club or band isn't associated with a particular genre or because the type of music at the club changes from night to night. In this case, you can try to contact the club by phone for more information or visit its Web site, if available. If you can't find the information you need through a phone call or online, your best bet is to go to the club and find out for yourself.

If the publications in your area aren't giving you all the information you need, or there simply aren't any listings, you'll need to go to where the musicians are to find out this information the old-fashioned way—by networking.

Networking to Learn More About Your Local Music Scene

There's no better way to learn about your music scene than by talking with the people in it. Musicians, booking agents, and even bartenders and waitresses at popular clubs are all in their own way plugged into the scene. It is up to you to meet, communicate, and then work with these contacts in hopes of learning and, potentially, prospering from them.

Fortunately for musicians, music, especially live music, is an extremely social experience, so it's relatively easy to talk with people about it. Even the shyest guitarist can summon the courage to go up to a guitarist who just finished a show and say, "Hey, man. Nice tone." Since guitar players generally love to talk about their sound, this simple start may quickly lead to a conversation about guitar tone, which leads to talking about the music scene.

To talk with musicians, you first have to know where they hang out. A show, of course, is an obvious location to find musicians, but there are more musicians there than just onstage. As a veteran of many club gigs, I can say that at any given show about one-third of the audience is musicians who are there either as a favor to the band, to check out the competition, or to network. Since you and these musicians already have something in common (being at the same show and check-ing out the same band), you should feel comfortable asking questions like, "Have you seen this band before? Where else do they play? Does this club book a lot of acts like this? Are you in a band?" Answers to these questions can help you learn more about your music scene.

Another great place to network is in your local music store. Music stores are a mecca for musicians who want to hang out in the store, jam on the instruments, and network (and occasionally buy something). Most music stores let prospective shoppers play for hours and never ask them to leave because it turns their store into a musical breeding ground, which ultimately translates into business. Walk into any music store and it's likely you'll hear a guitarist jamming Jimi Hendrix or the latest guitar-rock tune. Chances are this person, or any other customer in the store, has some knowledge of the music scene. In addition to the customers, the store employees are great resources. Most music-store employees are musicians who work at the store as a steady day job and then perform during nonworking hours.

Musicians also hang out at music schools, rehearsal studios, recording studios, and in online chat rooms. It is up to you to seek out these musicians because networking with them may lead to other useful information about bands seeking members, upcoming auditions, affordable recording studios, great engineers for hire, and other music-related news.

All of the above are essential activities that constitute the groundwork for any aspiring musician. As you start surveying the music scene and get a better sense of what's happening locally, you'll begin to see how and where you might fit.

MEETING THE BASIC CRITERIA FOR BEING A MUSICIAN IN A BAND

Attempting to launch a music career without first achieving certain basic minimum standards is like entering a car with no wheels in a race. It's pointless. Before you can consider joining a band, you must reach a working proficiency level on your instrument and establish your personal commitment level. Then you must obtain reliable equipment that will help you meet your goals and be taken seriously. Finally, you'll need transportation to get where you need to be.

Committing Yourself to Being an Active Member of a Team

Pursuing a music career, whether for fame, fortune, or for the satisfaction of playing once a month at the neighbor's backyard barbecue, requires time. You need to maintain a certain degree of commitment to consistently play with a band. Life can sidetrack even those with the best of musical intentions. This is to be expected. You have to determine how music fits into your life and find musicians with similar commitment levels to form bands. Your goal in a band context should be to play with musicians who prioritize their time similarly. That is, you want to find a situation where each member allocates enough time to band-related activities to ensure that all involved are on the same track to achieve common goals.

It's up to each musician to decide how much time to dedicate to his or her craft. Every situation and circumstance differs, so it's impossible to chart specific parameters for every personality type and goal.

As a musician, you should seriously think about how much time you're willing to dedicate to at-home practice and band rehearsals. Although this sounds obvious and perhaps even trite, the importance of practice cannot be overemphasized. When you first jam with a band, you need to come prepared—with skills honed and enough talent to contribute to the project and succeed within it. Superior musicians study their craft—at music school, through private lessons, and by way of self-teaching tools, including books, videos, and computer software tutorials. Every musician learns in a different way, but the good ones all share a common trait: a dedication to practice and to becoming better players. Talented players are rarely born that way.

Many "musicians" do not subscribe to solid practice habits, yet they attempt to join the music scene regardless of their absence of skills. Why would anyone want to start or join a band without musical talent? The answer is on MTV and VH-1 every day, as well as on the pages of *Rolling Stone* and *Spin*. Some see the rock 'n' roll lifestyle shown in the media and crave the musician's lifestyle. Sold-out shows, adoring fans, free food, free drink, easy access to drugs and sex, trashed hotel rooms, constant attention, and, for those at the top of the music food chain, private jets—all of this has tremendous appeal. As you progress through your music career, you inevitably will encounter people who seemingly epitomize this rock star life but have no real ability and are unwilling to put forth the effort necessary to become proficient at a particular instrument. Through hard work and dedication, and by sharpening their ability to handle any musical situation, good players separate themselves from these posers.

In addition to practice, criteria for being a musician in a band include reserving time for gigs and other band duties (making contacts, preparing press kits, booking shows, etc.). It helps to consider your life commitments (family, friends, job, exercise, leisure, etc.), prioritize music within that framework, and then plan a music career that fits accordingly.

Musicians who rank music at the top of their priority list find plenty of time to dedicate to succeeding in the industry; players who make it their fifth or sixth priority will have far less time, obviously, and as a result will be far less likely to achieve the goals of musicians who rank music as their number-one priority. This prioritizing is neither right nor wrong; it simply fits the individual and factors into the decision-making process. Musicians who honestly rank their priorities will benefit, because they won't ignore the things that matter most in their lives. And they won't waste anyone's time (including their own) when seeking musical opportunities.

It's important to play with people whose commitment to music falls into the same or a similar priority level as your own. In this way, if you rank music high in your life's ambitions and select your bandmates accordingly, you'll be less likely to find that your drummer has blown off rehearsal to watch a Julia Roberts marathon on cable. Band histories are full of stories of bandmates differing on priorities and separating as a result. Musical groups consist of people who grow apart as life experiences change them. This is normal and is to be expected. Bandmates lose their musical focus when they get promotions in their day jobs, fall in love, or begin raising a family. Through similar goals and commitment, bands can grow together and succeed.

Providing Yourself with the Right Equipment to Meet Your Needs

Performing with quality equipment means, at minimum, playing with guitars that stay in tune, amplifiers that don't burn out, and keyboards that do not need duct tape to hold input cables in place. In other words, equipment that will perform under rigorous use for an extended period.

Playing with the right equipment is important for two reasons. First, musicians are judged by the music equipment they use. It doesn't matter whether it's a guitar, a saxophone, a microphone (mic), or a keyboard amp. Equipment defines the musician. Every good player knows musical gear and knows that most gear is suited for specific ability levels. There's a direct correlation between equipment and musicians.

For example, Fender Instruments builds some guitars and basses in Mexico. These are great inexpensive beginner instruments, but medium- to advanced-level players find their inferior quality restrictive. Bringing one of these instruments to a record company showcase gig for an original band would be the equivalent of driving a standard factory-equipped Subaru on a NASCAR track. Such a vehicle, although fine for everyday use, would not belong on a racetrack. Other drivers and knowledgeable racing fans would rightfully expect little of this car in a race. Musicians and music fans would have similarly low expectations of a player with lesser gear.

On the other hand, if a player shows up at a gig with an American-made Fender, the perception reverses, since this instrument is highly respected. Musicians would most likely reserve judgment on the owner's ability as a guitarist until they heard him or her play, but at least they'd know there's a respect for quality.

Imagine this scenario: A successful special-event band is auditioning for a female vocalist. It's clear from the ad that the singer is to bring her own microphone to the audition. The singer shows up to the audition with a $19.99 Radio Shack mic that has a permanently attached mic cable—a sure sign of low-quality equipment. Based on that microphone, the bandleader will likely question the singer's commitment level before hearing what may be a great voice. After all, how serious could this musician be if she has invested only $19.99 in equipment that wasn't even purchased at a music store?

This is not to suggest that the singer needs to overextend on credit to buy expensive equipment or that she is without talent. There's plenty of quality gear available at affordable prices. In the case of this vocalist, the industry standard Shure SM58 costs less than $100. A used mic is even cheaper.

There's another reason quality equipment is so necessary, and that's because it will be used for a long time, through multiple rehearsals and shows. It's important to invest in equipment wisely, because it has to be reliable enough to stand the rigors of extended use. That $19.99 microphone is likely to malfunction over time—and that time may be soon! Think of gear like a car that's needed to make a hundred-mile commute every weekday for a job. If you buy an unreliable clunker that might not make the trip consistently, you're putting your job in jeopardy. Similarly, using shoddy music equipment that runs the risk of malfunction during a show puts your ability to gig in danger.

Money, or the lack thereof, is a significant factor that goes into selecting musical equipment. Every musician would love to own the best gear on the market, but often this is impossible due to financial realities—like needing the money you could be spending on a new guitar for food, for your rent or mortgage, for gas for your car. There are many inexpensive acceptable alternatives to the finest musical equipment. It is up to musicians to do the research to find them.

Say, for example, you're a bass player with an affinity for exotic hardwood bass guitars, but you can't afford an F Bass or a Ken Smith, basses that can cost several thousand dollars. After conducting some thorough research you discover that several bass manufacturers like Peavey, Carvin, and MTD make instruments out of the same woods that are offered new at half the price or less. If the Peavey is your choice, you'll want the Cirrus Bass (a perfectly acceptable and reliable American-made instrument) that costs about $1,400.

If the new Cirrus is still out of your price range, you can seek out used models by scouring the classified sections of local newspapers, going to pawn shops, searching eBay, and checking with music stores that sell used or consignment gear. Prices here can drop by as much as half from the store price, since Peavey basses don't hold their value very well. The average Cirrus bass on eBay sells for around $600, a discount of more than 50 percent.

If even the used Cirrus is out of your price range, you can dig even further. You'll find that some Peavey basses made from exotic hardwoods, such as the Peavey Dyna-Bass Unity Series, have been discontinued. This bass used to be Peavey's top-end model, listing at more than $1,000 fifteen years ago. Now on eBay, you might be able to purchase it for a winning bid of around $300, an amazing deal for a solid American-made instrument, with neck-thru construction, made of Hawaiian Koa with an ebony fingerboard—highly sought-after and expensive features in today's market.

Whenever possible, make an investment in durable gear. It will pay tremendous dividends in terms of reliability and peace of mind, not to mention perception. When a speaker blows up at your first gig, you won't be thinking about the $150 you saved by converting your old stereo system into a public address (PA) system. More than likely, you'll be lamenting the wasted performance opportunity and hoping your bandmates can be convinced to give you a second chance.

Ensuring You Have Transportation to Get to Where You Need to Be

Your ability to transport yourself and your equipment to shows and rehearsals is vital to a successful career in music. If you don't have your own vehicle, you may be fortunate enough to be in a band with a gracious bandmate willing to chauffer you to rehearsals and gigs. Without reliable and consistent transportation, you're forced to rely on the kindness of family and friends to take you to your destinations. This is both taxing for the driver and awkward for you, having to grovel or call in a favor just to get to practice or a show.

Free rides eventually dry up. Friends and family will tire of hauling you and your gear on schedules that are often inconvenient for nonmusicians. Relying on an older brother with a 7 AM construction job for rides to and from rehearsals that last until 11 PM or gigs that go into the wee hours of the morning will be short-lived.

Even relying on a bandmate for rides can become problematic. I was once in a band during a period when I had no car. Fortunately, the drummer in the band was willing to cart me, as well as the also vehicle-less guitar player. This worked well for a few weeks until the driver developed a pattern of being thirty minutes late. The guitar player and I both appreciated and really needed the ride, but sitting and waiting with all of our equipment on a corner for half an hour was really frustrating.

After one episode in which we waited for more than an hour, tempers flared. The end of the band came soon after.

Reliable transportation is as important as reliable musical equipment. Musicians have to attend auditions, rehearsals, and performances in order to be successful, and dependable transportation is necessary to get to and from these locations at the set time. Excuses involving flat tires and wasted alternators only work once before the band starts looking for a replacement player or the club crosses you off its list for gigs.

Before you can run you've got to be able to walk, and before you can seriously begin thinking about starting or joining a band you need to have done the necessary up-front preparations and met the basic criteria discussed in this chapter. Once you've taken this first step, then your next step is to define yourself as a musician and begin to consider what kind of band you want to be part of and are able to join or form.

CHAPTER 2

CONSIDERING WHAT KIND OF BAND TO FORM OR JOIN

Being in a band takes considerable time and energy between rehearsals, learning new songs, and playing shows, not to mention performing a host of nonmusical duties, such as booking and marketing shows, creating Web sites, and recording. A year can virtually fly by before you and your bandmates may be ready to play your first show. The decision to join or form a band is a significant one, because it's a choice that will cost you months, if not years, of your life and musical career.

To make the best possible decision, you've got to first look inward to determine what kind of musician you are as well as what your priorities are in music. You also need to consider what kinds of people you want to be playing with, and what qualities in your fellow bandmates are important to you. Once you've answered these questions, you need to decide what kind of band appeals to you, whether it's a cover or original band led by a bandleader, some of the members, or every member of the group. All of this requires both self-evaluation and a knowledge of different band situations before you're able to make an informed decision as to joining or forming a band that is worthy of your efforts.

DEFINING YOURSELF AS A MUSICIAN AND ESTABLISHING WITH WHOM YOU WANT TO PLAY

When musicians first band together, their new alliance generates a lot of energy and excitement, not unlike a first date. But also like that first date, they might look past potentially troubling issues and ignore warning signs while caught up in the euphoria of the situation. This is followed by the inevitable breakup over "musical differences," a wasted six months or a year down the road when reality hits.

It's important that you enter into a band relationship honestly and with eyes wide open to avoid a disappointing conclusion. You must present yourself accurately and your priorities up front to ensure that you and your bandmates are a good fit for a long-term relationship. You also need to consider the personalities of your potential bandmates to avoid working with musicians you don't like or whose actions impede the band.

Identifying Your Priorities

So what are your goals, dreams, and aspirations as a musician? These are questions every musician or bandleader you ever hope to play with is going to ask or wonder about you, and you will want to know the same of them. Once you establish your priorities, you'll be better able to effectively root out opportunities and then articulate these basic facts about yourself. This leads to finding compatible musicians to play with, without whom having a productive band is impossible.

A good example of knowing who you are and what you want comes from Sebastopol, California–based drummer Matt McGlynn. Matt explains, "For starters, I have a 'no jerks' policy. I want to be in a band with people I get along with. Second, I look for players better than me (I want to get good, not complacent). Lastly, I want bandmates who know how to listen so we are all on the same musical page."

When all band members share similar priorities, they become more than just individual standards—they become the band's philosophy. For instance,

McGlynn has particular needs that include playing with down-to-earth people who are talented and understand the importance of listening. If McGlynn's entire band has the same priorities, then the next time an opening in the group arises, there will be a shared understanding as to what's essential in bringing in a new member as well as what to guard against. If McGlynn's band auditions a bass player who can't lock into what the group is doing because he isn't listening to anyone other than himself, the band knows to move on in their search.

The best way to address your priorities is to write a candid personal inventory. Approach this exercise as you would a résumé or a marketing piece that includes key facts about yourself (although this document will most likely never be shown to anyone). Here are some examples of band-related priorities that may be shaped and expanded depending on the individual or the band:

1. I want to join a band.
2. I want to form a band and be a bandleader.
3. I want to be a member of a band that works as a team.
4. I want to be a member of a bandleader-driven band where my only responsibility is to attend rehearsals and perform.
5. I want to play with musicians in my age group.
6. I want to play with musicians of my gender.
7. I want to play with musicians of both genders.
8. I want to play with musicians who share my commitment level.
9. I want to play with musicians who match my level of experience.
10. I want to play with musicians who are friendly, respectful, and polite.
11. I want to play a certain style of music.
12. I want to be paid for every gig I play.
13. I want to be paid for every rehearsal I play.
14. I want to practice a set number of times per week.
15. I want to gig a set number of times per week or month.
16. I want to be in a band that plays original music.
17. I want to play cover music.

18. I am willing to work with a band on nonmusical projects (e.g., promotion, marketing, booking).
19. I am willing to pay a share of costs involved with running a band (e.g., rehearsal space, recordings, promotion).
20. I am willing to commute up to twenty miles for rehearsals and gigs.

You can adapt this list of priorities to your own musical goals. Say, for example, you're a professional musician with no other income and you desire steady, paying gigs regardless of any other criteria. Your list might include the following:

1. I want to play only paying gigs.
2. I want to gig as often as possible.
3. I will play any style of music.
4. I will play original or cover music.
5. I'm willing to drive to wherever gigs are, providing the compensation increases for gigs further than fifty miles away.
6. I will only do unpaid rehearsals if they do not conflict with paying gigs.
7. I am not willing to contribute financially to a project (musical or nonmusical endeavors).

If you would prefer to join a band that writes its own music, your list might include:

1. I want to play with people with a fierce musical drive.
2. I want to play with people who can read music.
3. I want to play original pop music.
4. I want to contribute to the writing of original music.
5. I am willing to contribute my time and effort in both musical and nonmusical endeavors to further the band.
6. I am willing to rehearse as often as the band as a whole deems necessary.

If, on the other hand, you want to run your own band, your list might include:

1. I want to be the bandleader of a rock group.

2. I only want to play with musicians who are responsible adults with successful lives outside of music and who are available to perform on weekends.

3. I am willing to pay musicians a fixed rate per rehearsal and per gig.

4. I want to play cover songs and an occasional original song that I write.

5. The musicians in my band must sing background vocals.

6. The musicians in my band must be able to tour extensively.

7. The musicians in my band must be respectful of each other, personally and musically.

8. The musicians in my band must adhere to the rules of the band (be punctual, be prepared, and be sober).

If you're honest about who you are as a musician and what you're looking for in other musicians you'll be able to find bandmates who are similar in terms of musical priorities. Finding people who share all of your priorities may be asking a bit much, since they vary per individual. However, musicians with varying priorities can coexist, provided compromise is in their vocabulary, although not at the expense of meeting most of their objectives. If your ideal band pays you for every gig and rehearsal, but the only option within your grasp doesn't pay for rehearsals, do you walk because of that difference? That depends on how important paid rehearsals are to you. If you're a professional musician and every dollar you earn goes toward providing for your family, this will be a bigger issue than if you view the band as a good way to make extra money to buy equipment. You need to have a clear understanding of what is meaningful to you.

I currently play for a bandleader who was originally interested in hiring a bass player who also could sing background vocals. After he heard my vocals at the audition (imagine a cat being played by a violin), he was less interested in me as a potential hire. But later, after he learned that I was a committed and responsible musician who could play all of the bass parts (other important criteria he was looking for), he backed off of his initial vocal requirement and invited me to join the band. He was able to compromise because I met a satisfactory number of his priorities.

Understanding that Personality Counts as Much as Talent

While musical proficiency, style, and commitment are important to musicians seeking to join or form bands, personality and traits such as being respectful, supportive, kind, and patient are equally relevant. (These are most likely qualities your closest friends share and are the main reasons you choose to spend time with them, so it makes sense you'd look for similar qualities in your bandmates.) If band members can't get along, it really doesn't matter how amazing a soloist a guitarist is or how long a vocalist can sustain a note, because the band will fail due to its internal feuding. San Antonio, Texas–based guitarist and bandleader Paul Mitchell sums up this point, saying, "If you spend enough time with bandmates you don't like, you forget about their talents and end up focusing on their problems."

I was once in a band where the singer hated the guitarist's oversized ego and the guitarist couldn't stand the singer's lackadaisical attitude. Their feud eventually spread throughout the band, as each demanded that all of the members take sides. I was caught in the middle, and probably spent as much time on the phone trying to mediate their issues as I did practicing our songs on my own. Ultimately, we ceased making music and became a soap opera. As you probably guessed, the band didn't last very long.

Playing in a band with people you enjoy being around makes it much easier to get through the rough parts of being a musician. There's nothing enjoyable about hauling a ten-piece drum kit up a flight of stairs. No one likes to argue with a sound person about the monitor mix, and no one wants to spend Friday night e-mailing flyers to a mailing list. But if you can find compatible bandmates, you'll discover that having them to help you carry your drums, to commiserate with after a bad sound check, and to sacrifice their Friday night as well makes the hard parts of being in a band more tolerable, and even fun.

Being in a band with people you respect and are compatible with can make you a better musician too, because you can reach a comfort level with your fellow musicians that allows you to gain confidence in yourself. Los Angeles–based drummer Eric Hoemann explains, "I like working with confident musicians who are cool, patient, and supportive, because they tend to be good team players that bring out the best in others, and they make me a better drummer. We only sound good when we work together and respect each other, and a good bandmate will do this and make the gig as fun and easy as possible."

When I'm auditioning musicians or considering joining a band, there's one personality trait that stands out above the rest as incompatible with me—being unrealistic. There are people who talk a great game about how talented they are or how they're going to form the band that just kills. I find these boasts barely tolerable even if they can be backed up by ability or facts, but when these players demonstrate that they have no desire to put forth the effort necessary to accomplish these goals, it's proof they aren't grounded in reality.

Early in my musical career I played with many people like this. One drummer wanted me to drop out of school because he was sure we were "The Next Big Thing." That belief never jibed with his penchant for skipping rehearsals to get high. Another guitarist claimed he had a celebrity cousin (albeit distant) who would help us land a management deal. Not surprisingly, the celebrity relative never materialized.

California–based bandleader Doug Waitman of Fine Artists Entertainment, which books Southern California–based special-event bands, has an understanding of the traits he looks for when hiring players for his bands. "Equally important to talent is a person's individual integrity. This quality has nothing to do with music, but rather the way in which this person makes choices and conducts himself. Successful band members with Fine Artists Entertainment have to be dependable, conscientious, and hardworking. They also must be good at working with others and willing to sacrifice their own personal glory for the good of the team. They must be friendly and supportive of the other band members and respectful of the leadership. Above all, a member needs to be true to his word, honor commitments, and adhere to the deadlines, schedules, and standards set by the management."

31

Considering all that musicians have to do, succeeding in a band is hard enough without playing with people who are unrealistic, unable to pull their weight, or unwilling to contribute as a member of the project. This type of musician may not show his or her stripes immediately, but will soon enough, and over time will lead your band down a road of unmet expectations. Avoid musicians who have bad attitudes, out-of-control egos, or who offer quick solutions rather than logging the rehearsal hours needed to make the band the best possible. These people will waste your time and shorten your music career.

IDENTIFYING WHAT TYPE OF BAND YOU WANT TO FORM OR JOIN

There are several types of bands—both in terms of their internal structure and the kinds of material they play. One band structure features a bandleader who directs the group; another is democratic. Some bands play original-only music, others play cover songs, and still others play both. There are also democratic cover bands and original bands fronted by a bandleader, as well as other combinations. The best way to decide which type of band is the best fit for you is to understand their makeup and determine how each will affect you.

Deciding Whether You Want to Be a Leader or a Member of a Team

The differences between a democratic band and a bandleader-driven band are in how they're managed and how decisions are made. In a *democratic band* each member contributes to making decisions, shouldering costs, and completing non-musical work. In a *bandleader-led group* one person is the unquestioned leader with the other members simply expected to play their instruments and show up for rehearsals and gigs as directed. It's also possible for a band to be led by a pair of bandleaders. These bands usually are fronted by a songwriting team that calls the shots.

In a democratic band everyone is invested in the project. Any success the band achieves is shared among its members (this does not necessarily include song-writing credits, however, since that depends on the group's songwriting process).

When you form or join a democratic band, it's like investing in a stock with the potential of big gains. The longer you're in the band, or hold the stock, and continue investing in it, the more it is worth and the greater its potential. Musicians who have been in a democratic band for a long time find it hard to divest, since they have put so much time and energy into it. Bandleader-driven groups usually do not have this shared commitment level, since members are less invested in the overall success of the band, having not shared the burdens with the leader or the spoils if the band is profitable. Factor in a possible revolving door of membership when members are fired or defect for better (or better-paying) bands, and there can be very little, if any, loyalty in these kinds of bands.

One example of a democratic band was San Francisco's Staci Twigg, a now-defunct indie-rock band that featured singer/guitarist Julie Zielinski. In Zielinski's opinion, democratic bands work well. "When everyone is involved, the group becomes more cohesive and has a stake in the outcome of the band," Zielinski says. Staci Twigg shared expenses and wrote the majority of its music as a unit. As Staci Twigg's popularity grew, all members benefited in the form of increased revenues from CD and merchandise sales. They also all stood to gain if the band landed a record or management deal, as opposed to a bandleader-driven unit in which the band members can be unceremoniously dumped if the label, or management, or bandleader, wants to go with a different backing group.

Some musicians find not having to deal with the nonmusical aspects of running a band preferable, so they seek out bandleader-driven projects. In this way they don't have to stress about booking the band, finding places to rehearse, and keeping everyone's musical interests satisfied. Simply being responsible for showing up and performing at a high level is often enough to worry about without factoring in writing songs, holding auditions, and handling other musical and nonmusical issues. Many bandleaders sell this type of "hassle-free" gig to musicians, as it is tremendously appealing to players who are at a stage in their musical careers where they have commitments other than music to factor into their daily lives.

Los Angeles–based bandleader/vocalist Ted Heath, a veteran of many bands both democratic and bandleader-driven, agrees. "Sometimes the best part of being in a band run by a bandleader is that the players don't have to make decisions," Heath says. "They don't want a say about how the band is run. After all, if they didn't like the way the band was being managed, they wouldn't be in it in the first place. Bands with bandleaders tend to have far less bickering on how the project is run."

On the other hand, democratic bands must get everyone's input to make decisions. This may be a slow-moving process if members can't readily come together to discuss an issue, or they don't all agree on a solution. "It hurts when you have to make decisions on the fly, especially when everyone doesn't agree," Zielinski says. "It makes the process take a lot longer." If a band member doesn't agree with a certain course or idea, it's up to the band to convince him or her otherwise, put the issue to a vote, or make a compromise.

Democratic bands can delegate jobs among their members to prevent one person from getting bogged down with too many responsibilities. Once assigned, the band member—or "band contact"—is responsible for the task at hand and can move forward with decisions like booking, marketing a show, or lining up a recording studio without having to consult everyone in the group. For example, I was a member in a democratic alt-pop trio, and each of us had a role in various nonmusical duties. I was responsible for booking shows, creating flyers, and managing the mailing list. The drummer handled all Internet-related issues, and the singer/guitarist, a recording engineer, managed the group in the recording studio.

The only way a band contact can work is if the members empower him or her to act in the band's interest. For instance, if the band contact responsible for booking shows learns ahead of time that the group's July calendar is open except for the fourth week of the month, when the singer is out of town, he or she can book the show without having to contact everyone in the group to check schedules. A band contact trying to book without this information must ask the venue to hold the date for the group while he or she contacts the entire band to make sure that particular gig date is open to all. This can take time, and the venue may not be able to hold the spot, causing the band to lose out on a gig opportunity.

Bandleader-driven bands don't have the luxury of sharing the band duties—the duties all fall solely on the shoulders of the leader. Probably the biggest challenge a bandleader faces is maintaining the group's membership. As a bandleader, if you can't find (or don't want) musicians willing to play for free in the band, you must turn to hiring professional musicians to fill out the band's roster. This can be a hindrance, especially if you don't have any money coming in from gigs or merchandise sales to offset the expense, and you have to go out-of-pocket. Prices are determined by the professional musician, but the average fee is approximately $40 to $50 for a three-hour rehearsal and $100 to $200 for a one-set gig.

Cost notwithstanding, having paid players in a band offers two important benefits for bandleaders. One is that compensated players tend to get their parts right the first time; it's their job to do so. If they fail to do this, they find themselves out of work, because no bandleader wants to hire a player who comes to rehearsal unprepared, just like no employer wants an unproductive employee on the payroll. San Francisco–based singer/songwriter Liz Pisco explains that hiring professional musicians who get it right the first time leads to fewer, more productive rehearsals. "I find too much rehearsal can really suck the life out of a song. It needs to sound fresh to be fun," Pisco says. "Having professional players who take my music as seriously as I do because their job in the band depends on it means we get it right the first time."

The second benefit of hiring players is that they're easy to dismiss. Stop paying them, and their reason for playing disappears. I was once let go from a paid gig because the band's revenue had dried up and the bandleader was unwilling to go into his pocket to keep me in the band. The bandleader knew I was unwilling to play for free, so I accepted the dismissal, and he got off without an argument.

If you want to be paid to be in a band, you need to be up front about what you expect to be paid for shows and rehearsals. Money can be a sensitive issue among musicians, and the topic should be broached before both parties have invested any time in each other. If you ask your bandleader for $50 per three-hour rehearsal a month after playing with the group for free, he or she will be displeased. The band has already invested their time in having you as part of the band when they could have been seeking out a player who would not ask for money. Establish your price from the start, make it clear to the bandleader, and see if the terms are accepted.

Players seeking money in exchange for their services need to accept that this requirement will significantly reduce their number of opportunities with bands. Funds can be scarce in the beginning levels of music, since most bands are just fighting to get gigs that pay very little or nothing at all. I receive many calls to join bands, and as soon as I bring up my rates I hear crickets chirping on the other end of the phone line 25 percent of the time because many bandleaders not only can't afford to pay me, but they can't afford to pay anyone more than a fraction of the $75 they make playing a forty-five-minute set at the local coffeehouse.

There are other challenges for paid players besides finding a healthy payday. Idealistic bandleaders sometimes hire players to back them in a band and then find themselves frustrated when the working musicians treat the bandleader's dream of being a star like a job. Factor in having to write checks after every practice and gig, and it can be a bitter pill to swallow for some bandleaders. I have played in several projects where the bandleader happily accepted my terms at first, only to become resentful after a few months when I wouldn't waive my fee to work in the band as an unpaid member.

Deciding Whether You Want to Play Cover Music or Original Music

With regard to the type of music they play, bands break down into three basic categories: cover band, original band, and hybrid band that plays both varieties. *Cover bands* do not write their own music; they simply perform music originally written by other bands. *Original bands* write and perform their own music. For example, if Tom Petty and the Heartbreakers played Fall Out Boy's "Sugar, We're Going Down," that would be a cover song for them. If Tom Petty and his band played "American Girl," that would be an example of a band playing an original song. *Hybrid bands* usually are trying to get their original material noticed but play cover songs to get gigs at clubs that feature cover bands or because they just needed more songs to round out their set and didn't want to wait to write more original material. This kind of band may play an occasional original song during a set of covers, which can be a successful tactic to get a following for their original music if they have enough repeat fans at their shows. But the move may also backfire, leaving an audience annoyed that they're not hearing favorite familiar music and are stuck listening to the band indulge themselves with their original tunes at what was expected to be a cover set.

There are many different kinds of cover bands. Some play Top 40 music and use the radio charts as their set list. A traditional wedding band performs the hits of multiple generations, like Etta James's "At Last" and the Village People's "Y.M.C.A.," to appease a crowd of vastly differing ages. There also are bands that play jazz standards like "Wave" and "Misty" in hotel lounges across the country.

"Tribute" bands pay homage to certain bands or genres by playing their greatest hits. These groups target a niche market that wants to see its favorite band or genre covered live without paying a fortune to see the real thing at a stadium or large venue. *Tribute bands* include acts like the Neil Diamond tribute band, Super Diamond, which plays all of Diamond's hits like "Sweet Caroline" and "Cracklin' Rosie." Another example is the Iron Maidens, an all-female tribute band that covers the band Iron Maiden. Genre tribute bands like the Cheeseballs play both 1970s and 1980s music. These bands can go all out to honor their musical inspiration and typically match the original artist or genre in wardrobe and hairstyle and some-times even play the same brand and model instruments.

Musicians seeking work in cover bands that play clubs, weddings, or special-event gigs are typically looking for a steady situation with frequent gigs, quality players, stability, and good pay, or they just want to have fun playing music without the stress of songwriting. Many musicians have careers outside of music and want to play in order to make extra income and to have fun without sacrificing other life priorities. They're turned off by the idea of being away from their families or day jobs to spend four nights a week at rehearsal or even longer stretches on a tour. They might argue that the role of music in their lives is no less vital than it is to a player in an original band struggling to hit it big, but they aren't prepared to sacrifice other important aspects of their lives to become "rock stars."

Ted Heath is an example of this type of player. "On the cover music scene, people are generally doing it to get paid, although there are people like me who just love playing music. The money is secondary," Heath says. "I don't care if it's someone else's songs as long as they're good. I get to sing some of the greatest songs ever written, I get to play with great people, and I get to stand in front of an audience, play to people who really appreciate what I'm doing, and not starve to death doing it!"

Cover bands rarely take their acts outside of their local music scene, since each community usually has its own stable of competent cover acts. There are Top 40 bands in every scene looking for opportunities to play private parties, and there are special-event bands doing weddings in every community that hosts them. For players who want to tour, however, this is a major drawback to cover bands. Cover bands also do not get big record deals or radio play.

For better or worse, the ceiling for cover bands is lower than that for original bands. Cover bands aren't going to "make it" in the sense of getting mainstream radio airplay and sold-out shows at Madison Square Garden. That said, it's easier to get ready to perform in a cover group, because you don't need to write good songs. You simply choose great tunes, learn them, and submit your demo CD to a popular dance club or booking agent for private events, and you're on your way—much to the consternation of original bands.

There's an innate animosity between original and cover bands because of the easier road cover bands follow. Original bands can spend months writing music together before they're ready to perform. Cover bands simply pick their favorite hits, learn them, and they're ready for the stage. Plus, they already know their songs will get people dancing or applauding, since everybody already knows and loves them. Original bands have to hope their songs are good enough to even get applause. It can be disheartening for original acts to see a cover band instantly hit the music scene by playing other people's music rather than by honing their own creative vision.

I was a member of a progressive-rock trio that celebrated the release of our debut recording by holding a CD release party at a popular club. While our gig was well attended and received, it was partially overshadowed by the cover band that followed us on the bill. This Top 40 band had a solid following of attractive women who drank and danced, unlike our following of intellectual prog-rockers who couldn't hope to dance to our odd-time-signature rhythms. Plus, the cover band put on a really good show. As an original act that had just put our entire lives (and bank accounts) into the band and our CD, we were envious of the response to their performance and frustrated; we felt they hadn't done anything nearly as taxing as what we had just accomplished.

Although the gamble in an original band rarely pays off in terms of wealth and fame, the creative payoff begins with the creation of the first original song. Writing songs with other musicians is a unique and inventive experiment that is very rewarding. Take it a step further and it becomes a well-recorded CD you will cherish forever. Writing hit music may mean financial success and fame beyond anyone's wildest imagination, but the best musicians and songwriters do not play for the dream of hanging out in a limo with supermodels (although the idea is rarely shunned). They play for the chance to create a unique artistic vision. Singer/songwriters, or bands working as a unit, can tell stories, create moods, or inspire with one great song. Playing an original song for a live audience, especially an approving one, is tremendously exhilarating. The audience is responding to something *you* created.

"I have been in both types of projects, cover and original music," says Ted Heath. "Original bands have a different mindset. They're going for the gold. They want to become famous, make a lot of money, and go on tour. The band is their life;

it's what they live and breathe." This is the appeal of the original band and the reason musicians continue a centuries-old tradition of banding together to write and play music.

Once you know your musical priorities and what kind of band fits your needs, you can seek out the groups and musicians that match your goals. To find them you'll need to take your networking and presentation skills to the next level and understand how to get musicians' attention within your local scene.

CHAPTER 3

FINDING MUSICIANS OR A BAND

A music scene is organic. Musicians constantly cycle in and out of bands as groups form, change membership, and break up, dispersing their members to start all over again. This fluctuation means there are always available musicians looking for bands as well as bands seeking musicians to fill out their ranks. The challenge to finding bands or musicians is identifying the ones matching your musical aspirations and priorities. This can be difficult. It's likely that many of your goals are similar to those of other bands and musicians—most bands want to play with musicians who are talented, responsible, hardworking, and personable, and most musicians want to play with this same type of musician in bands that are popular and gigging—and this can lead to intense competition for the same musician or band.

To get the attention of the bands or musicians to help meet your musical objectives, you need to create an advertisement outlining your priorities, circulate it throughout your local scene, and find ads from those matching your goals and requirements. Once you have completed these steps, you can then communicate with interested bands and musicians to determine if they should be auditioned.

CREATING, CIRCULATING, AND FINDING ADS

To effectively market yourself or your band, you need to craft an ad representing your needs that appeals to bands or musicians with similar needs. Then circulate your ads in locations where bands and musicians can consider them. In addition to placing your own ads in these locations, you need to search for compatible ads from bands and musicians seeking to join or form a project with you.

Creating Your Ad

In Chapter 2, you established your musical priorities. Now you'll want to return to those priorities and articulate them in an ad that can be relayed to interested bands or musicians. To illustrate how to create your ad, let's imagine a fictitious bassist seeking a band and a fictitious band seeking a bassist. Meet Moe, a twenty-six-year-old male bassist who describes himself as follows:

1. I'm committed to music.
2. I want to play original funk music that I write or write with others.
3. I'm available to rehearse and gig anytime.
4. I have reliable gear and transportation.
5. I'm willing to share in the work and expenses of the band.

Here is Moe's basic ad:

I'm a 26-year-old male funk bassist with reliable gear and transportation seeking an ambitious and original gigging project.

The fictitious band, Funky Minnow, is a four-piece funk band currently gigging about twice per month and growing in popularity. Based on their priorities, the band describes itself as follows:

1. We are a funk band.
2. Music is our number-one priority.
3. We want the band to consist of members around the same age.
4. We rehearse three times per week.
5. We vote on all band issues democratically.
6. We split all costs and nonmusical tasks evenly.

Here is Funky Minnow's basic ad seeking a replacement bassist:

> *Our 4-piece funk band, Funky Minnow, seeks a talented 20-something-year-old bassist with no attitude to join us. Bassist must have reliable gear and transportation and be committed to the success of the band.*

Notice that both ads are missing certain priorities. This is because your ad doesn't need to spell out, or even include, every issue on your list. It just needs the defining ones that musicians and bands must have to make an informed decision as to whether to pursue the opportunity. Adding priorities like sharing expenses and mandatory rehearsals to your ad can dilute its impact or, worse, come across as demanding or rigid. This information can be delivered later, when the musician and band are communicating, or at the audition.

Notice how listing every priority deflates the message in this example of Funky Minnow's ad and message:

> *Our 4-piece funk band, Funky Minnow, seeks a talented 20-something-year-old bassist with great attitude to join us. Bassist must have reliable gear and transportation and be committed to the success of the band. We rehearse three times per week. We also split all of our costs and duties evenly throughout the band. Finally, everyone in this band has an equal say in how we run our group.*

To get a positive response from your ad, it must appeal to potential responders so that when musicians or bands sharing your goals hear or read it they will instantly believe you or your band fits their needs. The way to do this is to insert some "pop" into your ad to make it stand out from its potentially bland alternatives. An ad like, "I'm a rock guitarist with pro attitude and gear looking for a serious original band that wants to take over Boston," will resonate with serious original rock bands seeking a guitarist because its final three words give it a memorable kick. This ad will generate far more interest than "I'm a guitarist looking for a band," which will be glossed over by groups searching for a passionate member and an ad that offers more detail.

Your ad concludes with your contact information, usually in the form of a phone number, e-mail address, or Web site address. Keep these numbers and addresses current and active, and check your messages frequently. Musicians and bands will form opinions about you based on how organized and responsive you appear. If you're easily accessible, they'll believe there is a good chance you're responsible, someone they can count on. If your voicemail is constantly full and rejects additional messages, or you never check your e-mail account, those are clues that you aren't organized enough to be dependable.

When preparing your ad, keep it concise and articulate. The following example of a poorly written ad comes from an e-mail I received from a bandleader who saw my profile online. I have not modified it, except to change the phone number.

Yeah Hi!

I saw your add on musicians Contact and wanted to send you a quick note to touch base (no point intended . . . lol!) and see if what we are doing is something you would want to get involved with. My band is currently showcasing for labels and we are looking for a bass player who has the "Chops", looks, and a pro attitude to join in on the fun. The music is just solid, radio friendly, up beat, comercial pop/rock (we are definetly not re-eventting the wheel by any means . . . lol!) and has lots of room for you to get creative and put your own thumb print on it. And just so you know, my Guitar player and Drummer are world class musicians and as good as anybody you could ever hope to jam with.

Anyways enough said . . . lol! I would love to hear from you if you think this sounds interesting and would like more info. You can call me at #(310) 555-5555. I look forword to hopefully hearring from you soon and take care.

— J -

This ad has all the information a bassist needs to make an informed decision as to whether the band meets his or her needs. The problem is the way it's written. For anyone with a spell-check function, there's no reason for such egregious errors as "add," "comercial," "definetly," "re-eventting," "forword," and "hearring." This makes for a very painful read. The bottom line for me is that this e-mail gives the impression its author doesn't have the necessary organizational skills to run a band, and if he isn't running the band, then the band isn't savvy enough to assign the task to someone who can effectively deliver their message. Because the text comes across so poorly, it also suggests to me there are few, if any, label show-cases in their future or world-class musicians in their lineup.

When you create your ad for the classified section of a local publication or a flyer, it needs to be sized for the limited space available. Many publications offer musicians and bands free space in their classified sections as long as the ad is ten to fifteen words or fewer. Thus, ads are condensed to "Pro Band w/Major Label Interest Seeks You! Have Great Hair," "Working Jazz Quartet Seeks Pianist Weekdays, Cocktail Hour Restaurant Gig," and Motley Crue's Mick Mars's ad in Los Angeles' *The Recycler*, which read, "Extraterrestrial guitarist available for any other aliens that want to conquer the Earth." Flyers might hold one or two para-graphs, but they also need room for perforated tabs with your name, or band name, and contact information on them so interested musicians and bands can get your facts without having to write it down or remove the entire flyer. Using Moe and Funky Minnow, here are some examples of how they can adapt their ads to fit these formats:

Here is Moe's ten-word ad:

Funky bassist w/car, gear, great attitude seeks gigging band (303) 555-5555.

Here is Funky Minnow's ten-word ad:

Funk band seeks committed 20-ish pro bassist. www.funkyminnow.com.

Here are examples of Moe's and Funky Minnow's ads on a flyer.

Bassist Available

Twenty-six-year-old funky bassist with reliable gear and transportation seeking an ambitious and original gigging project. Contact Moe at moe4bass@hotmail.com Or call (303) 555-5555.

Moe	Moe	Moe	Moe	Moe
(303) 555-5555	(303) 555-5555	(303) 555-5555	(303) 555-5555	(303) 555-5555
moe4bass@	moe4bass@	moe4bass@	moe4bass@	moe4bass@
hotmail.com	hotmail.com	hotmail.com	hotmail.com	hotmail.com

Funky Minnow Seeks Bassist

Four-piece funk band, Funky Minnow, seeks a talented 20-something-year-old bassist with great attitude to join us. Should have reliable gear and transportation and be committed to the success of the band. We have upcoming bookings. Check us out and contact at www.funkyminnow.com

Funky Minnow	Funky Minnow	Funky Minnow	Funky Minnow	Funky Minnow
Needs Bassist!	Needs Bassist!	Needs Bassist!	Needs Bassist!	Needs Bassist!
funkyminnow.com	funkyminnow.com	funkyminnow.com	funkyminnow.com	funkyminnow.com

---

When you post your ad on a Web site, you typically have much more space to articulate your needs because you aren't limited to just ten words or fewer as in a publication or a single-page flyer. If you find the Web site you are using to advertise has restrictions on the amount of content you can post, you can simply provide a link to your own Web site. Since it's just a click away, it'll be easy for interested bands and musicians to follow the link to learn more about you or your band.

In the following example of Web site text, because Moe has more flexibility with space, he is able to elaborate a little more on his priorities and offer additional information about his equipment.

My name is Moe and I'm a 26-year-old bassist who loves to play funk music. I have been playing bass for five years and have been influenced by Larry Graham and Flea. I play a Music Man Stingray bass, and my amp is a GK 400RB combo (it's enough to fill most clubs and has a direct out, so I can go through the PA system for bigger rooms). I also have my own car.

I'm interested in joining a serious original gigging funk band that will allow me to be a part of the songwriting process. Music is my life and what I want to do for a living. I am willing to rehearse and gig anytime, and I can share the expenses of the band and the work involved in nonmusical activities, particularly booking since I have a lot of connections here in town. If you are serious about getting funky, and learning more about me, get in touch with me through my Web site, www.moe4bass.com.

Here is Funky Minnow's ad on their Web site:

Hello Funky Minnow Fans!

We are currently auditioning bass players. We are looking for a talented and fun 20-something male or female to join our group. You should have reliable gear and transportation and be committed to getting funky!

To learn more about us, cruise through this Web site, especially through our Audio, Band Biography, and Upcoming Gigs sections. If you think you'll be a great fit, contact Tracy through our "Contact Us" link on the home page.

Now that you have an articulate and appealing ad, you need to get your message out to find the right band or musician to help you achieve your musical goals.

Circulating and Finding Ads

Print ads for musicians and bands usually are placed in three ways: on bulletin boards in places where musicians hang out, in printed publications with classified sections like "Musicians Wanted" and "Musicians Available," and on Web sites that have online classified sections for musicians. When you find appealing ads that match your goals, you can just take or print a copy.

Bulletin-board ads feature flyers advertising everything from musicians and bands to recording studios and CD manufacturers. You can find these boards in music stores, music schools, and rehearsal studios. In California, Bay Area's H.I.T. Wall Studios co-owner—and drummer for the band DU★DS—Will Strickland says of the networking scene at his facility, "We have a foyer with a corkboard. Bands and musicians are free to hang flyers for their upcoming shows or advertise a need for a band, drummer, or other player. There are always plenty of musicians checking it out and talking with each other about music and bands." When you find a flyer that matches your goals, remove a tab or write down the information.

These boards do have drawbacks. First, there's no guarantee your flyer will stay up. Musicians, or the owners of the board, may tear it down or place a flyer over yours. Sometimes the complete opposite is true, and flyers stay up for months, rendering their information useless. I've responded to flyers on bulletin boards only to find the spot in the band had been filled weeks before.

If you want to place your ad on a board, check with its owner to get permission. Some music-store owners and employees want to screen your flyer or give it a literal stamp of approval (if your ad doesn't have this stamp it will be removed) before it's posted. If you're able to place your message on the board, be courteous and don't cover up or tear down someone else's flyer. Not only is this rude, but it's likely that whoever placed the flyer is going to come back to its location and check on it at some point, at which time they'll most likely tear yours down as well.

As mentioned in Chapter 1, cities often have weekly or biweekly publications that feature calendar listings. These same newspapers and magazines are also likely to include a classified section for musicians, offering not only musical equipment but ads looking for musicians and bands. To post your own ad, contact the publication (the phone number or e-mail is usually printed at the top of this section) and check the parameters on pricing and content. If you're perusing the classifieds for opportunities, highlight the ones that appeal to you.

In addition to helping you find musicians and bands, these ads are great barometers for gauging the number of musicians circulating in your scene: Just count the number of opportunities available for a particular instrument, and you'll get an idea of who and what's out there. If there are a lot of listings for your particular instrument, then you're in demand and will probably have an easier time landing auditions since there's less competition. When I moved to San Francisco, I picked up a copy of *BAM*, a local entertainment magazine, and instantly knew I was in a favorable city because there were three full columns of ads seeking bass players.

Using the Internet is another great way to bring people with common interests together, and musicians should take advantage of this terrific resource. Major search engines such as Google and Yahoo! are ideal for finding classified sections for musicians on the Internet. Simply search "Musicians Wanted" and dozens of online classified sections are just a mouse-click away.

There are three different types of online classified sites: free, paid, and sites featuring both free and paid content. Examples of these sites available to musicians wishing to join or form bands are www.craigslist.org, www.MusiciansContact.com, and www.musiciansconnection.com. All of these sites feature listings, but it's free to list on www.craigslist.org, while www.MusiciansContact.com is a paid service, and www.musiciansconnection.com lets users look at adds for free, but they've got to pay to place them.

Free sites like craiglist.org feature ads similar to what you'll find on the bulletin board at a rehearsal studio. The advantage for users of free sites is that they don't have to pay to list their ad. Drummer Matt McGlynn found his current gig through craigslist. Then the band used craigslist to find a replacement bassist. (McGlynn also noted that through the site he found his current day job and a crib for his baby!)

Paid services like www.MusiciansContact.com (based in Los Angeles, California, but serving the United States and abroad) charge a monthly or annual fee for their content. Since musicians and bands have to pay to gain access, the opportunities available on these sites tend to be more professional in nature than a free service. Most hobbyists simply aren't going to pay to be listed or to acquire other listings. The groups advertising on paid sites are usually cover bands, although some original music bands list on them as well when they are seeking professional or highly dedicated musicians willing to play for free. MusiciansContact.com founder Sterling Howard says, "The players that use my site usually are looking for paid work, primarily in cover bands, since those are the ones that pay. Most of the people who use the site are bandleaders looking for responsible, organized players. The more organized the band the better. Disorganized bands, they won't find anyone here. Out of the 150 bass players or so on here, none of them is going to want to join a disorganized program. They aren't at that stage. This is what makes our site superior to a free site—the talent of our players and the nature of our bands.

"Original bands do use the site, and they always comment on the great players that are registered here," Howard continues. "Their only complaint is that the players they meet are looking for paid gigs. Still, for some original bands, who are organized and have it together—but are not necessarily making money—there's a chance of finding a player on www.MusiciansContact.com. Let's face it: Every player is ultimately looking for a shot with an original successful band. Everyone is open for the right thing."

Musicians seeking professional opportunities should still check out free sites. They are a resource that occasionally will yield pro gigs. Los Angeles–based keyboardist Paul McDonald says, "The Internet is the main thing these days.

I like craigslist.org and musicconnection.com . . . free sites. In Los Angeles, it seems to be the way bands do things. I like the Web ads, since they specify what people are looking for in greater detail, as opposed to the newspaper, which is pretty limiting. People either call me from my ad, or I call them. When I first came out here from England, I used the *LA Weekly.* Now I just use the Internet."

An advantage to online classified sections is quantity. They can simply physically hold more information than what an ad on a bulletin board or in a printed publication can fit. In a two-week period on craigslist.org, for example, there were 780 posts in Southern California relating to musicians wanted or available. MusiciansConnection.com also offers hundreds of new listings monthly.

Bands and musicians also can market themselves on the Internet by preparing their own Web sites and referring interested parties to them in their message for more information. If you're Internet-challenged, sites like www.purevolume.com and www.myspace.com are free services that offer simple-to-create Web pages where you can upload audio and pictures to further appeal to potential responders. The Internet is so vast it's unlikely someone will stumble across your site without being pointed in the right direction, so you'll need to include your address on your flyer, print ad, or online musicians' referral service. Here's an example of a classified ad that includes a Web site:

> *Professional vocalist available for all styles. More information at www.purevolume.com/provoxs*

As discussed above, ads for musicians and bands may be circulated in a printed publication, in a flyer, or online. However, they also may be verbal communication exchanged during a networking conversation. To increase the number of responses, don't limit yourself to just one method: By using more than one you'll have a better chance of finding a band or musicians that meet your expectations.

Networking in person is more efficient than print advertising because it's direct, real-time communication. Both bands and musicians can ask and answer questions about their goals without the delay of placing print ads and waiting for return and follow-up e-mails and phone calls. You simply ask fellow musicians and bands questions like, "Is your metal band looking for a guitarist?" and follow up with, "Let me tell you a little about myself . . ." or "Would you be interested in auditioning for my jazz combo? Here's what we are doing now . . ." and get feedback right away.

Print ads can be a hassle for musicians and bands placing the ad. Conception to publication may take days or even weeks. There also might be a charge for this service. Plus, ads usually lead to auditions with strangers, which can be uncomfortable for some people. Some musicians simply avoid ads altogether and network within their circle of friends and acquaintances to find opportunities. If you're familiar with your local scene, this might be easy for you since you just have to e-mail or talk with your contacts to find leads. For instance, one night while checking out a band in a club, I ran into a friend. I told him I was looking for a new band, and he promptly directed me to a friend of his who was looking for a bassist for his band. We spoke and I got an audition. It was the easiest audition I ever landed.

If you're new in town, you'll have to find these opportunities to form or join bands by talking to strangers and hoping you'll catch a break. As discussed in Chapter 1, musicians have a lot in common and usually develop an instant rapport. Guitarist Paul Mitchell explains, "When I first relocated to San Antonio I took a job at a local music store, and part of my job was to setup guitars and amps for potential buyers. Often, during the setup, random people would come up to me while I was playing and ask if I was looking for a band. This is how I landed my previous gig with Versital. I setup an amp for a bandleader, and I played through it to test it out before handing it over to him. He liked my playing, and we had a lot in common. The next thing I knew, we were playing in a band together and recording an album."

As with your print and online ads, be articulate in stating your needs. If you ramble about irrelevant matters, verbally or in writing, you will either bore people or lead them to believe you are only interested in hearing yourself speak; either way, you'll cost yourself an opportunity to join or form a band. I was once hanging out with a bass-player friend at a popular music club in New Orleans when we were both introduced to a bandleader who needed to replace his bassist. We were both interested in the gig, but my friend wouldn't shut up about how great he would be for the band, how his bass was custom-made, and even how his great-aunt had inspired him to become a musician. By the time he was done he had talked himself out of the gig. When it was my turn, I told the bandleader who I was and what I was looking for in about thirty seconds and followed this up with my contact information. I had an audition the next week and my long-winded friend did not.

Many musicians network through music schools and private instructors. Schools can especially be great launching pads for musicians to join bands, since they often encourage students to form groups. Coast Music Conservatory in Hermosa Beach, California, features classes for players interesting in jamming with other musicians and is preparing to take it a step further by referring students into the musical community.

Coast Music Conservatory founder and keyboardist Matt Rhode (who has played with Queen Latifah and was a musical director for Kelly Clarkson and an *American Idol* tour) says, "We are offering ensemble classes to interested students to introduce them to the experience of playing with other musicians. The ensembles will be led by a veteran touring musician and bandleader who can offer guidance on issues like song selection, playing different styles, group dynamics, and improvisation. Because all of our instructors also are working musicians with contacts in the music industry, eventually we will be able to offer a more structured referral service for our students on a case-by-case basis."

Private instructors also can offer useful networking opportunities, but because they usually only teach one instrument, they can't create a band out of their roster of students. They can, however, refer students to bands or other students knowledgeable in the local music scene. A private teacher with twenty students is a valuable resource, since a few of those students, or even the instructor, might be in bands or know of cool opportunities. I once took lessons from Bay Area music coach Jock Rockenbach, after which he invited me to play bass in his band.

It was a great opportunity for me, and it wouldn't have occurred had I not taken lessons from him.

Another way for musicians, especially singer/songwriters, to network is at clubs where they can participate in an Open Mic event—and even briefly perform. Open Mic stands for "open microphone," meaning any singer/songwriter who wants to perform a song or two can do so without having to book the event in advance; they simply sign up on an attendance sheet and wait for their turn. The audience is generally made up of other open mic'ers waiting for their chance to perform and musicians who are there just to listen. I found my first gig in Los Angeles while performing with a visiting singer/songwriter friend on the Open Mic circuit. A guitarist/vocalist approached me after the set and invited me to jam with his band. On another occasion, I was in the audience at an Open Mic with a drummer friend and a talented singer/songwriter finished his song and announced he was looking for a rhythm section. My friend and I approached him when he left the stage, and we were jamming two days later.

After scouring the local club scene and printed classified ads, visiting local music stores, rehearsal studios and schools, and effectively using the Internet, musicians and bandleaders will have successfully distributed their message and also have plenty of leads to flush out.

RESPONDING TO ADS

Now that you've created and circulated your ad throughout your scene and identified bands and musicians that meet your needs, you've got to prepare to respond to musicians contacting you as well as prepare questions for those whom you'll contact. Once you've communicated with interested musicians, and both parties feel there's a chance their musical priorities can be met, you can then agree to schedule an audition.

Preparing and Anticipating Questions

Musicians and bands rarely reach the audition phase without first going through a question-and-answer (Q&A) session. Auditions take a great deal of time and effort, and there's no point in going through one without believing that a musician or band meets specific predetermined criteria. This Q&A is a preaudition screening process, where parties ask questions, exchange ideas, and weed out candidates who are not good fits. Bandleader Ted Heath says, "When musicians respond to my ad for players, I prescreen them over the phone. I can usually eliminate people who don't have the same interests and aren't of the same caliber of what I'm looking for pretty quickly." As a musician, bandleader, or band contact, your goal is to successfully navigate this Q&A session. To do this, you need to prepare questions to ask as well as to anticipate those you'll receive so that you can plan your response to them in advance or, even better, address them before they are asked.

There are two types of questions musicians and bands ask each other during the screening process: priority questions and insight questions. Priority questions are based on your individual priorities. For you to consider an audition, you'll need answers compatible with your goals. If one of your priorities is, "I want to join a band that pays me for rehearsals," then one of your questions will be, "Do you pay musicians for rehearsal time?" If the answer is "No," then you move on to the next intriguing ad on your list and hope for a better match. If the answer is "Yes," then this band is still in the running for your services, and you can continue down your list of questions.

Continuing with Moe and Funky Minnow as examples, here are priority questions each party will need answered before committing to an audition. Moe's priority questions are as follows:

1. Is music the number-one priority in the lives of the band members?
2. Does your band play original music?
3. Would I be able to collaborate with the songwriters and play some of my original songs?
4. How often does the band rehearse?
5. How are band expenses divided? Is everything equally split?

Now, here are the priority questions Funky Minnow would ask:

1. Is music your number-one priority?
2. Are you an experienced funk bass player?

3. Are you available to rehearse three times per week?

4. Are you available for at least two gigs per month?

5. Funky Minnow makes all decisions as a band. Are you prepared to join a group that operates democratically?

6. We split all costs (rehearsal studio, recording, marketing, etc.) and duties equally. Are you prepared to contribute your share to the band?

Once you've addressed these minimum requirements with your priority questions, you can then ask more insightful questions. These questions tend to address the personality, experiences, and expectations of the musician or band members. The response to an insight question will provide you with a clearer picture of the situation and might impact your decision to audition, though probably not to the same extent as a priority question, which are usually deal-breakers if not answered to your satisfaction. An example of an insight question from a band interested in auditioning a musician is, "Why did you leave your last band?" (The equivalent for a musician questioning a band is, "Why did your last singer leave the band?") If the answer is, "Because they were a bunch of stupid jerks," you may be on the verge of inviting an attitude problem to audition. If the answer is, "Because I was more interested in playing rock than metal," and you are representing a rock band, you'll feel much better about inviting this person for a tryout. Other insight questions include:

- *Is the band looking to fill other vacancies?* The answer to this question can provide insight into the status of the band. A group with multiple open spots will have a lot of work to do before it's ready to perform, because it takes time to acclimate new members. If you're ready to hop on the ground floor of a band and work as a group, learning or writing songs and establishing yourselves on the scene, then this is a good situation for you. If you want to perform right away, this may be a project to decline. The answer might also provide you with a clue as to how volatile the band is, because constant turnover can be a result of difficult band members.

- *How long has the band been playing together?* This answer hints at the chemistry among the existing members. A band that has played together for some time is likely comprised of members that get along well and share common goals. They may also already be performing and have a competent marketing machine in place, which could save you time if you want to perform as soon as possible. On the other hand, as addressed in the previous question, newly formed bands take time to build camaraderie and land shows, but starting from the ground up may be ideal for players who want to join something fresh without any preexisting baggage.

- *What musical experience does the musician or band members have?* The answer to this question will matter to players who want to play with musicians of a similar skill level. If you're a seasoned musician with plenty of performing experience, you'll want to know that the members of the band aren't novices. Conversely, if you're a beginning player, you might not want to play in a band of advanced musicians since they are beyond your level of musicianship, leaving you struggling to perform to their level.

- *Are you, or the members of the band, students or working (part-time, full-time)?* Asking what musicians and band members do for their livelihoods may provide an understanding as to the availability of players for rehearsals and shows. If a member of the group is a stockbroker, then it's safe to say that late-night rehearsals and gigs might not be an option since he or she has to be up with the market each morning. If members are in school, they may not be able to shoulder an equal share of band expenses if they aren't also working. If you want to join a band where everyone covers an equal share, this can become an issue, or the band may settle for doing everything on a very low budget, which also may be a problem.

- *Is the musician, or are band members, currently playing in any other projects?* This answer may be very relevant. Some bands are protective, not wanting their members to play side projects due to potential time and scheduling conflicts that arise from being otherwise committed. If you're playing with other bands, you'll need to be sure everyone in this particular project is okay with this. On the other hand, some musicians want to join projects where the members are in other bands because this gives them the space they need to pursue other musical interests.

Once you've established your questions, you can turn your attention to anticipating what questions you may be asked by interested bands and musicians. You already know your musical priorities, and can address them with ease, but to separate yourself from other responders you need to anticipate other questions so you can address them, possibly even before they are asked of you, leading the band to believe that you're the right person for their project before the audition even begins. To do this, you need to understand the subtext of the ad and get a jump on it. For instance, if you pick up on the possibility that a band you're interested in joining is looking for someone to participate in the songwriting process and you tell them that you want to help write the group's original material before they ask, they're going to feel as though you're on their same wavelength.

To figure out the subtext of a message, look and listen for key phrases such as:

- *No flakes.* This likely means that either the band or some of its members have had bad experiences with irresponsible musicians. Address this in advance by talking about how you were in charge of your last band's booking calendar, or by simply stating that you are someone the band can count on because you know succeeding in music takes hard work and dedication.
- *No attitude.* When a band lists "no attitude" in their ad, it's reasonable to assume they have had personality difficulties with past players and perhaps had to fire someone for this reason. You can take advantage of this by alluding to your positive traits, saying something like, "Hey, I'm an easy-going guy who likes to not only work hard, but also likes to have fun and laugh."
- *Reliable gear and transportation.* This often means that the band or some of its members have played with musicians whose equipment consistently malfunctioned or had difficulty getting to rehearsals and shows. To allay their fears, mention what musical equipment you use (musicians love to talk about gear!), that you have reliable transportation, and that you're always on time for rehearsals and shows.

- *Has upcoming shows.* If a band's ad notes that it has upcoming shows, they are probably concerned with finding a member soon so as to avoid having to cancel dates or to hire a substitute player. Bands with gigs on their calendar also cannot afford to wait for musicians who are slow learners. To negate this worry, mention that you're a quick study who can jump right into a band and master their repertoire quickly.

- *Have label and management interest.* Many bands' ads include the fact that record labels and management companies have an interest in the group, meaning the band thinks it's ready to become a professional operation and possibly tour. You can address this by affirming your dedication to music and your willingness to help take the band to the next level.

- *Experience in the genre.* Bands and musicians that want to play a specific genre of music want to play with people who understand how to pull off the style. In your response, convince the group you have musical credibility in the genre by mentioning a band or musician in the genre that inspires you. If you're a drummer interested in a progressive rock band you might talk about Danny Carey from the band Tool, and how he got you interested in odd time signatures. You also can address techniques of the genre to demonstrate your knowledge. A guitarist who wants to audition for a jazz gig with a 300-song repertoire can highlight his or her sight-reading abilities.

Using the above examples, here's how Moe and Funky Minnow would break down the subtext for each other's messages for their responses.

Moe would zero in on the following aspects of Funky Minnow's ad and try to proactively address them in his communication with the band:

Four-piece funk band, Funky Minnow, seeks a talented 20-something-year-old bassist with great attitude to join us. Bassist should have reliable gear and transportation and be committed to the success of the band. We have upcoming bookings.

Likewise, Funky Minnow would highlight the following from Moe's flyer and inquire further to determine if he would be a good match for their band:

> Twenty-six-year-old funky bassist with reliable gear and transportation seeking an ambitious and original gigging project.

Determining How to Respond to an Ad and Deciding Whether to Audition

You can respond to an ad for a musician or a band either in writing or orally. Each method has certain advantages and disadvantages. Written responses, usually in e-mail form, are beneficial to you, the responder, because they offer the opportunity to deliberately tailor your communication in the ways previously shown in this chapter, without having to respond off the cuff, which, if it's not your strength, can be a drawback to communicating live. Plus, while writing also may restrict your interaction, since you can't ask or answer any questions in real-time, you won't get stumped or tongue-tied, either. The problem with e-mail communication, however, is that it slows the process, and usually you'll wait hours or even days for responses. In addition, if you only correspond via e-mail you run the risk of being skipped over by a band or musician with an urgent need.

Live communication not only gives you a chance to interact and quickly gain information but allows you to get a gut feeling for the band or musician as well. Paul McDonald says, "Some people can talk up their gig over e-mail but cannot keep up the charade of a bad gig in person or over the phone. You can usually tell a lot about the project just by talking, including whether he or she is serious or a waste of time."

Los Angeles–based guitarist David Wood agrees. "It's best to talk with people over the phone before the audition, and get a few major questions out of the way. What kind of music do they listen to (and want to play), do they have time to commit to one or two nights a week (or more), etc. You also want to make sure that you feel comfortable with the person. If not, forget it."

The best way to respond to an ad is to reply in whichever method the musician or band placing the ad offers: e-mail or phone. Many times, bands and musicians only list one method, in which case you've got no choice but to follow that direction. If you have a choice, though, check to see whether the ad recommends a method. For instance, bands that find my ad on my paid online service can read that I prefer to be contacted by e-mail even though my phone number is listed too. If an ad doesn't state a preference, go with the method you prefer.

Here's a sample written response from bassist Moe to Funky Minnow:

Hello! My name is Moe, and I'm responding to your ad placed on MusiciansContact.com for a bassist for Funky Minnow. I'm 26 years old and have been playing bass guitar for five years. My ideal opportunity is with a hip and talented band with cool people where I can provide a steady groove and have the opportunity to step out and shine as a player. I'm an easy-going guy who likes to have fun, yet takes a lot of pride in my playing and professionalism. I'm also a quick study with a good ear. I can be ready to play those future bookings in no time.

Currently I play a Music Man Stingray Bass through a Gallien-Krueger 400RB combo amp. It has plenty of power, can fill a small room on its own, and has a direct out to connect to a PA for larger venues. I've got a great funky, low-end tone that really complements the kick drum. Moreover, if necessary, the bass's onboard equalizer can add a top-shelf frequency range that really cuts through the mix. Overall, I'm very flexible with my sound. I just like to find my pocket within the band's dynamic range and work that frequency.

Musically, I'm influenced by the Red Hot Chili Peppers, Tower of Power, Funkadelic, and James Brown, and I have learned much of their material note-for-note. I've got experience in the funk genre and have played in two funk bands that have had some success: one original band and one cover band.

I own my own car and am available for an audition at your convenience. Just let me know when, where, and what time. Thanks for your time, and I look forward to hearing from you soon.

Sincerely,
Moe
moe2u@e-mail.com
303-555-5555

Now here's an e-mail response from band contact Tracy to Moe's e-mail to Funky Minnow:

Hi Moe:

Thank you for answering our ad for a bass player.

I want to let you know exactly what Funky Minnow is looking for so you can determine if this is something you would still like to pursue.

Funky Minnow has been together for just over two years and is finally beginning to crack the regular rotations at some of the better local clubs. We have a small but loyal fan base that loves us for our great live shows. The whole band is committed to making music work on a grand scale. We want to be huge.

We are looking for a bass player who wants to be part of a fun yet hardworking situation. Funky Minnow needs someone who can really groove onstage, and do his or her fair share of what it takes to succeed on the business end as well. We rehearse twice during the week and once on the weekends, if we don't have a gig.

If this sounds like a situation you would be interested in, please call me at (303) 555-7777 on Monday. I prefer to hear from you by phone so we can get to know each other and discuss a possible audition. We have a gig September 3, so we are eager to find our next bassist soon and move forward to meet our goals. From your e-mail, you sound like a cool guy who could really fit in with us. I know the band is looking forward to jamming with you.

Best,
Tracy

In this scenario, bassist Moe received a detailed e-mail in return with explicit follow-up instructions. This is not always the case. Often, responses simply state the bare minimum for the next step. Here's an example:

Moe—Got your e-mail. Sounds good. We're holding auditions Friday at Sonic Studios, 123 Maple. We'll be in room #11 at 5 PM. Bring your gear.

In this example, there's very little information available to Moe and seemingly no opportunity to follow up with any additional questions. In such instances, you've got to decide whether the information provided is sufficient for you to commit to the audition. If not, respond to the band or musician by asking for more information about their goals to assure a match. If they don't get back to you, don't lose any sleep over it. You don't want to play with people who don't respect the importance of your decision to join or form a band anyway.

Here's the beginning of a sample call from Moe to Funky Minnow:

Moe:	Hello. My name is Moe, and I am a bassist responding to your ad placed in the Recycler for a bass player for Funky Minnow.
Tracy with Funky Minnow:	Hi Moe. Thanks for the inquiry. Let me give you some more information about Funky Minnow and let you know exactly what we are looking for in a bassist . . .

63

After this opening exchange they go through their priority and insight questions.

If their roles were reversed and Tracy were calling Moe in regard to his ad as an available musician, the phone call might begin as follows:

> Tracy:
>
> *Hello, this is Tracy from Funky Minnow. I'm responding to your ad as an available bassist. I'm hoping we can chat so I can learn more about what you're looking for in a band and let you know what our band is all about.*

> Moe:
>
> *Hi, Tracy. Thanks for contacting me. Let me start off by letting you know what I'm looking for right now . . .*

When responding to an ad, it's important to try to make a personal connection, so both parties feel invested in the outcome. You not only want to come across as cool and natural but also like you want to play with the musician or band. As a bandleader for an original funk project who was fielding calls for new drummers, I once spent twenty minutes chatting with a prospective player because of his people skills. By the time we were done talking, I was practically ready to offer him the gig! I ended up giving him the audition slot of his choice and then bragging about him to the rest of the band. Before he even walked through the door and performed, he was the front-runner for the spot in the band.

Deciding whether to accept or reject a musician or band's audition request is the final stage of responding to an ad. Ultimately, your decision is based on whether you believe the band or musician meets your musical needs.

If you reject an offer, be honest about where the gaps between your priorities and the group or individual's lie, and cite this as your reason for moving on. Musicians and bands understand that not every person or situation is compatible, and if your reason for rejecting an audition is based on a minimum requirement, there really isn't any point in trying to change your mind. For instance, if you're a band seeking a singer for weekend performances, you might tell your vocalist candidate, who works bartending shifts on the weekends, that you're looking for someone with a more compatible schedule. This reasoning is very clear, and both the singer and the band should agree. When everyone decides it's not a good match, they can amicably move on to their next options.

Rejecting a musician or band becomes more complicated when there are no easy outs like scheduling conflicts or other priority differences. In these cases, even if you think the musician or band is irresponsible or untalented, just apologize and say you've found a better match elsewhere, even if you haven't yet. There's no need for confrontation with someone you don't intend to play with and that you may run into at some point in the future.

If you're open and respectful (even if secretly deceptive to spare their feelings), you should be able to retain the band or musician as a networking contact for the future. This is wise, since in the music industry you never know when you'll cross paths with someone again. I once rejected a candidate who was interested in joining a Motown tribute band I was putting together because he said he had four other bands going at the same time, and I didn't feel he could dedicate the necessary time to my project. He understood and didn't take it personally, and a month later he called me back to audition for his Steely Dan tribute band.

Here's an example of a message Moe will reject for not meeting his priorities:

Moe,

My name is Vaughn, and I'm the bandleader for a 1970s tribute band named Booty Call. We have a regular Saturday night gig at Club 707 and are looking for a groovy bassist who can make the booties move on the dance floor.

Give me a call at (303) 555-8888 or e-mail me at 70sluv@e-mail.com if you would like more information. I'm hoping to have a bass player ready to play live by the end of the month.

Here's an example of Moe's return e-mail to Vaughn of Booty Call:

Vaughn,

Thank you so much for your interest in me for your band.

Unfortunately, I don't think we would make a good match, since I'm looking to join an original band. As much as I love covering old-school 1970s funk during my practice time at home, I don't think I can give up my Saturday nights and expect to be able to join the type of original project I'm looking for.

Best of luck in your search, and I'm looking forward to checking out Booty Call when I have a free Saturday!

Moe

Even when you know you aren't interested in a band or musician, take the time to get back to them with your intentions. It's discouraging for musicians to be left waiting for a response after they've initiated contact, especially via e-mail where the act of replying takes about twenty seconds. Musicians and bands should be respectful of people's time and energy and be courteous enough to reply politely to all inquiries.

Here's an example of a live interaction where a band rejects a musician who's apparently not well versed in their style of music:

Musician: *This sounds like a great gig. Are you scheduling auditions? If so, I'd really like to come in.*

Band: *We really appreciate your enthusiasm and interest. Unfortunately, we're looking for someone with a more established background in our genre of music. Thanks a lot for talking with me, and good luck in the future.*

Before accepting an offer to audition, musicians and bands should review their priorities one final time to ensure they are compatible. If they feel the group or player is a suitable match, then they offer to either host or participate in an audition.

Here's an example of an accepted offer:

Tracy: *Moe, thank you so much for talking with me on the phone today. You sound like what we're looking for in a bass player and bandmate. We'd like to schedule you for an audition.*

Moe: *Great! I'm very excited to play with the group. I think I can really add a lot to the project. I'm available at your convenience to come in to jam.*

When an audition opportunity is accepted, the band needs to establish when and where "the audition" will take place and what material will be covered, as well as any other information pertinent to the audition. Then, musicians and bands need to prepare for their performance and, hopefully, add a new member to help them meet their goals.

CHAPTER 4

AUDITIONING MUSICIANS FOR YOUR BAND OR AUDITIONING TO JOIN A BAND

Auditions are opportunities for musicians to demonstrate their talents and provide a sense of how they'd mesh with other musicians as they seek to form or join a compatible band. There are no second chances in auditioning. First impressions are everything, and making a good first impression requires preparation. Once you're ready for an audition, you need to act in a manner that shows the musicians auditioning for your band, or the band you're auditioning for, that this is the right opportunity for them.

Every musician in a band has at least two essential responsibilities: performing the music correctly and adhering to the group's priorities. When irresponsible members let tempos go awry, allow harmonies to slip off-key, or show up chronically late for rehearsals, the entire band suffers and the committed musicians in the group are left wondering why they tolerate those who seemingly don't care or just don't have the talent to keep up. These bands never fulfill their potential and often end up disillusioned, disheartened, and frustrated. Eventually, they break up and their members move on to other groups.

To avoid playing out this ill-fated scenario, you can use the audition process as a preview of your potential band, gauging the talents and attitudes of either musicians or bands to determine if they're the right choice to help you reach your musical goals. There's no guarantee the audition will reveal that the musicians or bands lack talent or have attitude problems—these may manifest themselves later—but after going through the audition process, you'll have a realistic experience on which to base your decision as to whether to form or join a band with these musicians.

PREPARING FOR THE AUDITION

To get ready for an audition, you or your band need to prepare a flawless performance that can be executed effortlessly. In this way, you can turn your focus to what the prospective musician or group is doing. If you aren't prepared, you risk not only leaving an irreversibly unfavorable impression but also missing out on the nuances of the audition because you're too busy struggling through the songs to really pay any attention to anything else. To get to the point of total preparedness, you, or your band, need to do your part. For the band, this means establishing and then relaying the parameters of the audition so the musician or musicians have the information they need to excel. For the musician, this means understanding the parameters and adhering to them. Once musicians and bands are on the same page, they can rehearse for the audition.

Establishing Audition Parameters

Before an audition can be set up, parameters need to be determined and confirmed. Since the band hosts the audition, it's up to them to determine these parameters and clearly communicate them to auditioning musicians so they show up at the same place, at the same time, to perform the same songs as the band. It's up to the auditioning musician to determine whether the parameters of the audition are acceptable so that he or she can then confirm the engagement and begin to prepare.

Audition parameters generally consist of the following:

- Audition date and time
- Equipment musicians need to bring to the audition

- Location of the audition
- Any specific load-in instructions to access the audition location
- Material musicians need to perform at the audition

To set the date and time of the audition, the following four variables need to be considered: what dates and times work for the band, the availability of the rehearsal studio, how long the audition will take, and the availability of auditioning musicians.

Your first step in determining potential audition dates and times is establishing a consensus among your bandmates and securing an audition location. Begin by contacting everyone in the band and suggesting a number of dates and times for auditions. You might ask, "Can you be available to audition musicians on August 10, 11, 12, and 13 from 6 PM to 11 PM?" Once you have several dates agreed upon, you'll be able to contact the auditioning musicians and settle on a date to hold the audition. Be sure to hold your auditions no more than two weeks from the time you contact interested musicians. Any more than two weeks and you risk losing potential bandmates to other projects. I've been in bands that dragged their feet, only to find that when they finally got around to bringing musicians in, those players had already found other bands to join. The sort of musicians you want in your band—players who are talented and responsible—aren't going to wait weeks for bands to schedule auditions.

To determine the location of your audition, consider your current rehearsal space. If you have daily access it's likely you won't have audition scheduling issues, because you either own or lease your space exclusively and can jam there whenever you like. But if your band shares a space with other bands, or with nonmusical businesses, you need to coordinate potential audition times with the other people in your space to avoid scheduling conflicts. Bands that rent rehearsal space by the hour in rehearsal studio facilities need to arrange audition times with the manager of the facility to ensure they can have a room at the desired times. Book the room as soon as you have your audition dates nailed.

Now that you have a location and potential dates and times set, you need to establish how much audition time to give musicians. To do this, you've got to factor in everything you want to accomplish during the audition and estimate its duration. This can include the time it takes for auditioners to set up and tear down their equipment (if you want them to bring their own gear), to perform your songs, and to interview. Be liberal when setting the time. If you want your auditioning musicians to play four five-minute songs, instead of allowing twenty minutes, plan for twenty-five minutes of performance time to give yourself a cushion in case you want to start a song over or repeat a section of the tune. Don't just set aside twenty minutes and assume you'll be able to play the songs you want to cover and to thoroughly interview each musician. Twenty minutes may feel like an eternity when you're stuck in traffic, but when auditioning it can fly by because of seemingly inconsequential things you didn't plan on. Errors in a song that must be addressed with a repeat performance, small talk between musicians, equipment malfunctions, or an out-of-tune guitar that needs attention consume time.

If you don't properly estimate audition time, you run the risk of failing to accomplish everything you want or running overtime with an audition, which delays everyone scheduled afterward. If this happens you won't be able to properly evaluate the musician because he can't do what you've expected in the time he now has. In addition, you'll have unhappy musicians waiting outside the studio for their turn, thinking that your band isn't well organized. When you build extra time into each musician's audition, you avoid this pitfall. The worst thing that can then happen is you finish with an auditioning musician a little bit early and have extra time to review the performance with the rest of the group.

Here's a sample audition schedule with extra time built into each item:

- Player sets up equipment (set up amps, tune guitars, etc.): ten minutes—should take five minutes
- Play through four four-minute songs: twenty minutes—should take sixteen minutes

- Read through two musical charts for four-minute songs: ten minutes—should take eight minutes
- Interview musician, three band members ask two questions each: ten minutes—should take six minutes
- Remove equipment: ten minutes—should take five minutes

Total audition time for one player is sixty minutes.

When you schedule multiple musicians for their audition on the same day, don't line them up one after the other without any time between auditions (first player at 6 PM, second player at 7 PM, etc.). Doing so may result in some overlap if you get behind schedule. You'll also want some time to discuss their performances with other members of the band while they're still fresh. Plus, auditioning musicians are in direct competition so it may be uncomfortable for them to pass each other outside the rehearsal space, or to have one musician set up while another is removing his or her equipment. Using the above audition schedule as the example, a band would be wise to schedule auditions for four players at 6 PM, 7:20 PM, 8:40 PM, and 10 PM. That extra twenty minutes can come in handy if the band wants to replay any of the material or ask more questions.

The final step in establishing the date and time of your auditions is to confirm auditioning musicians. You'll need to offer them the multiple dates you've identified to work around any potential scheduling conflicts. If your band has a rigid audition schedule, you may miss out on desirable musicians that can't make your proposed date and time because of school, work, or other unbreakable engagements. If you have a sufficient talent pool of candidates from which to choose, this may not be a concern. But, if you want to give all potential candidates a shot at auditioning, you'll need to be flexible.

Now that you've set a date and time, you need to determine what equipment they'll need for the audition. If you find you're short on time for auditioning musicians, you may choose to provide the necessary equipment so they don't have to bring their own gear. This can save you ten or more minutes of set-up and tear-down time per audition. If you plan on allowing the musicians to use your equipment, be sure to have gear that works properly, sounds good, and isn't falling apart. If you provide a drum kit with a rusty kick-drum pedal for auditioning drummers, you may think every drummer you've auditioned has bad time, when in reality it's the gear you've provided. Auditioning musicians on bad gear prevents you from getting an accurate representation of their talent; they'll be too busy coaxing an adequate sound out of it instead of concentrating on performance.

If you're providing the large gear like amps, keyboards, and drum kits, you may choose to allow auditioning musicians to bring some small pieces of gear that don't take much set-up time to augment your equipment so they are able to get a sound they're used to. A guitarist might bring his or her own effects or pedal board to run through the Marshall half-stack you're providing. A drummer might bring his or her own cymbals or pedals to use with your drum kit. This can help their per-formance because they can find their comfort zone and give you a better idea of what they will sound like with their own equipment. When I go to an audition where I can bring supplemental gear, I bring a D.I. (direct input) pedal with an equalizer (EQ) that can shape my sound so I'm not limited to just using the amp. This way I can get my tone and sound pretty close to how I would if I were auditioning with my own gear.

Many bands will insist that musicians bring all of their own equipment because, as mentioned in Chapter 1, they're not only auditioning the musician but also the musi-cian's equipment. Bands may want to be absolutely sure that musicians have the proper gear to get the kind of sounds they feel will fit the group. Bandleader Paul Mitchell says, "When I'm running an audition, I expect players to bring their own gear. I want to know what gear they have, because that factors into my final decision."

When you provide the audition location and directions to musicians, be precise so they can plan on arriving at the right place on time. Give the exact address, provide directions from their general vicinity, and, if necessary, encourage them to use Yahoo! Maps or www.mapquest.com to be certain they know where they're going. If you're holding auditions in a rehearsal studio that has multiple locations, be clear about which one you're using. In Los Angeles, there is a rehearsal studio chain called Sound Arena. There are two Sound Arenas within a few miles of each other in Van Nuys and Sherman Oaks, making it easy to confuse the two studios. I've auditioned musicians at these facilities and have heard plenty of them explain their lateness by claiming they ended up at the opposite Sound Arena.

You've also got to be able to provide musicians with load-in instructions, whether the audition is going to be at a studio or in your garage or basement. These instructions should include information on parking, gaining entry, and locating the room. For musicians coming to your studio or home for the first time, finding it may be complicated. To help keep them from getting lost, walk them through every step, from parking their car to getting to your door.

Parking conditions vary depending on the location. While larger professional studio facilities have onsite parking, others don't. Ones that do have parking may require a keycard or code to access it. If you're holding auditions in your home, musicians may be able to park in your driveway or garage, or they may have to find a space on the street, which may prove difficult if you live in a city like San Francisco or New York, where parking spaces are at a premium.

Parking conditions are especially important to musicians transporting heavy equipment to an audition. If they can pull right up to a home or a professional rehearsal studio, they'll probably only have to carry gear a few yards, which is a relief for a drummer bringing his kit. But if they have to park on the street, far from the studio, they could end up dragging their equipment for blocks. If your rehearsal location doesn't have an accommodating parking situation, be sure to warn musicians so they can arrive with plenty of time to spare to search for a parking space. Or, offer to meet them in front of the facility, help them unload their equipment, and guard it while they park. Then, have them meet you back in front of the audition space.

Once you've told auditioning musicians where to park, explain how to get to the rehearsal space. If your rehearsal studio requires a keycard or access code to gain entry to the parking lot, coordinate with musicians to help them get inside the space. Professional rehearsal studios can be tough to access, but home rehearsal spaces can be equally complicated if they have a difficult space to navigate. If your band practices in your attic, and it's only accessible through the side door on the garage—after which you need to climb a flight of winding stairs—you'd better explain this to auditioning musicians in advance in order to avoid confusion and delay.

In addition, you may choose to add some protocols to the load-in instructions for musicians to follow before entering the rehearsal space. This can be helpful for bands that want to run their audition session to the letter. Here are some examples:

- Wait by the entrance until you're let in. Do not knock. We'll let you in when we are ready.
- If you're more than twenty minutes late, don't bother coming at all.
- Make sure your bass is tuned up and ready to plug into our amp before you come in.

Putting it all together, here's an example of some load-in instructions for an auditioning musician to get inside a rehearsal studio in a professional facility:

- Park in the lot downstairs. The vehicle gate is always open.
- Once you park, go to the loading dock and use the intercom on the right of the door to contact us. Our number is #2332. Use the keypad to input our number. The in-studio phone will ring so we can buzz you in.
- There is a freight elevator to your right after you come through the door. Take it to the 2nd floor.
- Once you reach our room (#2332), knock on the door, and we'll let you in.

Here are instructions for an audition at a private residence:

- You can park on the street outside my house.
- Once you park, bring your gear through the black gate in front of the garage and wait by the front door. I'll have a sign posted on the door that reads "Auditions."

- Once you're there, don't knock. We'll be in the middle of auditions and won't be able to hear you. We'll let you in as soon as we are done with the preceding audition.

Finally, once you've outlined all of the logistics, you need to tell the musicians what songs to learn for the audition. Most auditions require a musician to learn anywhere from two to five songs, just enough for the band to determine whether the musician can fit in musically with the group but not so much that the musician can't learn them all prior to an audition a week away (or so much that the musician might balk at committing to learn an inordinate amount of songs when there is a chance he or she won't be invited to join the band).

When establishing the songs you want musicians to learn for the audition, pick tunes from your set list that challenge the auditioning musician. This helps highlight the players who can handle the more technically difficult songs and allows you to weed out the ones who can't rise to the occasion. If you're in a rock cover band auditioning guitar players, pick a song from your repertoire that's technically difficult for guitarists, like Hendrix's "Voodoo Chile" as opposed to the Troggs' three-chord classic, "Wild Thing," which even mediocre guitarists can cover with ease.

Once you decide on the songs to cover for the audition, you need to deliver them to the musicians. You can do this by sending a CD in the mail, e-mailing an audio file, or directing the musicians to your site to download the file. Mailing materials is riskier, because they can get lost or damaged—forcing you to resend them—while MP3s can be e-mailed or downloaded without these potential problems. If you plan on mailing materials, be clear about when the package should arrive and ask the musicians to confirm receipt. The last thing you want to happen is for an auditioning musician to contact you the day before an audition and ask where the music is.

If you're auditioning musicians for your jam band that improvises its music or for your band that requires its musicians to sight-read from charts, you won't need to provide any music. Just tell the auditioning musicians what genre of band you are and tell them to bring their creativity and sight-reading chops.

As a musician auditioning for a band, it's difficult to alter the parameters of the audition, because most of the items are nonnegotiable. The audition is going to be at the location the band chooses, covering the songs the band wants to play, and you'll have to bring, or not bring, your equipment, depending on how the group is conducting the auditions. Once the band gives you the key information about the audition, you can either accept it or try to work out alternatives.

Two items you might be able to influence are the date of your audition and your time slot on that day. As we discussed, it's likely the band has built some flexibility into their audition schedule to accommodate musicians with conflicts. If this is the case, you may be able to secure a date that better fits your schedule. Don't be demanding when you ask for a change of date. The band has very little invested in you at this point and will easily dismiss you as an option if they interpret your scheduling issue as a lack of commitment. If the band is unable to meet your request, you'll either have to decline the audition or rearrange your priorities.

If the band offers you a choice for your time slot, pick one that puts you in the best possible position to land a spot in the band. Some musicians feel that spot is last, because the band has a fresh impression of you when their audition process ends. Personally, I like to audition first, while the band is still energized. I've found that as auditions proceed, the band tends to get bored with their parts and noodle off on their instruments rather than give each time slot the benefit of their best performances. If you audition first, you have a chance to set the bar for every musician following you as well. Keyboardist Matt Rhode says, "I always try to schedule myself in the first available audition slot on the last day of the auditions. This way I have time to bring my own gear and set it up, so I am not stuck playing on the same crappy rental gear as everyone else. And being heard on the last day lets your performance stay fresh in everyone's memory."

Once auditioning musicians and bands have all of the information they need to conduct the audition, they confirm all of the audition parameters so there's no uncertainty. Any error or miscommunication will throw the band off schedule and could cost a musician a shot at joining the group. Once you've repeated all of the information, it's time for you or your band to start preparing for the audition.

Preparing Your Band for the Audition

To find the musician who's the best suited for your band, you need to set up an audition process that is identical for everyone so player comparisons are on equal terms. Have the auditioning musicians perform the same songs. If they audition playing different songs, it's harder to determine who's the better musician for the band, because you can't compare performances of different songs. In addition, ask the same interview questions. You can't compare a musician who said that he's willing to do a regional tour with one who didn't have a chance to field the same question.

Also, make sure your band knows its own material. It's hard to accurately judge, or make comparisons among, auditioning musicians when the band makes mistakes on its own songs. This causes auditioning musicians to make mistakes as well as they try to figure out what you're doing differently from the recording they received. You've got to provide the same correct and consistent musical backdrop for every auditioning musician so you can accurately compare everyone and make the best possible decision as to who to invite to join the band.

A band that doesn't know its own songs can leave a terrible impression on an audition candidate as well. I've been to several auditions where the band wasn't prepared to play its own material. It's very awkward to play with bands like this. Not only does it defeat the purpose of the audition, but when it happens everyone knows whose fault it is, and that's got to be disconcerting for the group. I participated in one audition where I was the only one in the group who could play through the audition songs. I could tell the band was humiliated by the experience by the way they hung their heads during the botched performances. After the audition, they called me and asked me to join. I declined. At that stage in my music career,

I saw no point in joining a group that lacked the discipline to correctly learn and perform its own material. Your band must know its material before the audition begins if they're going to make a positive impression and convey to candidates that the group is worth joining.

In addition to knowing their own parts, bands auditioning players must know the auditioning instrument's part. This knowledge doesn't have to extend to being able to perform that part on that particular instrument (or another instrument), but someone in the band must be intimately familiar with the auditioning player's part in order to determine the accuracy of the performance. Repeated listening to the part on a recording can achieve this level of understanding.

In bandleader-driven bands, the responsibility of learning the auditioning musician's part falls on the group leader. In democratic bands, a member must step up to be accountable for developing this knowledge of another instrument's part. Since some instruments tend to relate to other instruments, the job is easier for certain musicians. Because bass and drums frequently intertwine, bassists will memorize drum parts to help perform their own parts and vice versa. Guitar and keyboards also correspond, as do keyboards and bass, or keyboards and horns (keyboards match most every tonal instrument, since they have a wide frequency spectrum). Each band member can tell if the auditioning player sounds good with the group, but one member of the band should step forward to keep tabs on the technical details of the auditioning musician's performance.

If you're planning to conduct an interview as part of the audition, you need to prepare your questions in advance. These questions should be based on your priorities discussed in Chapters 2 and 3. If you've already covered your key priority questions (like those concerning style, commitment level, and transportation) during the communication in which you offer the audition, then you can skip the interview, ask other questions you feel are relevant to your band, or repeat every question you initially asked to ensure the responses are the same. This will be the last chance you have to ask auditioning musicians questions, so be sure to get all of the information you need.

It's up to your band to determine how it wishes to ask the questions. Democratic bands may decide to have one member of the group conduct the interview, or members may take turns asking questions. In these instances, it's helpful for each player to ask a predetermined question to avoid a free-for-all atmosphere that consumes too much time. If there's a bandleader running the group, he or she will run the interview and may decide to ask the questions in private, after the performance part of the audition, or invite the entire group to join in if the bandleader believes their input is needed. Interviewing in private is wise if there are questions that may be confidential, such as ones related to compensation, or that don't require the involvement of all band members.

When the band is ready to perform audition material and interview questions are ready, you want to physically prepare the rehearsal space for the auditions so the incoming musicians can easily load in, set up, and load out. If you're requiring them to bring their own equipment, clear a path so they don't have to carry their gear around, or over, your amps, mic stands, and cables. Have an open space for their equipment and an electrical power strip ready as well so they don't have to waste time searching for multiple wall power receptacles for their gear.

Finally, reconnect with the auditioning musicians in the days before the audition to confirm that they're coming, and know when and where they're expected and what they're playing. Keep it simple. There's no need to interview the candidate; you just need to repeat the specifics. It can be as brief and straightforward as "Hello, Jimmy. Just calling to confirm the audition tomorrow at 7 PM at our home studio at 1111 Maple Street. We look forward to hearing you play the songs from our demo CD." Once the candidate confirms, end the communication. Now you're ready to host the auditions.

Preparing Yourself for the Audition

Once auditioning musicians receive the songs the band is asking them to learn for the audition, they listen to them to be certain the music matches what they want to play. This is a crucial step for you, because if the music does not live up to your expectations—for example, if the music isn't the style you thought it was, or it's clear by the performances on the recording that the talent level of the musicians in the band is lacking—you'll have to contact the band and let them know you're no longer interested in auditioning. Here's an example rejection e-mail to the band from a vocalist who didn't think the band's music fit his goals.

Dear Jane,

I received your disc in the mail today. Thank you for sending it so promptly. I enjoyed the music, but it is not exactly what I am looking for right now. I do appreciate your time and consideration. Good luck in your search for a vocalist.

Mark

If the band's music meets your expectations, then you'll need to learn the songs for your audition. The first step is thoroughly listening to the songs. If you listen to them constantly—in the shower, while driving, exercising, at work—you'll find they become intuitive and you'll be able to recall them with ease during the learning process as well as the audition. Once you know your audition songs' key changes, lyrics, and dynamics as well as you can recall those of a common tune like "Wild Thing" or "Jingle Bells," you've listened well enough and won't make any major errors when you perform them for the band.

Once you've listened to the songs, you need to learn your parts. If you have a good ear, you shouldn't have any problem picking out your instrument or vocals and mastering it. If your ear isn't very refined, learning the tunes can be a greater challenge since you won't be able to hear what you're supposed to play. This could put you at a disadvantage compared with the auditioning musicians with good ears, so you'll need to find a way to overcome this hurdle.

You can begin by asking for help from a musical friend or teacher that has a good ear and can pick out your part. Don't be embarrassed to ask for assistance.

Even professional musicians need help from time to time. According to legend, when the original lineup for Kiss reformed in the late 1990s, guitarist Ace Frehley hired the guitar player from a Kiss tribute band to teach him his own guitar solos from past recordings. If Ace can ask for help, you can, too. There is no shame in doing whatever you can to prepare. I have a guitarist friend with a great ear who used to charge musicians who couldn't learn songs on their own twenty dollars per song to teach them their parts exactly like the original recordings. He made a few bucks on the side, and the musicians he helped had a better shot at landing spots in bands.

If you're auditioning for a cover band, and can't learn the songs on your own, there are other options for learning the material. You can purchase sheet music or a music book that contains either music notation or tablature transcriptions of the songs. Once you buy these, you can play along with the original recordings.

Tablature, or "tab," is a way to write music, without using notation, for guitar, bass, and drums that is easily decipherable. It depicts what string, fret, or drum or cymbal to play throughout a song. Tabs are available in music magazines like *Guitar*, *Guitar World*, *Bass Player*, and others. Free Web sites, such as www.e-tabs.org, www.tabpower.com, www.mxtabs.com, and www.tabcrawler.com feature tablature for popular songs, and many other similar sites exist. To find if there's online tab written for your instrument and your particular song, simply input the name of the song and the word *tab* into a search engine, and see what links pop up. If you're looking for bass tab to Stevie Wonder's "Superstition," just input "Superstition Bass Tab" into a search engine like Yahoo! and click on a link to direct yourself to the information.

While learning cover songs with online tabs can be beneficial to players who can't learn the music by ear, there are sometimes quality-control issues with the tabs that can lead you astray from the original recordings, affecting the accuracy of your performance. This occurs because the Web sites receive the tabs from musicians who have created them and don't check each one for accuracy. The site has no way of knowing if the tabs are correct. For instance, I searched and found three tabs for Stevie Wonder's "Superstition." Of these three, two were passable (although not 100 percent accurate), and one was in the wrong key and had other mistakes as well. Online tabs can be a great way to get the basic idea of a song but may not have the accuracy you need.

If the audition doesn't call for you to learn specific songs, but rather to be competent in a specific genre, then you must be adequately versed in the style if you're going to win the gig. If you're a bassist up for a blues gig and the audition does not call for specific blues songs, you'll need to delve into the style and be prepared to play the pentatonic scale in a I-IV-V progression over different keys, as is common in blues music. In addition to this, you'll need to understand 6/8 feel, swing, and be able to play through alternate changes over the second chord. (If none of this makes sense and you have a blues audition coming up, you'll need to study up fast!) As keyboardist Paul McDonald suggests, "Find out as much as possible about the style of music you're going to be playing and listen to recordings of the masters of that style."

If you have specific songs to learn for your audition, write notes on your part, or create a chart. Writing down the music will help you retain it as you're learning it because you won't forget any details over the course of practicing the songs before the audition. Plus, you'll have a permanent record of how to play the song that may be handy at a later time. I've written notes on cover songs that have served me for years (I have a "Mony Mony" chart that looks like it could be carbon dated to the American Revolution).

If you can't write music notation or tablature, you'll need another method to document the songs, one that allows you to reproduce a song as well as if you were reading sheet music. Here's a simple method of writing music parts without tablature or notations (shown for bass guitar) that works for me, provided you know the names of the notes of your instrument:

"Walking on Sunshine"–Katrina and the Waves
Intro: 8 measures (8 counts of "1, 2, 3, 4") of rest while drums play
Verse w/o vox: Bb—Eb—F—Eb x2
Verse: Bb—Eb—F—Eb "coming around"
Chorus: F—Eb—F—Eb—F—Eb
V:
C:
V:
Breakdown: Bass plays verse line
C:
V: Wait for bandleader cue to end the song

This method is just one example of a very simple road map to "Walking on Sunshine." It's a basic chart including verses, choruses, and a breakdown. It relies heavily on my having a solid recollection of how the song goes (one you can gain by repeated listening to the song), since it doesn't note how many times the verses or choruses play on each pass or have any rhythmic information. I've also inserted little clues to help me get through the song. For example, this chart has a note after the "Verse w/o vox" (meaning verse without vocals) that reads "x2." In this chart's language, that means those four chords listed after Verse w/o vox are played twice. Or, the quoted line in the first full verse, "coming around," is a note that the lyrics before the change to the chorus end on the line "coming around." Finally, I've noted that the song ends on a cue from the bandleader. This differs from the original recording, which fades out.

Using the same method, here's another one of my charts for bass:

"Rock Your Body"–Justin Timberlake
Verse   G G—A   **AA** E—E—E—EE   **EE** x6
Chorus: G **STOP** —**AA**—E—E—E—**EE**—back to main [V/C riff]
"Talk to me, boy" x4   **AA**—E **STOP** "Have you naked …"
Bridge: e—d B—C—D—E AA x3 C—C—D—D **STOP**
V/C: until "Talk to me, boy" x4 **AA**—E **STOP END SONG**

On this tune, I've put certain letters that correspond to notes in bold. In my method, bold equals octaves, so these notes are played an octave up from where I would normally play them. I've also added lyrical cues to help keep me on track. I've also put the word *STOP* in bold in a few places. This is to remind me when I'm reading the chart in the middle of the tune that there are rests in certain places that I need to catch. Again, these notes rely on my having a basic understanding of the rhythm of the bass and many of the vocal cues, since neither is entirely documented.

These are just two examples of charts that musicians might use as an alternative to music notation or tablature. Guitarists and keyboardists not wishing to write out the music may just use chord symbols instead of single notes like I do as a bassist, and there's likely a host of other methods musicians use to recall music. Find a method that works for you.

Once you have your notes completed, practice your part without them and work to commit it to memory. Performing at an audition with your nose buried in a chart makes you appear as though you're not engaged with the rest of the band. Written aids should only be used at an audition or gig if the volume of songs in the repertoire is so vast as to make aids necessary, or if you cannot remember parts any other way.

Some players don't like to ever use notes because they feel they become overly dependent on them to play their parts, or that notes distract from the feel and interpretation of the song. Drummer Eric Hoemann agrees with this approach: "I memorize all the songs I have to learn and don't use sheet music. Currently, I'm playing with dance bands, and I just play better when the songs are second nature and my focus is on the performance, groove, and jamming my parts with the other musicians."

When you learn your songs, concentrate on the part and how it's delivered so you can accurately replicate it. Practice your part slowly, mimicking the tones of the instrument or vocal. Don't gloss over any parts of the song, because it'll be evident during the audition when you fudge an important section or miss a vocal scat line. "If the music is difficult, practice the music slowly at first, really slowly," Paul McDonald says. "The key to playing fast is to practice slowly." Matt Rhode says, "It's absolutely essential to learn your parts as close to the recorded versions as possible. As a keyboardist, I also try to spend time on the sound design to match the recorded sounds as well. Most artists want to hear the parts they're familiar with, and there will probably be room to change the parts once the rehearsals start." Los Angeles–based guitarist David Metzner adds, "The secret to a successful audition is being confident, prepared, and professional. Make sure you're as familiar as possible with the material at hand, both on and away from your instrument. Don't just practice the material; spend time just listening to it as well to better absorb the music."

Once you've learned the songs and can play them with ease, prepare for unexpected changes to the songs. Mix things up by practicing standing up, sitting down, in your living room, and your bedroom to get out of your comfort zone. The rehearsal studio where you audition is going to be unfamiliar territory, so do your best to throw yourself off your game before you get there so you're prepared for a new environment.

In addition to playing in different locations, prepare for deviations from the recordings you've received. Bands don't always play their songs exactly like the recording. Sometimes they change the key of the song, or the tempo, or even the style. If you practice the songs in different tempos and keys and even consider other styles, you'll be better equipped to excel if the band throws you a curveball. I once had an experience where the band told me when I arrived at the audition that they played the classic "Brown Eyed Girl" with a calypso beat instead of the standard pop beat. Fortunately, I had rehearsed that song repeatedly before the audition using different beats on my drum machine and could handle the change.

When you audition for a band, they're interested in more than just how you perform the songs. They need to know that you can fit into the band's image as well. Look in the mirror and think, "Do I look like a member of this band?" If you're auditioning for a country act, wear a cowboy hat and stiff denim. If the band wants to be the next Foo Fighters, then avoid all hairbrushes, combs, and hair products like they were platform shoes at a polka concert. Do these things without sacrificing your own personality, though, because the band will likely see through it to the real you. "Attire and your overall 'look' are more important than you might think," says Matt Rhode. "Dress appropriately for the gig, but be yourself; it's painfully obvious when someone is dressed in a way that's not comfortable for them."

Don't pretend to be a different person, but do try to fit into the group. Part of being in a band is having uniform members—no one person in the group stands out too much from the rest (unless it's intentionally for a lead vocalist). The Beatles started out wearing the same black suits, skinny ties, and mop haircuts. Alternative pop band the Hives all wear white jackets, black shirts, and white string ties. They all fit their own standard. When you walk into the rehearsal studio for the audition, you must make an impression of belonging to the group identity. When in doubt about what to wear, go with black clothes since they match just about any genre.

PERFORMING AT THE AUDITION

Now that you have spent countless hours preparing for your audition with the band, it's time to follow up that effort by executing your plan and putting yourself in the best possible position to find a group that matches your musical goals. To do this, you need to get to the audition and nail your performance. When the audition is over, the band will decide whether to invite you to join the group, and you choose whether to accept the offer.

On the day of your audition, leave home well in advance of your start time. You can't predict traffic congestion or confusing directions, but if you allow a cushion of thirty or more minutes to get to the audition, these obstacles won't matter. Being late to your audition will likely eliminate you from consideration. As Matt Rhode explains, "It's crucial to get to the audition early. Nothing looks worse than somebody stumbling into the audition room five or ten minutes late, drenched in sweat and mumbling incoherently about the traffic."

While you're driving to the audition, review the material again to keep the songs fresh in your mind. I like to burn the audition songs to a CD to play in my car so I can sing along with their bass lines as I drive. This action reinforces my parts and simulates the performance so that, in a way, I've already played the songs with the band before I've even walked into the studio and set up my gear.

When you arrive, unload your equipment (if you need to) and follow the band's instructions to get to the room where they're holding the auditions. If you're early, just wait for your time slot and try to relax. It's normal to be nervous before an audition. After all, you're performing in front of a group of judgmental strangers! To keep your anxiety in check, remember your preparation. You've spent hours rehearsing these songs or practicing in this genre and should know the material as well as the band and any other auditioning musicians.

You can pass the time by listening to the songs again on a portable audio player or by tuning your instrument, setting up a drum rack, or singing vocal exercises. Even if there are no auditions preceding yours, and you think the band is just sitting around waiting for you to arrive, don't try to enter the room. It's likely the band is setting up, rehearsing, or talking among themselves. They won't want to be thrown off schedule by your arriving early.

If the band is auditioning other players while you're outside the room, try to listen through the door to hear how the band and the auditioning musician sound. Doing so can give you an edge because you can get a feel for how the band plays live before it's your turn to perform. If your audition is based on improvising or reading charts, listening in gives you the opportunity to think about certain rhythms, chord changes, and time signatures in advance. By the time the previous audition is over you'll likely have a better idea of what you want to accomplish. Another reason to listen to the audition before your turn is that you can hear how your competition is doing. If they're performing well, you'll know you need to be on top of your game. If they're struggling, you'll know you're already better than one musician vying for the spot, and this can be a big confidence boost since you've prepared to the point where you won't have any major problems.

At one audition, I could hear the bassist before me wrestling with a weird wiry bass tone and not locking in to the drummer. None of it sounded like the songs we were supposed to be playing and I imagined the band was probably in agony waiting for the audition to end. When it was my turn, I went with a simple, low-end frequency bass tone and concentrated on grooving with the band. Twenty seconds into the first song of my audition, the huge smiles on the band members' faces let me know I was the frontrunner, which only made me play better.

When it's time for your audition, enter the room and introduce yourself to the members of the band. Don't belabor the introduction process: a friendly hello and handshake will do. The band will then provide you with any information you need, like where to plug in your power cord, where to set up your mic stand, or even some information about the group. Bandleader Ted Heath says of beginning an audition, "I try to loosen players up a bit by talking about the band, and I introduce them to the members and then go right into the music."

Try to remember everyone's name. It will make a favorable impression during your audition when you can address every musician personally, rather than calling them "Drummer" or "Hey you." To land the gig, you need to impress the band with more than just your musical talent; personality counts. Being friendly and polite, in addition to musically proficient, can help solidify you as the favorite in the auditions. No one wants to be in a band with a member who's rude or unfriendly, regardless of talent.

After the introductions, set up your gear and wait for the band to start the audition. If there's any dead time after you set up, don't use it to show off; just wait patiently for the performance to begin. The band doesn't want to hear every chop and lick in your repertoire; they want to hear how well you perform their material while they're playing it, not as a solo effort. When the band calls the first song, perform it like you've been playing it in your sleep—because you practically have been.

If you've memorized the songs, you won't need your notes. Still, it can be a good idea to have them handy in case you need to refer to them. Since many bands don't use music stands, find a discrete spot to place the notes. I put mine on top of my amp, a spot where a quick backwards glance will remind me of a four-bar rest after the second chorus, or the location of a key change in a particular song. You may also consider putting them at your feet by drum, or effects, pedals. If you think your notes may end up on the floor, use big block letters so you can read them.

Expect to make some mistakes during the course of the audition, since you've learned new songs and are playing them with the band for the first time. The band will probably be shocked if you don't make at least a few errors, because it's unusual for auditioning musicians to play every song perfectly. Of course, if you can pull off an error-free audition, it's a great thing. Minor slip-ups, like rushing a drum fill, won't doom your audition, but they can start you down a path of bigger mistakes if they distract you to the point where you can't focus on the rest of the songs. Understand that mistakes happen and try to develop a selective, short-term memory that does not dwell on them. If you become preoccupied with something like being late on the key change on the final chorus of an audition song, you might not recover in time to accurately perform the next tune. When a mistake occurs, just nod in acknowledgment of the error (because the band knows exactly who committed the blunder) and move on. Don't stop playing, and don't ask the band to restart the song. If you head down this trail, the band will think you fluster easily and may not offer you the gig. The band wants to know you're capable of overcoming errors mid-song, just like you'd be expected to do during a show.

If the band asks you to perform a song you haven't prepared for, don't panic. They aren't expecting you to play it to the level you did the planned audition material; they just want to know if you can be creative on the spot without freezing. "I like to start by playing the songs I asked them to learn in advance and then move into a tune or two that they didn't expect," bandleader Ted Heath says. "I like to put auditioning players on the spot to see what they're made of."

I've done auditions where the keyboardist was yelling chord changes to me during the songs, and others where the guitarist expected me to figure out what to play based on the chord positions on his fretting hand. Handle these occasions by keeping things simple, not by panicking, and by relying on the skills you've developed on your instrument to get you through the song.

Don't overplay during the audition. If you want to add the occasional complementary fill or riff, you may do so, but don't forget that your basic task is to perform the songs as they are on the recordings. The audition is for someone to join a band, not for an egomaniac who wants to use the band solely to showcase his or her own abilities. Los Angeles–based drummer Robert Smith says of his audition with his band, 2nd Rate Citizen, "The band wanted someone who could fit in and immediately mesh with the atmosphere and the music. The audition came down to me and one other guy. Apparently he blew it by coming in and just pounding away like crazy. I went in and was more concerned with getting through the songs, making sure the endings were all solid, and holding the beat. In the end, the band knew right away that they liked me over the other guy."

Once you've performed the songs, the band may choose to interview you. This interview is a follow-up to the questions you answered before they decided to audition you. As before, the majority of questions will be designed to assess your commitment level to the project and to ensure you're a match for their goals. Be candid and honest, and give the band the information they need, even if it seems irrelevant to you, because it may be important to them. I was once turned down at an audition because the bandleader didn't want a married man in the band. I assured him that my wife understands and supports my musical aspirations, but the bandleader couldn't get past his preconceived notions that married people don't have adequate time to pursue a music career and that they just aren't cool. I could've lied, but how long could I have kept my marriage a secret from the band? It would've come out at some point, the band would have been displeased, and it probably would've cost me the gig—making the hours of audition preparation, days of rehearsals, and gigs a waste of time for all concerned. I know he made a mistake by rejecting me, but I had to accept his view and move on to my next audition.

Before your audition ends, you should ask several questions of the band to gauge your chances of being invited to join the group. These questions are:

- How did I do?
- Is there any reason you think I couldn't be successful with your band?
- What's the next step?

"How did I do?" is a tough question to ask, because it exposes you to criticism if the band bluntly says you did poorly. It's worth asking, though, because it's important to determine how the band views your performance, especially if they didn't like it. No one wants to hear that they won't be considered for a band, but if you do hear this, at least you can then move on to the next audition completely focused and unencumbered by hopes of landing this gig. You can also learn from your performance, and the entire audition experience, and be better prepared in the future. If you learn that the band feels you did an excellent job and are the leading candidate, then you can feel good about your performance and keep practicing the audition material in anticipation of joining the band.

If the response is the generic, "You did fine," you should push a little further to connect with the band. This also lets them know you were fully engaged during the audition and that you care about how you performed (and about getting the gig). Pick out a specific area in one of the songs that you can comment on and ask for their feedback. For instance, you might say, "I really enjoy the groove in 'Deer in the Headlights.' Was my keyboard effect what you were looking for?" Or a statement such as, "I love singing over the energy-build after the chorus of 'The Glass Is Half Full,'" might get the band to talk about the song and what they liked, or disliked, about your performance.

"Is there any reason you think I couldn't be successful with your band?" is another question that puts you in a vulnerable position, but if you have the courage to ask it, you can give yourself an opportunity to respond to the band's concerns. If you don't ask, the band might dismiss you for a reason that doesn't apply to you, or one you can easily refute. If you want to join the band, you need to challenge any negative views.

A band may say, "We like your playing, but we aren't sure your guitar tone fits with our music." If you really want the gig, you won't find this an insurmountable obstacle. You can respond with, "I was trying to match the tone on the recording you gave me with the audition material as best as I could. I have plenty of tonal options with my equipment. I'm very open to the idea of you helping me modify my tone to best fit the band."

Positively responding to criticism lets the band know you're easy to work with and flexible. Responding negatively or defensively turns the band off. A response like, "Well, you must be tone-deaf if you think I have the wrong tone," will cost you a gig. No band is going to want to invite someone into the group who thinks their guitar tone is more important than the music.

The band may respond to this question with a reason that might be characterized as lifestyle difference. Perhaps you're in school at the time of your audition, and the band might think that will conflict with their rehearsal schedule. Or, as in my experience, the band might think that a married player won't have time for the band. Address these issues with facts, as well as a positive and cooperative attitude, and you may be able to convince the band that their fears aren't relevant in your case. If you're in school, a response to a band that expresses concern over your availability can be, "Yes, I'm in school during the day, but I have all of my evenings free for rehearsals and shows, and I'll be graduating in six months so my calendar will really open up." If your limited experience in a genre is cited as an issue, you might say, "I'm still learning the genre, but I love the style and am committed to practicing the material on my own for as long as it takes for me to get up to speed with the rest of the group."

Your final question of the band should be, "What's the next step in the audition process?" You need to know when you can expect to hear from the band with an invitation for a second audition, an invitation to join, or a rejection. It's crucial that you leave the audition with some sense of when you'll hear from them so you don't end up waiting weeks to hear, all the while not knowing if the delay is because you haven't been chosen, or if it's because the band is on tour, or it's suffering through some kind of emergency. The typical response from the band will be something like, "We'll get back to you when we complete our audition process early next week." Technically, this is all the information you need, but to avoid being stuck in limbo if you don't hear from them "early next week," ask the band if it's okay for you to contact them if you don't hear back from them a few days after the date they said they'd contact you. By getting permission from the band, you won't appear desperate or impatient if you do contact them to check on your status. The band may also appreciate this in case they're delayed in their process or they lose your contact information.

If the band says they plan to hold a second round of auditions, anticipate that you may get a call to return. When you get home, take notes on everything that transpired during the audition, including what songs you performed, improvised, and whether the band expressed any concerns that you can better address on your return visit. If you get called back for a second round, impress the band by picking up right where you left off. You'll be expected to play any songs you may have performed, or learned, during the first audition, so make sure you don't repeat any mistakes you may have made during the first audition.

I once had a second audition for a band that taught me two songs after we jammed the predetermined material at the first audition. Fortunately, I took good notes on those songs, so when asked to play them again I was prepared and able to play them straight through without any problems. After I landed the gig, I learned it was this effort that pushed me ahead of my competition for the gig. It's also useful to write down the names of the band members, along with any other key information that may help when the second audition occurs, such as how to gain access to the rehearsal space or where the band prefers you to set up in the room.

When the audition is over, thank everyone for his or her time. A simple, "Thank you for your time; I really enjoyed myself," and a smile go a long way toward making a positive impression on the band. Even if you've already decided you don't want to join the band, being aloof or rude is uncalled for and might come back to haunt you if you later change your mind or end up sometime in the future auditioning for another band that includes a member of this current group. If you're interested in joining the band, make it clear that you're interested, yet not desperate. A comment like, "I really enjoyed myself and I hope we get to do this again soon" is fine. Going over the top and saying, "You guys are the greatest! I was born to be in this band!" is a little too much and might turn them off because they're looking for a bandmate, not a fan.

Don't dally or try to hang around to chat with the band after the audition. This is an awkward time in the process, as there's nothing left to say, and the band is probably anxious to evaluate your performance in private. There may also be musicians waiting their turn to audition and they won't be able to set up with you still there. Just pack up your equipment, say a polite goodbye, and exit quickly. Stammering endlessly, or nervously, can leave a bad impression. "Do not talk too much at the audition," Matt Rhode cautions. "The band really doesn't care that their hit ballad helped you to score with your girlfriend at the high-school prom. I know lots of people who have literally talked themselves out of a gig. Chances are the less you say, the more professional you'll come across."

FOLLOWING UP THE AUDITION

When the audition is over, musicians and bands evaluate the experience and determine whether to accept, or offer, an invitation to join the group. Once you or your band has made this decision, you follow up the audition by contacting the other party and making your intentions clear. Only bands can make the decision to invite a musician to join their group, so if you are an auditioning musician interested in joining the band, you need to drive home the fact that you're the right fit for the group. When a band has determined if a musician matches their needs, they contact the musician and deliver the news.

Following Up with the Band

After your audition, you need to decide whether the band matches your musical goals and if you'd consider joining the group. If not, move on to the next audition. When you hear back from the band with an offer you wish to decline, simply thank them for their time and tell them you don't feel like it's a good fit. Be direct and don't offer any room for argument so you don't have to go into detail about why you don't want to pursue the opportunity. This can only lead to animosity, because the band won't agree with your reasoning that they're irresponsible or don't know their own songs. Here's a sample e-mail rejection:

Hi Troy,

Thanks for e-mailing me about the second audition opportunity. I really appreciate your interest, but after the first audition I'm not sure we're a good match. Good luck in your search.

Ben

If you decide you're interested in joining the band, let them know by following up the audition with an e-mail, or phone call, that stresses the following three points:

- You want the gig.
- You share the goals of the band and are a good musical match.
- You're looking forward to hearing back from the band when they've made a decision.

Be positive and upbeat in your communication, even if you feel the audition performance was lacking. It's possible the band thought you were just fine. There's more to being the best candidate for a band than musical prowess. Personality counts too. If you can demonstrate you have a great attitude, the band will consider it a plus, and it might separate you from better musicians who have questionable character.

Here's a sample follow-up e-mail from a musician reiterating his interest in a band on the corporate party circuit:

Hello Janet,

Thanks so much for all of your hard work in putting together this audition process. It's been a model of professionalism that's a credit to you as a bandleader.

I had a great time jamming with you and the band last night. You've put together a really good group of people, and I hope I have the opportunity to work with the band. I feel I'd be a great fit.

I look forward to hearing from you when the audition process concludes at the end of the week.

Michael

Here's a sample voice message following up a pop-band audition:

Hey, Bobby. It's Mark, the singer you auditioned last night at 8:30. Thanks for having me over. You guys really have it together. I had a blast, and it sounded awesome. I can't wait till we can do it again. Give me a call next week when you guys have made your decision. Thanks.

Now that you've followed up the audition, wait to hear from the band.

Following Up with the Musician

When a musician leaves the audition, your band is free to chat about his or her performance, and about how the musician might fit into the group. Your criteria for judging a musician are your musical goals. You have to ask yourself: Does this musician fit our band? Is he or she talented enough to handle the musical aspects of our group? Does he or she have the temperament and attitude to mesh with the band? Once you've asked yourself these questions (or possibly before), you'll develop a gut feeling about who's best for the band. Bandleader Julie Zielinski makes her decisions about who to invite to join her band based on instinct. "You just have to go with your gut feeling," she says. "When I meet a player I like, I can just tell if it's going to work out. I'm not necessarily looking for the greatest player. I just want them to fit in."

If you're the bandleader, then you make the final decision on who joins. If you're part of a democratic band, then you'll need to build a consensus among your bandmates to determine who to invite into your band. In most democratic bands I've been in, there's been an obvious candidate that stood out through attitude and talent, and in those instances there's no disagreement. If the band members can't agree, then they can either continue debating the musicians on their merits or invite them back for a second audition, until a true frontrunner everyone can agree on emerges.

When you've decided whom to invite into the band, you'll not only have to inform the chosen musician, but you'll also have to let the other candidates who auditioned know that they'll not be asked to join the group. However, before you reject any musicians, make sure your first choice candidate wants to join. If they don't, you'll have to considering offering the spot to your second or third choice, or maybe even starting a new audition process to find suitable musicians. If your band is rejected by a musician, ask why he or she is no longer interested. It's likely the musicians will make the generic claim of stylistic differences; but if they are candid, you may learn valuable information on how your band is perceived.

Rejecting musicians, especially those who clearly worked hard to prepare, is a difficult task. No one likes to give, or get, bad news. Still, you need to contact these musicians, because to not do so is both unprofessional and disrespectful considering the amount of time and energy they expended to audition for you. The very least their effort deserves is a phone call or e-mail with their status in the audition process. Be direct and offer no room for argument so you don't encourage the musician to fight for the spot in the band.

Using Funky Minnow and Moe, here's an example of an e-mail rejection:

Moe,

Thank you so much for coming in the other night. Everyone in the band really liked you, and it's obvious you're a great player. Unfortunately, we've decided to invite another player to join the band. We believe he's a better fit for us right now.

Thanks again for your time and effort. Best of luck to you in the future.

Tracy

On the opposite, and more enjoyable, side of the coin is offering a musician a spot in your band. When you do this, reaffirm all of your needs and tell the musician why you've chosen him or her. Doing so will make your reasons for wanting the musician in the band absolutely clear and establish it as a priority of the band's. If one of the reasons you invite a female vocalist to join your band is because she's available to gig three nights a week, and you mention this when you make your offer, you're giving her a chance to say, "Wait, I don't have time to gig that much," meaning you now have to go back to the drawing board to find a singer. If her response is, "Of course … your gig schedule is one of the main reasons I want to join the band," then there's no confusion in regards to the goal of the group.

Here's an example invitation for Moe to join Funky Minnow:

Tracy: *Hi, Moe! Are you ready to join the band?*

Moe: *Yes! Thanks, Tracy. This is the best news I've had all year!*

Tracy: *Great! Just to be clear, we need you to be totally committed to the band, available for three rehearsals per week and at least two gigs per month. We also need you to contribute financially to the band. Our rent and Web-hosting fees aren't free!*

Moe: *I understand completely, Tracy. I'm your bass player. Let's get funky!*

Now that your band has a new member, or you've joined a new group, you're ready to begin rehearsing with the band and taking the first steps toward playing shows.

CHAPTER 5

PULLING YOUR BAND TOGETHER

Bands schedule rehearsals to bring their members together on a regular basis, whether it's to determine which songs to play, to practice their music, to prepare for gigs, or to organize their mailing list or develop strategies to promote their shows. Regularly scheduled rehearsals are critical, because it is through them that bands learn to work together. There's also a personal and musical tightness that can develop, which helps bands to achieve their goals of playing the most popular clubs, commanding the highest fees and energizing their fans.

All bands work at getting *tight*. Tight bands know their music and bandmates so well they're able to anticipate each other's moves and to respond accordingly. When musicians achieve this level of familiarity, they can minimize mistakes as well as improvise solo sections and song endings and change tempos mid-song. Being tight is one of the elements that separate great bands from merely good ones, and the only way to achieve this level of consistency is through productive rehearsals.

ESTABLISHING A REHEARSAL STRATEGY

Before your band begins rehearsing, you need to develop a strategy that maximizes your practice time. An effective rehearsal strategy determines where a band will rehearse, what they wish to accomplish during their rehearsals, how often they'll rehearse, and what ground rules they'll follow to ensure their rehearsals are efficient and effective. A rehearsal strategy is only as good as the members' ability to adhere to it, so the commitment of each band member is essential.

Finding a Rehearsal Space

The first step in pulling your band together should be finding a place to rehearse. Rehearsal spaces vary from professional facilities and multi-use warehouses to a band member's garage. It's up to you to find a space that's both affordable and will meet your needs.

The optimal rehearsal space is a *lockout*, which cannot be accessed by anyone without the band's permission. Lockout studios are often located in large complexes that specialize in housing music groups, but since they can be anywhere that's exclusive to the band, they include a band member's garage or a rented room in a warehouse.

The major advantage of lockout space is that your band can safely leave their musical equipment when not rehearsing. There's no carrying heavy amps, drums, keyboards, or guitars to and from the studio. This can be a big time-saver, because a band, particularly one that has a drummer with a large kit, can take up to twenty minutes to set up and another twenty to tear down. If your group has several members with lots of equipment, having a lockout space can significantly increase your productivity during rehearsals.

"It's best to have a place to leave your gear so you don't have to drag it around to every practice," says San Francisco–based guitarist Peter Smith. "You can just walk in, pick up your guitar, and start playing. I can't say enough about having a set rehearsal space if you're in a serious band, because you can get a lot more done. It adds to the cost of the band, but factor it in. It's important."

Lockouts in professional rehearsal facilities often feature amenities that can make your band more efficient. You don't have to worry about blowing an electrical circuit; there will be more than enough capacity to power your band. Professional facilities might also have drum risers, sound panels to limit noise, carpeting, air-conditioning, free parking, and even broadband access. In addition, when you rehearse in an environment that's geared toward bands, you don't have to worry about a neighbor calling the police because your band is too loud or providing restroom facilities for your bandmates (not to mention cleaning up after them). In California, fully equipped rehearsal facilities with lockout rooms include Los Angeles' Downtown Rehearsal and the San Francisco Bay Area's H.I.T. Wall Studios.

Not every professional rehearsal studio is equally well furnished. Some are simply empty rooms with four walls and a few power outlets. It's up to your band to accessorize them with carpeting, shelving, or a drum-riser. One example of a simpler lockout facility is Varna Street Studios in Van Nuys, California, which offers empty rooms, electricity, a unisex restroom, and some parking. That's it.

Many lockouts are nonspecific buildings that contain empty shells intended to support multiple purposes, including rehearsal spaces, construction warehouses, and T-shirt factories. New Orleans' Overhead Door is a complex featuring a set of large, hangar-like buildings with individual spaces available for rent. I've rehearsed there in various rooms and have had artists, furniture refurbishers, and construction companies as neighbors.

To lease a lockout space, one band member will need to sign a lease, a legally binding contract between the band and the facility. Be forewarned that the facility will most likely check credit history and references, so be prepared with this as well as with references from previous or current landlords. If you're going to sign, be prepared to meet the lockout's requirements, including paying rent in a timely manner—which may mean having to nag your bandmates to provide their shares.

Your contract will focus on two key issues: liability and the payment of rent. The clauses in the lease protect the facility and are nonnegotiable, because no studio wants to be held liable for stolen or damaged equipment. As H.I.T. Wall Studios co-owner Will Strickland says, "We can't control who's given an alarm code or key by a member of the band. Because of this, we cannot be held responsible for any theft in the rooms. If the band made the mistake of trusting the wrong person, I can't be held responsible for replacing a guitar amp or a kick drum."

In addition, the contract will give the owner the power to evict if, for example, you're continually late on your rent. Carefully read through and be sure you understand your lease before you sign. There can be damaging ramifications if you fail to comply with the terms. Make sure your bandmates understand and agree to all of the terms as well. You don't want to be left on the hook should problems arise.

Professional lockouts are usually rented on a monthly basis, depending on the location and leasing philosophy. Cost varies by market and region. I've seen prices range from $100 to $900 per month. To find rehearsal facilities in your area, check the Internet and the Yellow Pages. Most important, check with your network of musicians. Ask where they, or bands they know, rehearse, and whether they'd recommend the facility. As Will Strickland says, "Musicians are fairly computer savvy, so I make sure our Web site is included in search engines such as Yahoo! A Web site can help answer a lot of questions ahead of time and be a selling point if it's well organized. Our best means of advertising is, and will probably always be, word of mouth. The reason for this is we're dealing with musicians' recommendations rather than something in print. Still, we also have line ads in both the San Francisco and San Mateo County directories [Yellow Pages]."

The most affordable lockout rehearsal space is your garage or basement. The advantages of home rehearsal spaces include the cost and convenience. You don't have to pay rent, and at least one of the band members doesn't have to commute. The disadvantages can include insufficient electrical capacity to power the band's equipment, neighbors that complain about the noise, and having to clean up after your bandmates. To determine how loud your band can be and what hours it can play, check your city's municipal code (usually available online) to review the noise ordinance. Most residential areas operate under a "good neighbor" policy, where neighbors give each other advance warning of parties or other loud events. Despite the potential problems and hassles, the cost of rehearsing at home can't be beat, which is why it's preferred by so many bands.

There are other spaces available for bands as well, but you'll have to be creative to find them. Using atypical rehearsal locations can work well, as long as they are secure, affordable, and able to handle loud noise. I once played with a band that rehearsed in the back of an old theater. The group could play anytime after 7 PM, jamming next to cool old theatrical props.

You may have an "inside" contact at a business that doesn't mind a band coming in for practice every week or two, provided it's after business hours. In another band I played with the bandleader befriended the property manager of his building. Through this contact, our band was allowed to use the residential complex's storeroom to rehearse. We couldn't practice there regularly, because of noise issues with the building's tenants, but when the band needed to learn a song or two, we could jam for a couple of hours for free. Guitarist Paul Mitchell occasionally jammed at a defensive driving school run by the father of his band's drummer. "There was plenty of space for us, ample parking, and the price was right ... free!"

If you don't have access to a free space and the price of a private lockout is beyond your means, you can offset the cost of a rehearsal space by finding another band to go halves on the room and rent. The best way to do so is to ask the establishment's landlord. They're likely to encounter other parties who either want to share a room or have turned down a room because the cost was too high. Another approach is scanning bulletin boards in rehearsal studios for postings of bands interested in sharing space.

Keep in mind that a room need not be shared only between bands. Your group might be able to share with a professional musician who needs a place to give lessons, or with a solo musician. I was once in a band that shared a space with a musician who needed a place to practice because his wife didn't want him blasting his Marshall half-stack in the house. A band can share a lockout with a business as well. I once shared a room with a welder. Whenever you share space it's important to find someone trustworthy, because your lockout partner will have access to any gear you choose to store there and he or she will be asked to share in the rent.

If you do share a space, you'll need to set up a rehearsal schedule that enables both parties to take advantage of it. One band might use the room Mondays, Wednesdays, and Sundays, while the other band uses the room Tuesdays, Thursdays, and Saturdays. They can alternate Fridays and make changes for gigs or other necessities as required. Or you might arrange to share by time of day, taking either day or evening.

Even with a partner to share the space, many bands cannot afford a lockout room. Some groups simply don't practice often enough to justify having a dedicated space. Renting a room in a professional rehearsal studio by the hour, or a time block, is the best alternative. This considerably lessens the expense when compared to a lockout facility with a monthly or annual lease. There are other benefits, too. The band can rehearse in a professional environment, with a PA system, and possibly other equipment, such as amps and a drum kit placed there by the establishment. This also avoids your having to sign a lease, which can be beneficial if your credit rating is a problem or you aren't sure your bandmates will be good for their portion of the rent.

Although the cost of renting a practice room varies by the facility and the market, for professional facilities you can expect to pay approximately $12 to $15 an hour with a possible minimum of three hours. At these rates, if your band rehearses twice weekly—six hours total—you'll pay about $360 per month to practice.

This might be comparable to a lockout studio, so you'll need to determine whether the benefit of having a by-the-hour space outweighs leasing a space. If $360 per month is significantly lower than the cost of a lockout in your area, then you have to decide whether the cost savings offsets not having a dedicated space to store your equipment and rehearse at your convenience. Two rehearsal studios that book hourly are Southern California's Sound Arena (with locations in Van Nuys, Garden Grove, Hollywood, and North Hollywood, as well as other cities throughout the region) and Ultra Sound Rehearsal in New York City.

There's one key drawback to renting a room by the hour or time block. Depending on the demand for rehearsal space in your area, you may not be able to find an available room. If your band needs a room on short notice for an emergency rehearsal or showcase event, you may be in trouble. Professional studios are often booked weeks or even months in advance.

Whether you find a lockout studio, share a space, or rent by the hour, you may want to take extra measures to secure your musical equipment. Gear can be stolen out of your car when it's parked, out of your hourly rental when your band goes outside for a breath of fresh air, or out of your lockout when it's broken into during the middle of the day.

Being victimized by theft is a terrible experience, but it doesn't have to cripple your musical aspirations by leaving you unable to replace your gear. Many insurance companies will allow you to take out a policy on your gear, or you can attach a policy rider to your homeowner's or renter's insurance. I use a company called musicproinsurance.com. My annual cost is 1 percent of the total cost of replacing all of my gear. Be clear with your insurer about whether you are a professional or amateur musician, because it will make a difference as to what kind of coverage they can offer you. Coverage for a professional is more costly than that for a hobbyist, but if you try to pretend you're an amateur and are identified otherwise, you'll end up dropped without a cent reimbursed. If you can afford insurance (and I don't think you can afford not to have it), you should get it. In addition to providing you with money to replace stolen or damaged equipment, it'll give you peace of mind the next time you leave your gear at your studio or in your car while you stop at a convenience store.

Determining What Needs to Be Accomplished at Rehearsals

Once your band has found a rehearsal space, you've got to decide what needs to be accomplished at rehearsal. This will help your band decide how often it needs to rehearse in order to meet its goals.

Bands use rehearsals to work on both musical and nonmusical activities. Musical tasks include songwriting, jamming your song list, and honing the nuances of your band's music like nailing harmonies or drilling a challenging section of a song. To determine what your band needs to accomplish musically, evaluate your group. If the band is newly formed, or has a new member, you're going to spend your rehearsals building a song list, either by writing or learning the songs. If the band is established, your musical tasks will primarily consist of maintaining your song list and adding to it (though probably at a lesser rate than for a newly formed band).

Nonmusical tasks include all band-related activities that don't involve playing music. They're as essential as musical tasks because they can lead to playing more shows, to more fans, for more money. These tasks may include:

- Creating a mailing list
- Creating a strategy to book shows
- Drafting e-mail notifications to fans
- Taking a band photograph
- Assembling a band press kit
- Writing copy for a band Web site
- Writing a set list for a gig

Nonmusical tasks tend to be need-driven. For example, if your band has a gig coming up, you'll need to write a set list for the gig and draft an e-mail notification to alert your fans of the upcoming show. You don't need to do these things at every rehearsal; they're only necessary when the need arises.

Deciding How Often to Rehearse and Creating a Rehearsal Schedule

Once your band has determined what needs to be accomplished at rehearsals, the next steps are to decide how often to rehearse and to create a workable schedule to accomplish your goals. Three factors should be involved in your decisions: your band's degree of commitment, its level of talent and discipline, and what it wishes to accomplish during rehearsals.

It's important that every member of the band agrees on the frequency of rehearsals so you all feel your time is well spent. If some members of the band feel the group practices too much, they may become resentful, while those committing to the schedule might question the others' dedication. This conflict can divide a band, so total agreement is important.

If your band consists of talented and disciplined musicians, you may be able to get away with fewer rehearsals. Talented musicians can learn and master songs quickly, while novice players may struggle to do so. As a novice bass player early in my music career, I played in bands with musicians of similar skill levels. I remember riffs like the guitar and bass intros to Guns and Roses' "Sweet Child o' Mine" being nearly insurmountable, taking weeks of rehearsal and at-home practice time for the guitarists and me to master. Today, as a more experienced player, riffs like that are simple to learn and require one pass to master.

If the musicians in your band are disciplined, they'll also be more productive and will require fewer rehearsals than players who are unable to devote themselves to personal practice time. Disciplined musicians practice on their own, making rehearsals more efficient because their parts will have been learned in advance. Rehearsals then become a place to practice entire songs instead of having to go over separate parts again and again because one or more members didn't learn their parts.

If the entire band is prepared, learning a five-minute song may take one or two run-throughs. If all members aren't ready, you'll struggle and waste valuable practice time, which will also add to the amount of time you'll need to be gig-ready.

If your band is working quickly to build a repertoire so you can begin booking shows, you'll need to practice often, perhaps three or four times per week. If you've taken on a new member and need to get him or her up to speed on your music, you'll again need to practice often, at least until the new member knows the set, at which time you may decide to cut back, since everyone knows the tunes. If your band rarely gigs, and when it does it's always the same songs, you may be able to get away with practicing once before every gig. Every group consists of different personalities and goals, so it's impossible to suggest every possible type of rehearsal schedule. Ultimately, your band needs to determine this for itself based on its commitment, abilities, and goals.

To maximize your rehearsal time, you can create a calendar and to-do list that includes future rehearsal dates and times as well as future to-do items. Assignment sheets and rehearsal calendars provide band members with a road map to prepare certain songs and nonmusical activities before your first, next, or future rehearsal. They help the band take full advantage of its time together.

Bands can create their rehearsal agenda with a simple message delivered in person or via e-mail. For example: "Hey guys, next practice is this Monday at 8 PM at Downtown Rehearsal. We'll go over those two new song ideas we jammed yesterday." Or, "Our first rehearsal will be Sunday at noon. We'll start with the material we covered at the auditions and then just start writing new songs after that." The members of the band now know exactly what lies ahead, and they can work on new song ideas or practice the audition material at home to be prepared to contribute to an efficient and effective rehearsal.

If you prefer a more detailed approach, you can create an assignment sheet that includes information like date, time, and location as well as a more comprehensive account of what the band will cover at rehearsal. You can then hand-distribute the assignment sheet at the end of a prior rehearsal, or mail or e-mail the information to band members. Assignment sheets may also include music to learn from a CD or an MP3 attachment if the band needs to prepare to rehearse certain songs.

The greater the level of detail in the assignment sheet, the more helpful it will be. A sample assignment sheet for a band that performs original material might include comments such as, "Prepare to work on harmony vocal parts for the songs 'Shiny New Penny' and 'Raining Tears.' We'll also cover the bridge section on 'Joke's on You.'" If your assignment sheet includes nonmusical items as well, they might include, "Chris: Bring your camera. We're going to take headshots of each band member for the Web site. Everyone be ready to have your picture taken." Upon reading the sheet, Chris knows to bring his camera, and hopefully all members remember to comb their hair (or not!).

Here's a sample assignment sheet for fictitious original rock band Scissor Lift:

Scissor Lift Rehearsal Assignment Sheet

Date: Sunday, Dec. 4
Time: 1 PM to 4:30 PM
Location: Dave's garage

Assignments

1. We need to write copy for a new e-mail flyer for the January 3 gig.
2. Thirty-minute free-form jam to generate new song ideas. This will be a recorded session.
3. Two hours working out four new song ideas from November 28th rehearsal (see attached MP3 with this audio).
4. Remaining time will be spent rehearsing existing material. In particular, we're going to rehearse the solo section in "Cherry Picker."

Based on this assignment sheet, Scissor Lift band members know they'll spend the bulk of their practice time working on the new material they recorded at a previous practice session, and they'll have the audio to properly prepare for it. They'll also have advance warning that they will spend some time on existing material, specifically the song "Cherry Picker." With this knowledge, the members can individually focus more of their personal time on this song and its solo section before rehearsal begins. They can plan ahead as well by beginning to think about the text for an upcoming gig flyer that's listed on the assignment sheet. Then, when the group gets together again, each member can volunteer ideas about the flyer. If Scissor Lift follows the assignment list on the sheet, the band will effectively use their time to complete all the listed tasks.

Here's another sample of an assignment sheet, this time for fictitious cover band Tons O' Funk:

Tons O' Funk Rehearsal Assignment Sheet

Date: Tuesday, December 21

Time: 8 PM for vocalists; 8:30 PM for all other players

Location: Van Nuys Sound Arena, Room D

Assignment

Rehearse set list for January 5 gig at Club Stone. The set is as follows.

1. "Play That Funky Music"—Wild Cherry
2. "Boogie Oogie Oogie"—A Taste of Honey
3. "Le Freak"—Chic
4. "What Is Hip?"—Tower of Power
5. "Brick House"—The Commodores
6. "Think"—Aretha Franklin
7. "Last Dance"—Donna Summer
8. "I'll Take You There"—Staple Singers
9. "You Should Be Dancing"—Bee Gees
10. "That's the Way I Like It"—KC and the Sunshine Band
11. "Let's Groove"—Earth, Wind & Fire
12. "I Feel Good"*—James Brown

* Possible encore song

Comments: VOCALISTS—arrive at 8 PM for harmony work on "I'll Take You There," "Let's Groove," and "Boogie Oogie Oogie." EVERYONE—plan on running through the set twice. On the second run-through of the set, we're going to play without stopping—just like the gig!

The Tons O' Funk band members will receive their assignments before the rehearsal and have plenty of time to practice the proposed set list. Plus, the members who sing will have an opportunity to work out their individual harmony parts in advance so they can finish their work by the time everyone else is ready to play. If the Tons O' Funk singers show up unprepared, they'll eat up a lot more than just the thirty minutes of rehearsal time specified on the assignment sheet. The rehearsal will take much longer than it needed to, and the other band members will stand around with nothing to do except to complain about their time being wasted.

Once you've worked with assignment sheets, you may find they're so helpful you'll want to write a month of them to keep the band focused on its goals. To do this, you can create a rehearsal calendar.

Take, for example, a monthly rehearsal schedule for fictitious pop band Black on Red. They've purchased a large whiteboard, some markers, and created a rehearsal calendar hung in their lockout rehearsal facility where they can all see it and add to it.

Black on Red consists of four members: Lulu on vocals and bass guitar, Mack on drums, Bobby on keyboard, and Seth on guitar. Lulu is a part-time student; the rest have full-time day jobs. Black on Red have set their calendar so they have time to write new material, practice existing tunes, and take care of nonmusical projects, as well as accommodating the members' personal needs. Here's their practice schedule for a month:

Black on Red Rehearsal Schedule

Monday	Tuesday	Wednesday	Thursday	Friday	Saturday	Sunday
1 7–11 PM Songwriting Session, Play set	**2** Off	**3** 8–11 PM Songwriting Session Review, Play set, Write gig for mailing list	**4** Off	**5** 8–10 PM Play set twice, Prepare for gig	**6** Gig at the Wolf Den, 6 PM Load-in	**7** Off
8 7–11 PM Songwriting Session	**9** Off	**10** Off Lulu's Exam	**11** Off	**12** Off	**13** Off	**14** 7–11 PM Songwriting Session
15 7–11 PM Songwriting Session, Play set	**16** 8–9 PM Take band photo for Web (Seth— bring camera)	**17** 8–10 PM Songwriting Session Review, Play set	**18** Off Lulu's Exam	**19** Off Mack is on vacation (through 23rd)	**20** Off	**21** Off
22 Off	**23** Off	**24** 8–10 PM Play set	**25** Off	**26** 7–11 PM Write gig e-mail for mailing list, Play set	**27** 8–10 PM Play set twice, Prepare for gig	**28** Off
29 Gig at Kennel Joint 7 PM Load-in	**30** Off	**31** Off				

Let's take a look at another monthly rehearsal schedule and calendar, this time for fictitious Tom Petty and the Heartbreakers tribute band, Damn the Torpedoes. This group is a side project consisting of professional players who love Tom Petty's music. Group members e-mail the bandleader their schedules, and he creates a calendar around their ever-changing schedules. He then mails members the monthly calendar of events. With hectic schedules, they don't have much free time to rehearse, so they need to learn and maintain their set on their own time. Since the group has no home-base lockout studio, they rent by the four-hour block to rehearse. Here's their practice schedule:

Damn the Torpedoes Rehearsal Schedule

Monday	Tuesday	Wednesday	Thursday	Friday	Saturday	Sunday
1	2	3 Rehearsal at Van Nuys Sound Area 7–11 PM Play set	4	5 Gig at Howling Willie's 8 PM Load-in	6	7
8	9	10	11	12	13 Gig at Mick's Bar 6 PM Load-in	14
15	16	17	18	19 Gig at Howling Willie's 8 PM Load-in	20	21
22	23	24 2 PM Interview with Santa Monica *Daily Courier* Meet at Starbucks, 1356 Third St.	25	26	27 Gig at Mick's Bar 6 PM Load-in	28
29	30	31				

Establishing the Rules of Rehearsals

Once a rehearsal schedule has been created, it's important to agree on some simple rules to keep your band on track. Any number of rules may be implemented, from coming to rehearsal prepared to not coming high or drunk. Base the rules on the personality of your band. If the band is serious and structured, you'll probably have several rules for its members. If the band is laid-back, there might just be one or two.

Bands differ on the repercussions for breaking the rules. Some bands institute fines for infractions like being unprepared or late, and these can be quite effective. Legend has it that the Godfather of Soul, James Brown, used to fine his band members $50 for each mistake during a live performance. If a member of his band made multiple mistakes, he or she could end the gig running a deficit with their boss, paying James at the end of the night instead of the other way around! As you can imagine, this got the musicians' full attention.

Most band members, however, can't afford, or won't agree to, a financial penalty when they break the rules or make mistakes. This is understandable, especially in democratic groups where there isn't a bandleader to strictly enforce the rules and collect the penalties. In these instances, it's up to the rest of the band members to hold the rule breaker accountable for his or her actions and insist they abide by the rules of the band. If one of your band members consistently breaks the rules, stand up to the offending musician and ask that he or she be more responsible. It's never easy or pleasant, but it must be done before his or her behavior drives the group apart. If you're the musician in your band who's constantly breaking the rules, be forewarned. Ambitious bands won't tolerate you due to the detrimental effect you'll have on the entire band, and you'll soon find yourself fired.

One rule that ought to be on every band's list is that members need to show up on time for rehearsal. Unless you plan on breaking your rehearsal into segments that involve just some of the members (e.g., vocal harmonies for singers, rhythm section rehearsal for bass, drums, guitar, and keyboard), beginning a band rehearsal without everyone in attendance is pointless because their instruments won't be represented. I've been in several bands with chronically late members (especially drummers), and it's very frustrating to practice without them. The music doesn't sound like it should, defeating the whole purpose of rehearsal. Then, when the late musician does show up, the band has to start the songs all over again.

Having members who are chronically late brings down the morale of the rest of the band. It's such a selfish act. Psychology 101 tells us that people who are continually late, either consciously or unconsciously, believe their time is more valuable than anyone else's. If you're stuck with a bandmate who can't arrive on time, you'll eventually find yourself angry and frustrated by the tardiness. Worse, you may begin arriving late yourself just so you don't waste your own time waiting. Either action is a rehearsal killer and can be detrimental to a band's future.

There are other rules that can be implemented as well. Common rehearsal rules also include no alcohol, no drugs, no food, and no visitors. Keep in mind, though, that creating too many rules can alienate band members who don't want to be in a band that doesn't know how to have fun or that takes itself too seriously.

Vocalist Julie Zielinski once played in a particularly strict band that had the following rules:

- No hands in pockets at rehearsals.
- No coasting during rehearsals; be spirited.
- Don't watch other members for cues.
- Keep up-to-date on all songs on the master list and be prepared to rehearse them.

"The rules really took the fun out of practice and the band, especially the rule about being spirited," says Zielinski. "Forced spirit at an 11 PM rehearsal is just not me. After dealing with these rules for about six months, I was not at all disappointed when we parted ways."

When conducting, or participating in, rehearsals, remember to be respectful of your bandmates, even if they break the rules. Yelling and becoming hysterical will only divide the band into two camps: you and everyone who thinks you're a tyrant. I've played with tyrants before, and the bands never last long. No one wants to be verbally abused at rehearsal. Replacing band members is time-consuming. You don't want to go through placing ads and hosting auditions again if you can help it. It can set you back weeks or months. If your bandmates like and trust you, you'll have a better shot of getting them back on track if you treat them with respect than if you treat them with contempt.

All bands have members that do things that will drive you or other bandmates crazy. The guitar player might always be too loud, the singer might forget lyrics, and the drummer might have the annoying habit of constantly bashing his or her drums when you are trying to talk about a song. You can't control everything. If a musician is effective at fulfilling his or her role in the band and is a decent person, try to accept any quirks and annoyances, or at least bring them out into the open where the band can discuss them openly before they become divisive. Don't fire a bandmate for something that isn't a significant issue with the group. If you let band members go for minor infractions, you'll never be able to keep a group together.

Despite all of the rules, agendas, and calendars, keep one thing in mind: This is supposed to be fun! Chances are you didn't get into music to treat it like a nine-to-five job. Aside from practicing, songwriting, and all other items on your schedule, rehearsals are opportunities for bandmates to get to know each other and hopefully become friends. Keep things as light and fun as you can and your rehearsals will become a more pleasurable experience for everyone involved.

PREPARING YOUR SONG LIST

Once bands have established their rehearsal strategy, they'll begin meeting to work on their songs (as well as attending to nonmusical responsibilities like promoting the band, promoting upcoming gigs, and preparing for those gigs, which we'll cover in Chapters 7, 9, and 10). The songs will either be written by band members, be covers selected by the group, or be a combination of the two.

Writing Original Material

Bands create their own music either by writing songs as a unit or by one or more members of the group writing the music and bringing it to rehearsal for the rest of the band to learn. Each approach has its advantages. Writing as a team can build unity through group involvement in the process, creating songs that represent each member's contributions. On the other hand, writing songs independently can sometimes produce a more cohesive result because there are less ideas or egos involved. This approach may also be preferable if a certain member, or members, of the group excel at songwriting.

If your band writes as a team, there are two basic approaches that can be taken. The first is for you, or a member of your band, to bring a song idea to rehearsal. The song idea might be a lyrical phrase or an instrumental line. The band then uses it as the foundation of the song and builds other parts from it. These parts are usually flushed out by jamming until the other members work out complementary ideas on their instruments. Once everyone in the band has his or her part established, you have a completed song.

Aerosmith's "Janie's Got a Gun" is a good example of a song written using this method. Bass player Tom Hamilton brought his initial bass idea to the group during a jam session. Upon hearing it, singer Steven Tyler worked out a vocal melody. As they continued to work on the piece a song began to emerge and the rest of the group added their parts. This ultimately created a hit tune for the band.

If your band uses this approach, you may find that your ideas are taken in directions you never imagined. Hopefully, you'll be satisfied with how your idea develops. Peter Smith says, "I really like feedback from the band when I bring in song ideas, and I've had my best successes come from tunes cowritten with other people. I'll come up with a rhythm pattern or chord changes that I like, and some general ideas for the melody, and ask the other members to contribute to the song with complementary parts of their own."

Drummer Robert Smith says, "Our songwriting sessions are pretty much an open forum, but our guitar players and singer bring in most of the ideas that we expound on. Right now, whoever is the most excited about a part jumps in and takes control during rehearsal, and we start working our parts out. Everyone participates, and it works well."

A second approach that can be used to create original material is to free-form improvise, or jam, music until song ideas develop. All members of the band play their instruments and draw ideas and inspiration from each other. Eventually, bits of melody come together, followed by counter-melodies and harmonies, drum parts, and bass lines. Before long, a song is born.

The 1970s band Chic has a funny example of this approach on one of their biggest hits, "Le Freak." The tune came out of the band's frustration at not being admitted into the famous New York nightclub, Studio 54. Denied entry, they angrily returned to their rehearsal studio and began jamming. Soon, a rhythm developed, followed by the one-phrase lyrical passage and title, "Fuck Off," dedicated to the Studio 54 doorman. The band quickly realized they had a great song idea and deleted the expletive—changing the lyric to "Freak Off," which eventually became "Freak Out." "Le Freak" became a huge success and breakthrough song for the group.

If your band likes to write songs based on jams, record those free-form sessions to save any worthy ideas. You'd be surprised how often you can overlook interesting ideas that develop during a jam because they don't pique your interest at the time. When you listen again later, though, they may stand out. I was once a part of a trio that spent the first twenty minutes of every rehearsal jamming with the mics rolling. After listening to the tapes a week or two later, we often found bits and pieces that would eventually evolve into songs in our repertoire.

More often than not, groups driven by singer/songwriter bandleaders don't write music as a team. The leader brings a complete, or nearly complete, song idea to the band to learn. In these instances, any number of approaches may be used to relay the song idea to the band.

One approach is to record the song and then distribute it to the group to learn. In some instances, your song will be brought in fully fleshed out, with each instrument and part already set, perhaps performed by you or other musicians you've worked with. In these instances, there's no need for your band to create their own parts to the song. You're simply asking them to play their parts exactly as recorded. It's up to you whether you want to give the band some discretion to slightly or drastically alter parts within the framework of the song.

I was once a member of a band that was run in this fashion. The bandleader was a singer/songwriter who first created his musical vision in the recording studio with a producer and hired studio musicians. He then distributed the finished recording to his band so we could learn our parts. Occasionally he would ask or allow a player to deviate slightly from a recorded part, but, unless he instructed differently, the music was considered set. The result was a live product that mirrored his studio creation.

Another option as the principal songwriter is to bring your band a song idea, either live at rehearsal or prerecorded, and look to your bandmates to create their own parts based on your direction. This is similar to the approach where a member of a band that writes as a unit shares an idea with the group, except that here the principal writer has veto power. If you're introducing a song to your band in this fashion, simply start playing and begin directing your band. If, for example, you're a guitar player/vocalist, start playing your part and ask the drummer for a beat with the kick pounding four-on-the-floor and the snare drum doing a second-line pattern. Then, ask the bass player for a polka-style line in the key of your song. Keep directing until you have all the parts you envision, at which point you'll have your song.

Wisconsin–based singer/songwriter Buzz Meade teaches his band songs in this fashion, using a prerecorded CD. Meade is the leader and principal songwriter, yet he leaves the music somewhat open for interpretation by his bandmates. "I want to give everyone in the band an artistic say in a song," Meade says, "but I don't want it to stray too far from what I originally wrote. I find making practice

CDs for the group enables the musicians to work on songs at their own speed before rehearsal. Plus, having the CD gives them a reference point if they find they're having trouble remembering their parts later. I rarely work on new material without a prerecorded CD unless it's a very simple song. I find musicians tend to forget the new song forty seconds later anyway, and spending time this way takes away from practicing other songs on the set list."

Selecting Songs Written by Others

If you're selecting songs written by others for your band to perform you'll do so based on three issues: you or your band's passion for the music, the demand for certain types of material, and your band's ability to perform the songs you choose.

If the band has a passion for certain songs, you may choose to perform them regardless of how they might impact your ability to land shows. Bands that create a song list based on their passion for the songs will rank having fun playing music as a high priority since they aren't necessarily interested in playing to the current trends. I once played in a band that covered progressive rock songs from bands like Rush and Pink Floyd. We loved the music and were able to secure some gigs, but for the most part we couldn't play regularly because there wasn't a demand for the music in our local music scene. Music isn't always about performing every weekend or making money, though.

If you're more interested in gigging frequently than in playing your favorite songs (which is not to suggest you might not really enjoy some of the selections), your song choices will be based on filling a demand for a particular genre of music. As special-event bandleader, Doug Waitman says of choosing songs for his set list, "It doesn't matter if you can do 'Bohemian Rhapsody' or an entire side of the Beatles' *White Album* if no one will dance to it. A special-event band's job is to provide the audience with fun activities, primarily dancing." If you're a special-event band and you can't get your audience to dance, the group isn't very good or you've chosen inappropriate music—meaning you'll have a hard time getting gigs.

Your band's ability also comes into play when selecting songs. If you're trying to land gigs as an act that replicates specific songs or genres, you need to accurately cover your material. If the band is moderately talented, tunes like "Louie Louie" by the Kingsmen and "You Really Got Me" by the Kinks won't be a problem. They're simple songs and shouldn't require a lot of practice. If, on the other hand, you want to cover songs by Tool or Dream Theater, your band better have amazing chops, because these groups write technically challenging music.

Doug Waitman agrees. "The songs you choose should incorporate and complement the talents of the musicians and vocalists," he says. "Performing specific songs that have an uncanny resemblance to the original artists often gives the audience a pleasant surprise and exploits the uniqueness of your band that separates yours from all others. If you can pull off something that most other bands would not attempt—an operatic ballad, singing in a foreign language, a complicated classic funk tune or salsa music—your band will be memorable. Likewise, if your particular band cannot do justice to a song or style of music, leave it alone."

There are cover bands that put their own spin on their songs. For example, Los Angeles–based the Dan Band features a male vocalist singing unique and entertaining versions of female empowerment songs like Bonnie Tyler's "Total Eclipse of the Heart" and Kelis' "Milkshake." If your band provides its own interpretation of cover songs you have some leeway to recreate them in a fashion that may not require the same technical skill as the original artists. Still, if the band doesn't have the ability to make the song somewhat recognizable, you'll defeat the purpose of covering it.

Once it's understood why specific types of songs are to be chosen, either the bandleader or the band makes the selections. Bandleader-driven cover bands rely on the head of the group to choose material. It makes sense that the individual running the band and footing the bills makes this decision, since he or she is most invested in the group and the process. Band members will join for various reasons (gigs, money, fun, etc.) and accept the song list as a nonnegotiable part of being in the band.

If the band makes the song selections, then each member should bring ideas in for feedback and approval. As with songwriting, it's useful for cover bands to include their members in the selection process so they feel invested in the group.

I was once in a cover band that specialized in 1980s music. Only the vocalists and I were interested in choosing the material, so the three of us pooled our ideas and created our song list. We all knew we wanted "We Got the Beat" by the Go-Gos and "Mickey" by Toni Basil on the list, but in other instances we had to compromise because we couldn't fit all of the songs we had chosen into our initial forty-song list. We finally went through each remaining song and discussed its pros and cons, whittling the list down to a manageable number. Then we worked through this list again with each of us having a veto if one of us truly couldn't stand the song. The process didn't take long, and by the end of it we had forty songs we all agreed on.

REHEARSING YOUR MATERIAL

Now that you've prepared your song list, you've got to practice your material until the band has it down pat. Drilling your song list is a staple of most band rehearsals.

Some bands, typically newly formed groups or bands with a limited repertoire, are able to rehearse their entire song list in a single practice. The only drawback to running through the same songs at each practice is that you run the risk of burning out on them. If this becomes the case, take a break until the next rehearsal and work on something fresh.

If your band has too long a song list to practice each tune at rehearsal, you can practice only some of your songs each time you get together. I've been in bands that would open and close each rehearsal with just a few songs from our set so we could maintain them. We then spent the bulk of our rehearsal time writing new material. You can also set aside one rehearsal every week or two to cover your song list while using the others to write or learn new material. If you need to run through your complete repertoire at rehearsal, but don't have time, try practicing just the first and last thirty seconds of each song. This can get the band in the groove with regard to tempo and feel, as well as what is usually the most challenging part of a song, its beginning and ending.

When rehearsing songs, examine their details and nuances to make sure they're being performed correctly. If you're the writer (or one of the writers), make sure it meets your expectations. If the song is a cover, make sure the song is faithful to the original recording. If you're revising a cover song with your band's own spin, make sure your version represents what you are trying to accomplish. The best way to analyze your existing material is to record it and then play it back. If you don't want to record yourselves, then make mental notes of your performance and share them with your band afterwards. This approach can work, but it's not as effective as listening to a recording, because recordings always tell the truth, while memories can be misleading.

Also, just because your band knew the songs at one point in time doesn't mean mistakes can't seep in. Staving off this *mistake creep*, which occurs when errors slowly enter into the makeup of a song and become permanent, is key for bands that want to maintain the integrity of their songs. When you play a song the wrong way for too long, you begin believing it's actually the right way.

When I played in a blues-and-swing band in San Francisco, we covered Elvis' "Jailhouse Rock," which has a very recognizable set of snare drum hits in the introduction. Somewhere between learning the tune and playing it live for many months, our drummer forgot that the snare hits went one, one-two, and instead was playing them in reverse. This went unnoticed until the bandleader heard the original version during a second listen months later and brought it to our attention. It was a simple slip but a great example of how mistake creep can alter the elements of a song without the band realizing it.

When your band hears mistakes in their material, they should speak openly about them, as well as discuss how to correct them. No one should feel awkward pointing out errors. Rehearsals are times for making corrections and tightening your set, not simply repeating it without analysis. Band members should also feel free to offer constructive advice on how to fix problems in the songs so their points aren't taken as insults. A comment like, "You just can't keep time, can you?" isn't going to help your drummer hold the beat steady. "I think the time is wavering a bit. How about we run a click track through the PA so we can all play the song together at 140 bpm?" will be a much more constructive comment. Now that the mistake has been identified and a course of action has been established to correct it, the song can be performed again, or you may choose to make a note about it for a later rehearsal assignment sheet.

Once your band is able to play through all songs without error, you're ready to take them into the studio to record a demo.

CHAPTER 6

RECORDING A DEMO TO GET GIGS AND MARKET YOUR BAND

A demo *is an audio recording bands create to showcase their music to bookers, special-event planners, music industry professionals, and even fans. A band's demo (short for "demonstration") is not a full-length album; it's a sampling of two to six songs from a band's song list that represent the band. A demo's quality doesn't have to be on par with major-label-produced songs you hear on the radio. It can be a rough approximate of a band's music. Bands distribute their demo in hopes that they'll land gigs and create a greater awareness of the group and its music.*

Recording a demo is a challenge. For one thing, recordings are brutally honest. Any flaws in a band's performance, such as an inability to sing consistent harmonies or keep time, will be exposed in the recording process, rendering the demo far less effective. For another thing, recording studios can be expensive, and the recording experience itself intimidating and stressful.

To prepare for cutting a demo, you need to first understand the different recording options available and their respective costs. You also want to establish a budget to determine what kind of recording you can afford. Preproduction demos should then be made by the band to ensure that the music is as tight as possible. After following these steps, if you can afford a recording studio, you'll seek one out that fits your needs and budget. Once you're ready to record, you'll track, mix, and master your music to complete your demo.

KNOWING YOUR RECORDING OPTIONS AND ESTABLISHING A BUDGET

There are a few approaches to recording a demo, and each has a price. Your responsibility is to know your options and what each costs before establishing a budget.

Understanding Your Recording Options and Their Costs

There are three basic recording options: There's the small-budget do-it-yourself recording. There's the midsize budget, semiprofessional recording, often produced in a modest one-room studio by an engineer with limited professional experience. And there's the large-budget recording produced in a professional studio with seasoned engineers.

If your budget is restricted, don't worry. Advances in recording technology have leveled the playing field. Today, it doesn't take much money to create an impressive-sounding recording. With a mixer and some microphones, a personal computer, and software like Pro Tools and Sonar, you can record a great-sounding demo.

Remember that you're not trying to record a Grammy-winning album. Your goal is simply to produce a functional demo to help your band land gigs and to distribute your songs to your fans. My first band had a recording budget of $10. We used it to buy one high-quality Maxell cassette tape, which we inserted into a portable cassette player with a built-in microphone. Although the sound quality wasn't great, it was what we could afford and it got us gigs in several local clubs and one town fair.

On a budget of $200 or less, you've got to already own, or be able to borrow, a computer with recording software, a four-track recorder, or even a handheld digital recorder. You may also need other items like a mixer, an effects processor, and software plug-ins. To record on this budget, you'll just need enough money to cover important recording accessories like recordable CDs, one or two inexpensive microphones with cables, and perhaps a mic stand.

The major problem with working on a small-budget recording is expertise. Unless you, or someone in your band, have recording experience, you won't be able to maximize your recording potential. Engineering is a skill that takes years to acquire. Without it, your demo can still be an effective tool for landing gigs and marketing your band, but if you don't know where to set up microphones, how to use effects, and how to tweak EQ, it won't be on par with those coming out of studios run by capable engineers.

A do-it-yourself recording does have one key advantage over one produced in a semiprofessional or professional studio: You're able to take your time. You can record in your own rehearsal space for as long as you want without worrying about going over budget.

I've been involved in many studio recordings where the looming threat of additional recording costs has created a lot of stress, turning what should have been a manageable experience into a frenzy of activity as the clock ticked. None of these experiences ever produced overly satisfying results because we were rushing to beat the clock instead of concentrating on our performances. If you're recording yourselves, the only deadline you're beholden to is the one you set.

With a midsize recording budget of $200 to $1,500, you ought to be able to record with a semiprofessional, or professional, engineer in his or her own studio. A semipro studio should feature all the basic necessities, like a mixing board, sound monitors, and enough microphones to properly mic a drum kit. What these studios usually lack—and what separates them from larger, more expensive studios—are items like great pre-amps and effects processors, as well as a superior tracking room to capture great acoustics and natural reverb.

The engineers at these studios may not necessarily be professionally trained, but they'll have learned recording techniques (possibly by recording their own bands), and through repetition, they may have become very proficient engineers. At rates ranging from $15 to $50 dollars an hour, with a budget of $1,000, you can afford five days at a $25-per-hour studio, which should be plenty of time to record and mix a demo.

While all studios are dependent on the quality of their engineers, smaller studios live or die by their expertise. Matt Strickland, co-owner of H.I.T. Wall Studios, as well as vocalist and guitarist for the band DU★DS, professional recording engineer, and producer in the San Francisco Bay Area, says, "An engineer with a great ear can make all the difference in a recording." If you're able to find a small studio with an engineer who really knows how to get the best out of his or her limited equipment, you can end up with an impressive demo.

With a larger recording budget, $1,500 and up, you can have the luxury of recording in studios that feature first-class equipment, tracking rooms with great acoustics and natural reverb, and trained engineers. Your budget should adequately cover studio costs, but be forewarned that you may also have to pay for engineering fees in such facilities. Studio time is typically billed at $50 to $100 per hour but can go as high as several hundred dollars per hour, depending on the facility.

Many large studios don't employ staff engineers, but will recommend independent engineers who have worked with them before. When it comes time to pay for the recording of your demo, you'll write two checks—one to the studio and the other to the engineer.

Before you write off the possibility of recording at a larger studio for budgetary reasons, keep in mind that many large studios are feeling the pinch of losing business to smaller professional and home studios with digital recording capabilities that rival their own. As a result, you can sometimes negotiate a reasonable rate with a larger studio that isn't completely booked.

Recording studios, especially those with high overhead, need to operate as many hours of the day as possible to maximize their revenue. These studios often have premier clients recording at top dollar prices during traditional operating hours so they can offer smaller projects a discounted rate to record during off-hours. A former band of mine was able to secure studio time at one of the top studios in San Francisco by agreeing to work from 11 PM to 8 AM. We were hopeless coffee junkies by the end of the session, but we were able to work at a very reputable studio for an affordable price.

Examples of larger, more expensive studios include TOAST studios in San Francisco, the Plant in Sausalito, the Village in Los Angeles, and Electric Lady Studios in New York. These studios have recorded artists such as the Beach Boys, Metallica, Snoop Dog, Third Eye Blind, Pat Benatar, Steely Dan, and Jimi Hendrix. If your band can afford the cost and believes this level of recording quality is what you need for your demo, you can follow some well-known acts into these recording studios.

Regardless of how much money you can afford to spend on your demo, there's no substitute for a great performance, and no recording equipment that can compensate for a bad performance. The Beatles, the Jimi Hendrix Experience, Cream, and most Motown acts recorded using only four or eight tracks on devices that, by today's standards, are the equivalent of driving around in a Model T. They made great recordings because they captured great performances on tape. If you and your band have your act together, your performances can transcend budget limitations.

Creating a Recording Budget

A *recording budget* establishes how much money you can afford to spend on a demo or CD. By setting a budget before you begin researching studios, you can avoid the heartbreak of learning that a facility you've fallen in love with is out of the band's price range.

If it's your own group, prepare to foot the entire bill. When musicians are either paid members of a band or just playing for fun, they won't have the same stake in the band's success and may not feel the demo should be their financial responsibility. If you're in a democratic band, the group will most likely split the cost of recording equally or come up with a suitable compromise that accommodates all members.

To determine how much money is available to record your demo, you need to identify potential sources of funding. There are two kinds of funding sources: ideal and usual. Ideal sources are benefactors, such as a parent who's willing to help with the recording costs, and producers willing to pay in exchange for a financial stake in the band. In these instances, bands don't have to shoulder the costs alone. Los Angeles–based vocalist Erica Canales says of her recording experience, "I only had money to pay the musicians who played on my record. I couldn't afford studio time. I had to find a producer who believed in my music and was willing to partner with me to cover these costs in exchange for a percentage of my earnings."

The usual source of funding for recordings, however, is members of the band. This is the more likely scenario for bands and it includes a budget comprised of earnings from the performances, the band members' disposable income, or a combination of the two.

Needless to say, it's preferable to fund your demo with band earnings than to go out-of-pocket. Paying out-of-pocket can be tough if you're living paycheck to paycheck. If the band doesn't depend on its earnings for living expenses, then it's extra money and ideal for band expenses.

The problem with paying for projects like recordings with band income is that gigs, especially for beginning groups, tend to pay anywhere from zero to $50. It can take twenty gigs or more to earn enough to cover a midsize recording budget, and unless you're performing regularly this could take a year or more. It's like filling a swimming pool with an eyedropper.

Groups that have this fortitude place their performance income into what's commonly referred to as a "band fund." The fund operates like a bank account, although it's more likely held in a shoebox in your rehearsal studio. Regardless of where it's physically located, a band fund only works when it's allowed to grow. It's difficult for bands to avoid spending their earnings, especially after a show when they've just been paid, have a post-gig buzz, and want to celebrate. It's tempting to use the money to pay for drinks, or to buy burgers at a late-night diner. A small amount of earnings won't seem like it will make much of an impact if you need significantly more to make a dent in studio costs. This is where many bands abandon the fund and just disperse the money to members.

"I've found the band fund doesn't work. It always seems to disappear on beer and food after the gig," says bandleader Paul Mitchell. "Sure, everyone talks about replacing it later, but it never happens. Now I collect the money from the club, disperse it, and forget about it. For my band, $50 here and there doesn't impact the fund when we need much more than that to do a decent recording."

For a band fund to succeed, it needs to be allowed to grow. The best way to do this is to immediately put your earnings in an envelope and hide it in a safe place like an instrument case or the back of an amplifier. Since you won't have these items handy when you're mingling after the show, there's no chance you'll "accidentally" reach into your wallet and spend your earnings.

If the group doesn't have a fund and has to pay for the recording out of each member's disposable income, you need to determine what you can afford to spend. The ideal recording budget is divided equally among the members. However, each member of the band is likely to have a different financial situation that dictates what he or she is able to contribute. This can make it difficult to come to an agreement on each person's financial contribution. One member may have a day job that nets a healthy paycheck, but another may be a student who relies on help from his or her family. Finding common ground can be challenging.

To avoid an uncomfortable situation, it's best to cater to the finances of the band's poorest members by finding the lowest financial common denominator. If one member of the four-piece band can contribute $1,000, two others can contribute $750, and the remaining member can contribute $500, then your budget should be $2,000 (4 × $500). This approach can help you determine the budget without forcing a bandmate to eat ramen noodles every night for the next six months.

If some band members are completely broke, it's tough to reach a compromise that involves everyone's equal financial participation. Some members will have to pay more than others. This is a difficult situation that can create tension within a band, and it may lead to some members feeling they should have more say in the recording process because they paid more.

If your bandmates can't split the costs equally, either work out a scenario where those unable to cover their share pay back the ones who are over time, or agree that the debt can be forgotten entirely. As financially taxing as this might be, it isn't a bad idea. Haranguing bandmates like a loan shark isn't a role to which a band member should aspire.

Finally, be honest about how much you can afford to spend. Don't allow yourself to be pressured by those who want you to kick in more than you're comfortable with or who are willing to let you go into debt to cover your share. The recording may be the most important thing in your life at the moment, but it's still not worth what may amount to years of compounded interest to pay off a debt. And in many cases, the debt you accumulate will outlast the band. I've made the mistake of going into debt to finance recordings, and years after the bands had broken up, I was still paying it down.

PREPARING TO RECORD YOUR DEMO

The best way to prepare for recording your demo is to record. This session is called *preproduction* because it's done in advance of the recording itself. Bands use preproduction to identify any kinks in their music that must be corrected before they record their demo.

Recording Your Practice Sessions

The first step in preproduction recording is for band members to prepare individually. Each member practices and records his or her parts independently to ensure flawless reproduction. The benefit of practicing alone is that you can hear what you're doing independent of the other instruments.

It takes discipline to practice alone. When playing with the band you can lean on them to help you get through the songs. This is especially true when it comes to following a song's structure. If you aren't exactly sure when a pre-chorus or bridge occurs, you can wait for the vocalist's cue through his or her body language or lyric, or wait for a drummer's cymbal crash to signal the change. When recording, you may not have these crutches to get you through the songs, especially if you're in a different tracking room, recording your part, or you don't have a good viewing angle of your bandmates. If you're relying on cues, and don't get them, you'll make mistakes while recording and you can throw off the rest of the band. Practicing on your own forces you to thoroughly understand the structures of your songs.

To practice effectively, you need to play in time, and this means you'll need a timekeeping device like a metronome or drum machine, which will keep your performance true to the song's tempo. Practicing without such a device can result in your rushing or slowing down your instrument's parts.

If you're singing lead or harmony vocals on the demo, you'll also need an instrument with perfectly tuned pitch to sing against to ensure you're on pitch. This can be a keyboard or even a guitar. As long as the instrument can match the dynamic range of your vocal part, and is in tune, it will work. Vocalists typically practice against perfect pitch to make certain they're in the right key and to check their pitch on notes they aren't confident they can consistently hit. You can take your preparation to the extreme by recording your entire vocal melody on a keyboard or guitar and then singing along with it.

After recording yourself, play it back to see whether you've played your part accurately. If you didn't, identify the problem and keep working to correct it. If you can't play a certain musical pattern fast enough, perform it with a metronome at a slower speed until you're ready to move it back up to correct speed. If you can't consistently hit the vocal notes, move the note down the scale until you can, and then over time slowly bring it back up to the correct note.

Recording Your Band in Preproduction

Once band members feel confident about their ability to perform their parts, everyone is ready to record the preproduction demo with the band. "I like to make sure I have everything down before going into the studio," says Paul Mitchell. "I'll bring a cheap recorder or a four-track to the rehearsal studio. Then we'll throw out a couple of mics, turn on the click track, press record, and determine if the songs are down pat. Once they are, I know we're ready to go into the studio."

Since the band has been practicing these songs during regular rehearsals and has just finished an extensive preproduction exercise, everyone should have the song structures down and be able to perform the tunes without error. Everyone's focus should now be on the nuances of the songs, particularly drum fills, guitar, bass, keyboard, and horn licks, as well as vocal riffs that typically come in transition sections of songs such as before or after a chorus, or bridge, or during the ending of a song.

It's likely that the band has improvised many of these riffs and fills in the songs. If the band excels at improvising, there should be no musical clashes between instruments. If there are, stop improvising. If you record a section where multiple instruments are filling, and it's not syncopated, your music is going to sound disorganized. Establish in advance who's filling where.

When your band has completed its preproduction recording, play it back to hear how it sounds. Listen to hear whether the band is playing in time, the harmonies are in key, and the drum fills are in sync with the guitar and bass licks. If you hear problems, identify them and discuss how to resolve them.

SELECTING A RECORDING STUDIO

If the band is able to afford a recording studio, the next step is to select one that fits your budget and provides the best possible facilities for the money. Begin by locating studios in your area. Then, you need to interview them to determine whether they match your band's needs. Once you've narrowed your list to a few studios, set up a tour of their facilities before making your final selection.

Finding Recording Studios in Your Area

To find studios in your area, use the same techniques you employed to find musicians and bands. To generate leads, search print advertising and the Internet and speak with fellow musicians.

The size and quality of the information in ads you'll find will depend on the advertising budget of the studio and where the ad is placed. Small semiprofessional studios may not have the money for color print ads or complex Web sites. They may only be able to afford ten-word ads or Web sites with few pictures and no audio. Large professional studios can afford to place large ads with photos and client testimonials in local music publications as well as have elaborate Web sites with various audio samples.

Effective ads, big or small, provide the same basic information, which will include the studio's recording capabilities, the engineer's experience, and the rates. Ads do exaggerate, so temper your expectations when you see hyperbole like, "Best sounds in town or your money back!"

Some studios won't advertise their rates because they either prefer to negotiate each deal separately or they don't want to lose potential clients before being able to show off their facilities. I once called a professional recording studio to ask about the rates and instead of giving me an answer, the manager asked what my band's budget was. After sharing the information and doing some negotiating, we agreed on terms. I've also contacted studios whose representatives turned into proverbial used-car salesmen, attempting to convince me the facility was worth the extra money because someone famous had once worked there, or because their equipment was used on a top-selling album.

Here's a sample of a stripped-down print ad you might find published in the classifieds or on a bulletin board in a rehearsal studio:

RECORDING STUDIO
LOW RATES—TOP QUALITY
Experienced in Rap, Hip Hop, Punk, Latin Styles.
Starspot Productions; (323) 555-5555; blakeD@mystudio.com

The ad isn't fancy, but it provides enough information for you to contact them if they're a good fit for your music.

Word of mouth is an excellent means of finding studios as well. In addition to identifying studios in your area, you can get first-hand information on cost, experience, capabilities, and rates from bands that have recorded in them. Ask musicians in your area if they would recommend the studios where they recorded their demos. If so, get the information and add the studios to your list. Also, ask to hear their demos to judge the recording quality for yourself.

Interviewing Studios

Once you've made a list of recording studios, you want to interview them to determine whether they fit your needs. Each studio should be evaluated based on four criteria: cost, the experience of the engineer, recording capabilities, and their plan for recording your band. Be sure to talk with someone who can answer all of your questions. If you're calling small semiprofessional studios, the owner and engineer are likely the same person and can answer questions about rates and recording techniques. If you're contacting large facilities, you may need to speak with both the owner (or their designate) and the engineer to get your questions answered. Take detailed notes on each interview to help you and your bandmates decide whether to follow up with a tour of the facility.

Cost is the most important of the four criteria. If you can't afford a studio's rates, there's no point in continuing the interview. However, you can ask the studio to lower its rate or possibly recommend a studio that's within your price range.

When discussing rates, explain what kind of music your band plays, what sort of budget you have, how many songs you want to record, how many instruments there are in the band, and the purpose of your recording. This information will help the studio determine whether they can meet your needs within your budget.

"The best thing a band can do is have a dialog with the engineer before the session," says Peter Slankster, professional producer, recording engineer, and owner of Creamy Sonic Studios in Dublin, Ireland. "Tell the engineer exactly what you want to accomplish and see if he or she can help you do it within your budget."

If you've determined you can afford a studio, find out how the billing will work. There are three ways studios can charge for their services: by the hour, by the day, or by the project. Hourly and day rates are calculated by setting a cost per hour or day and multiplying it by how many hours, or days, the band is in the studio (a day rate usually covers an eight-hour period). A project rate is a one-time cost that encompasses the entire recording process.

Each rate structure has its advantages and disadvantages. Hourly rates can be ideal if you're able to quickly track your songs without rerecording, and you may not need to spend an entire day in the studio. If you have to choose between an hourly rate of $30 an hour or a day rate of $240, and you feel you can finish your project in six hours, you'd be able to save $60. The drawback is that you may find yourself racing against the clock, trying to finish the project before the next hour begins. On the other hand, if you choose a day rate, you may wind up not using time you've paid for if you finish the demo before your day ends. If you accept a day rate, be sure to ask how many hours equal one day's studio time.

Project rates are rare because studios don't want to be stuck with a band that's recording in slow motion. This can cost studios money, because they can't take on new clients if the old ones are still working in their facility. Project rates are offered for three reasons. If the studio is able to keep the project moving, they may be able to make more money than if they'd charged by the hour or day and finished sooner than anticipated. Project rates can alleviate some stress as well if an engineer faces a daunting project and doesn't want to be pressured to finish in a specific number of days or hours. Project rates may also be attractive to bands that don't want to stress about time. If you find a studio willing to offer this rate, see if they have a cap on the number of days you're able to spend in the studio before your time expires and additional fees begin accruing.

You may find that each studio has only one rate structure. However, most studios today, especially small ones, are run by entrepreneurs willing to negotiate and make deals with bands to keep their facilities active. Be firm if you have a rate preference and the studio might comply.

Before making a final decision on which rate structure to accept or pursue, give some thought to how much time you'll need. There's more to recording than simply entering a studio, plugging in, and playing your songs. You and your bandmates will spend a lot of time setting up and testing equipment. This is especially true of drums, which can take a long time to mic properly. I've been in recording sessions where the entire first day was spent getting the right drum sounds.

After setup, there's *tracking*, which is the term for the actual recording of the instruments. This can either be done with the whole band recorded at one time or with each instrument recorded separately. Once tracking is complete, you move on to *mixing*, which can take as long, or longer, than tracking because it's the phase where you and your engineer make crucial decisions regarding compression, equalization, panning, and volume that will profoundly affect your songs. Finally, there's *mastering*, the process of preparing audio to be transferred to a media format like a CD or MP3 file.

Included in these phases are many nonmusical tasks the engineer will manage during your session. There'll be hard drives to format, files to import and back up, and mixes that need to be transferred from one format to another. These tasks can take anywhere from several minutes to hours to complete.

To get a better idea of how much time your band will need in the studio, ask the engineer for an estimate. He or she should be willing to give an opinion on how long the process will take and how you may be able to maximize your time and money.

"The engineer working on the project will have more experience with the industry and the process than you and will be a valuable guide," says Peter Slankster. "The engineer should be able to tell you how to get the most out of your money. The engineer also will have a better idea of the time involved with the recording process—how long it will take to set up, mic, and get tones for a drum kit. With this knowledge, the engineer will help you with things, such as how much time should be booked in the studio and the schedule for the musicians."

The second criteria in evaluating a recording studio is the experience of the engineer with whom you'd be working. You want to know how long he or she's been an engineer and how the engineer learned the skill. The answers the engineer provides can give you insight into his or her abilities. If you're not speaking with the proposed engineer for your project, ask to schedule an interview to occur in the future.

You also need to learn whether the engineer has experience in your kind of music. This experience can lead to greater efficiency and a better-sounding demo because the engineer will be able to forgo a learning curve. If your engineer has experience recording rock bands, he or she will understand how to compress drum sounds to make them sound more aggressive and how to layer distorted guitars without having them sonically cancel out each other. If the engineer is experienced in recording light jazz, he or she will know where to place microphones to pick up the natural reverb of the tracking room. A lack of experience in this area can lead to a poorer quality recording or one that takes longer to produce, costing you time and money.

If you're satisfied with the engineer's experience, ask to hear some of the demos he or she has recorded. This is a standard request. If the engineer balks, he or she probably hasn't produced anything worth listening to and you need to move on. If the engineer agrees, ask him or her to invite you to the studio to listen, direct you to the audio portion on a Web site, or send you a sample by mail or e-mail. Listen to these demos with your band. If you're able to hear each instrument, the engineer understands the concept of separation and equalization, as well as how to place music within a mix so that it has a full sound. Be sure the music is balanced and there are no odd volume swells that don't match the song's dynamics. Also, listen to whether the demo enhances and complements the songs. Does the recording come alive during catchy choruses, or does it lack energy? Ultimately, if the quality of the recording excites you, then the studio should be added to your short list. If not, move on.

The third criteria is a studio's recording capabilities. You want to know what sort of equipment and how much room they have in their facility. You also need to know how the engineer envisions his or her equipment and tracking space helping your band record the best possible demo.

The more equipment a studio has, the more options you'll have when recording. A studio with multiple compressors, effects possessors, pre-amps, microphones, and even guitars, basses, and amps can give you more options than a studio with one compressor, no effects processors, and just a few microphones. If the recording equipment is top-notch, you can achieve a better sound. For example, if your studio uses an Avalon compressor, you'll get a better result than if you record at a studio with a Behringer unit—provided the engineer knows how to operate the compressor. A disadvantage to an abundance of gear is that you may spend too much time experimenting and fall behind schedule.

If the studio has multiple tracking rooms, each instrument and its amp can be set up in a different room and band members can record at the same time without having to turn down their volumes or finding ways to deaden their amp's sound to prevent the sounds of other amps from seeping into their mic (when other instrument sounds are audible through another instrument's mic it's called *bleed*). With multiple rooms, your band can test each one's different acoustics to determine which room works best for recording instruments like drums and voice, which benefit from the natural ambiance of the room.

Don't be enchanted by a studio simply because there's enough gear to record an orchestra or a tracking room with cathedral ceilings. Remember, great equipment doesn't necessarily make for a great recording. A good engineer can produce an excellent recording with average equipment, but an average engineer can't do the same with great equipment.

When you ask an engineer about a studio's capabilities, he or she will likely respond by addressing which medium they use: *digital recording* or *analog recording.*

Digital recordings convert your music into binary numbers and are made with Macs and PCs or digital recording devices like mini-disc recorders and ADATs. They can be stored on a CD or hard drive. Analog recordings capture your music as a continuous sound wave and are typically made with tape machines that vary in size to handle tape from .25 inch to 2 inches. Analog waves are stored on tape, which can be expensive.

Recording purists say analog is the better medium because it offers a warmer sound. They claim instruments like the human voice and cymbals translate better on analog than digital because their sounds don't artificially trail off as they become quieter. If this were true, it's less likely to occur now with the constant development and improvement of the software on digital recording mediums.

If a studio offers you the choice of recording in analog or digital, ask the engineer for samples of the work they've done in each medium and let your ears be the judge. If you decide to record in analog, you'll need to factor the cost of analog tape into your budget. Depending on what kind of tape you use (standard tape is sized from .25-inch to 2 inches in width) and whether you use pre-used tape, the variance in cost can be hundreds of dollars. Analog recording and tape machines are becoming increasingly rare. They're often old and in need of calibration and maintenance. To ensure the best sound quality, your engineer may insist that his or her machine be tended to before your recording. This cost may be passed on to your band.

When you ask about recording capabilities, make sure the studio can *multi-track* (each instrument recorded on its own track). With separate tracks, musicians have the opportunity to correct any mistakes made during the tracking phase by recording over them at a later time. This is called *"punching in."* Without multi-tracking, the engineer won't be able to effectively mix your songs. If your band's instruments are bunched together on one or more tracks, any effects, panning, or equalization you put on a track will impact every instrument on that track. If you have drums and bass on a track, you'll end up having to mix them as one unit and won't be able to use equalizer (EQ) to focus on getting great definition on cymbal crashes because it will distort the bass.

The final criteria key to evaluating a recording studio is how the engineer plans to record the band. For your demo to assist you in landing gigs, it needs to capture your live performance so bookers and special-event planners know exactly what kind of band they're considering.

To recreate your live sound in the recording studio, you'll need to either record with the same equipment you use for rehearsals and shows or with equipment that can approximate your sound. If you plan on using your stage setup, bring your instrument and everything else that contributes to the way your band sounds onstage. If you're a guitar player, there's more to your sound than just your Gibson SG guitar. There's your amp, your effects, and the cables you use. You should also consider your picks, strings, and what stage of their life you prefer them. Many guitarists prefer to record with brand new strings. Others—like Eddie Van Halen—have been known to record with completely dead strings, because they feel they're more consistent sounding than fresh strings. In addition, standing or sitting impacts how you fret and strike the strings, which affects the sound of your instrument, so you might even consider being on your feet while recording to mimic they way you play with the band.

Unless the studio has an instrument you want to use for your demo, you'll use your own instrument to record. Amplifiers are another matter. If you use an amplifier, you may choose to approximate your amp's sound by using an amp modeler. These are direct boxes that feature complex circuitry that enables them to simulate the sounds of mic'd amplifiers. Line 6 makes a modeler called the POD for guitar and bass that's become very popular. Its sounds can be manipulated tonally with the flip of a button or the click of a mouse. These sounds can be more consistent than amps, plus you can send the output directly into a recording medium without having to worry about your amp bleeding into your vocalist's microphone or disturbing the studio's neighbors. They're also very convenient. An amp modeler like the POD is about half the size of a shoebox and a lot easier to carry than a Marshall stack. It's even more convenient if the studio has modeler software built into its system. If so, you'll just need to bring your guitar and effects.

Different instruments can be recorded in different ways, depending on the instrument and the desired sound. If you're a guitar or bass player, you and the engineer may decide that the best way to capture your live sound is to mic your amp. You may even decide to use two mics, one placed an inch from the speaker and another ten feet away to record your amp's sound mixed with the natural acoustics of the room. Or you may choose to use an amp modeler as previously described. If you're a sax player, you'll have to mic your horn, since you can't send a signal from an acoustic instrument without a pickup or a line output (like a horn or voice), as those found in digital keyboards, guitars, and basses.

Talk with your engineer about what kind of sound you need and listen to his or her recommendations. An experienced engineer should have ideas. I recently worked with an engineer who positioned my conga player on plywood and then mic'd the surface of the conga as well as the wood on the floor. He then mixed the two signals and got a great tone. I would never have thought of that, but I'm not surprised he did. He's an expert. I'm in the studio a few times a year and rarely with a conga player.

Many studios have their own equipment. Because of this level of familiarity, they're able to consistently get good sounds. If the band agrees with the engineer's direction, and the tone either matches or closely resembles your own, take advantage of the studio's gear. This will save time and the need to lug in your equipment. For example, Peter Slankster believes his G&L L2000 bass—strung with Elixir strings—gives him a great sound and tremendous flexibility. He practically insists all bass players use it in his studio. Bassists traveling to his studio can travel light!

You'll also need to address how the engineer intends to track your band. This can be done in three ways (and each can be done with multi-tracking). The first method is to record the entire group playing together, as they would during a live performance. The second is to record each instrument separately, one at a time. The third is a hybrid of the two, where some band members record live while others record their parts separately.

Each method has advantages and disadvantages. If your band records at the same time, you can capture a "live" feeling. The drawback to recording together is that a mistake impacts the entire band. One error can ruin a take, and the band will have to record the song again. This can get pretty frustrating, especially if one member is continually making mistakes.

Some studios can't provide bands with the option of recording at the same time due to their size. If the studio is one room, there might not be enough space to have the entire band tracking at once. The studio might also be in a house or an apartment with noise restrictions. In these cases, the band will have to record separately.

A disadvantage of recording separately is that it takes longer to complete the tracking phase. It's simple math. If a five-piece band records a four-minute song as a unit, it'll take four minutes to complete. If band members record the same song individually, it'll take twenty minutes. If time in the studio is an issue for budgetary reasons, you may want to consider tracking at the same time.

If you choose the hybrid technique, you can break down your recording session by sections. Your bass and drums can record their parts first. Then your vocals, guitar, and keyboard can record individually on top of the bass and drums. If the band features layers of guitar and keyboards, as well as multiple-harmony vocal parts, this method can be beneficial because these instruments wouldn't be able to complete their tracking in one pass anyway. And if the bass and drums are grooving, it'll provide a foundation with a live feel that can make the whole song sound as though it was recorded live. The drawback is that it takes longer to complete and may be slowed further if the earliest recording musicians are error-prone.

Touring Studios and Deciding Where to Record

Once you've completed your interviews, you and your band need to select the studios you want to tour. This will be your last step before deciding where to record. Go back through your notes to see which studios were within your budget and met your four criteria. Then give them a call and ask to tour their facilities. If they're interested in your business, they'll accommodate you.

There are many reasons to tour potential studios. Obviously you want to see the recording facilities, check out the tracking room, and have the engineer walk the band through his or her vision for your demo. But most important, you want to feel assured that what you were told about each studio is true. When you're considering spending hundreds or thousands of dollars you want to know you aren't being conned. Before digital recording, even small studios had to invest thousands of dollars or more in recording equipment, and no one makes that sort of investment without having some recording knowledge. Today, all you need is a computer and some software and you can be the proud owner of a recording studio—whether you know what you're doing or not.

When you arrive at the studio, try not to pass judgment on it if it's in a bad neighborhood or a grungy building. One of my favorite facilities, Hyde Street Studios, has recorded numerous major-label bands, yet it's located in the Tenderloin District in San Francisco, a very rough neighborhood. Appearances on the outside of the studio don't matter. Your concern is what's going on inside.

When you enter the studio, look around to see if it seems organized. Check to see whether there are cables, mics, and headphones strewn around the floor and pre-amps leaning against the wall or holding open a door. Recording equipment is delicate. If there's lack of care about gear, the engineer probably isn't going to put much into your demo either.

When you've finished the tour, ask the engineer to play some of the studio's work through the studio's sound system. If the engineer pulls out a finished CD, you can gauge what a completed project sounds like, which can be beneficial, but ask to hear a project that hasn't been mixed to CD yet so he or she can solo the audio on certain instruments and tracks. Hearing specific instruments isolated will allow you to judge the quality of the sound without being influenced by the other instruments. If you want to hear the engineer's recorded drums, listen to them soloed to hear if there's a big kick drum sound, a crack to the snare drum, and a clear wash to the ride cymbal.

Afterward, ask the engineer to listen to some recordings you'll have brought. These should include your band preproduction recording and a CD of an artist whose sound you would like to emulate in the studio.

Playing your band's preproduction audio gives the engineer a better sense of your style of music, your instrumentation, and your skill level. During this listening session, discuss what's sonically important to your band. If you're in a punk band with a signature overdriven guitar sound, explain that you want the guitars prominent in the recording. If you're in a pop band, let the engineer know that the vocals and melodic hooks must have prominence. If you're a hip-hop band, discuss the need for a healthy dose of sub-bass frequencies on your demo.

Once you've finished playing your preproduction recording, play the CD of that other artist. Peter Slankster says of this approach, "This is very effective and gives the engineer an idea of what you are looking for. You can even make a mix CD with ten to twenty songs that you think sound great in the genre that represents your music. Also, when it comes time to mix your music, you and the engineer can compare your mix to the songs on this CD."

Matt Strickland agrees. "I usually calibrate my brain to the bands that I am working with to see what they perceive as a good sound. I listen to CDs they like and pick out what they like about the music and why. People are so different when it comes to 'good sound.' Once we are all on the same page, the next thing is to think about how to get the music there. Do we need to borrow certain drums, rent bass gear? I do whatever it takes get the session comfortable and sounding right."

When listening to the tracks, explain why they appeal to the band and ask if, and how, this sound might be achieved in the studio. Speaking in the language of the engineer is not essential; use layman's terms. If you're in an alternative rock band and you've brought *Hot Fuss*, by the Killers, you might simply say that you like how the drums really stand out or how the bass sounds big and "in your face." After hearing the music, the engineer can confirm that you like distorted bass in the front of the mix and heavily compressed drums. You can then discuss how this sound can be achieved.

Keep in mind that if you've chosen music from a major-label artist, the CD is likely to have had hundreds of thousands, if not millions, of dollars invested to make it sound incredible. Unless you're recording in a large studio with major album credits and have a very large budget, your engineer won't be able to duplicate the recording. But since most studios use similar digital technology, you might be able to get close.

When you're done listening, the tour is over. Even if the studio seems like a great match, don't make a decision until you've completed your due diligence and toured the rest of the studios on your list. You'll be impatient and your inclination will be to want to finalize a deal with the studio right away. This is understandable, but a few more days of studio visits will be worth it if you're able to find a facility you like better.

Once you've settled on a studio, contact its representative to finalize the deal. Reaffirm the cost, determine the time and date of the session, and ask for everything in writing. Then review any load-in procedures. Finally, thank the studio and tell the engineer or manager you've been negotiating with that you're looking forward to working there.

RECORDING YOUR DEMO

Once you're ready to record, your first step is setting up and testing your equipment. From there it's on to tracking your songs and mixing and mastering your demo.

Setting Up at the Studio

If you're recording the band in your home or a rehearsal space, you're responsible for setting up everything. This includes your instruments to any microphones, direct boxes, input cables, and recording devices you plan to use. Each member can set up his or her specific gear, but designate a member of your band to be the "engineer." This person will be responsible for making sure everyone is set up properly and that audio levels have been tested, in addition to running the recording equipment itself. If you're working at a recording studio, your engineer will show you where to set up your gear (unless you're borrowing the studio's equipment) and he or she will handle everything else.

How you set up your gear depends on how you plan to track. If you're recording using just one microphone, experiment with both mic and musical-equipment placement to find the "sweet spot" in the room where you'll get the best sound. The *sweet spot* is recording jargon for the location where you hear the best separation in the room. *Separation* is another piece of audio jargon. It describes being able to hear each frequency and instrument clearly, with minimal sonic overlap. If you don't have separation, every sound washes together and is unappealing.

There isn't a sweet spot that works in every room for every band. The spot depends on the band's instrumentation, where musicians are positioned, and the way the room is constructed. If you're in a ska band with a horn section, a booming bass, and a trebly guitar, and you're recording in a concrete room, with the drums placed in the center, your sweet spot might be in a corner. If you move the horn section five feet in any direction, your sweet spot might change. If you place mattresses against the walls of the studio to deaden the room's sound it might change again.

It can also change if the guitar player switches amps. The sweet spot is entirely variable, which is what makes it so difficult to find.

The only way to find the sweet spot is to experiment with different mic, amp, PA, and drum placements. You'll need to record each time you change the mic or gear and play it back to hear whether it sounds better or worse than your previous spot. This is time-consuming, but necessary if you want to get the best sound possible.

Your equipment must be set up in a way that prevents bleeding when you're recording the entire band playing at the same time using multiple tracks. If you're using direct boxes, you don't have to worry about this because the signal is contained. You can avoid bleeding by setting up your gear in a separate tracking room to isolate the sound, or you can arrange a wall of baffles around the amp. *Baffles* are heavily padded panels of wood used to muffle, or mute, sound. They can be expensive, costing hundreds of dollars. If you're recording in a studio, the facility should have them. If you're recording on your own, and don't own (or can't afford) baffles, you can use mattresses, cushions, a couch, or anything else that has enough fabric and padding to prevent sound from easily transferring through it. If the baffles or separate tracking room don't entirely mute your sound, they've probably done enough to prevent bleeding. Once your band has completed a test recording, listen back to each track to be sure they are free of bleed.

In a recording studio, especially one that gets a lot of work, engineers have certain rooms, or areas within a room, where they like to position specific instruments. For example, a studio may have a special soundproof room for vocalists to record, or the engineer may prefer that the drums be set up in a corner of a one-room studio. Through experience, the engineer knows where to put each instrument to get the best possible sound. The vocalist in the soundproof room works because vocal mics are very sensitive and the engineer can't risk other instruments bleeding onto this track. The drum kit in the corner of the room is there because the walls are padded to minimize echo. It's also likely that if your engineer has a preference for placing instruments in particular locations, he or she has input cables and mics already in place.

Ask your engineer where to set up equipment. Don't expect him or her to remember what you play. If you feel you're being asked to set up in the wrong spot, say something. When the engineer is ready, they'll set up any baffles you need, confirm you've connected to the right input cable, and set up your mic if you're using one.

While you're waiting to be set up or track, don't play. Nothing annoys an engineer more than having his or her ears blown out by an overanxious musician. "It's challenging to work on projects with inexperienced players," says Peter Slankster. "Once I had a drummer start banging on his drums and it shot my hearing for the rest of the day. And on a day when I needed to really listen to get proper drum tones, it was very difficult to accomplish with my ears not at full capacity."

Sessions are notorious "hurry up and wait" periods. One minute you're recording and actively involved in the process. The next minute you're sitting around watching your engineer turn knobs or format a drive. Plan on spending a lot of time waiting for the engineer to complete tasks. And try to stay out of the way.

Before you can begin tracking, your engineer needs to test the volume level of each instrument's signals. If the level is too low, it'll be difficult to hear the instrument once it's recorded. There are tricks to raise the level at a later time, but it's preferable to get it right during the tracking phase. If the instrument is too hot (loud), it will distort. To test the signal, you'll be asked to play or sing for a few moments while the engineer tries to find the proper volume.

While you're having your signal checked, play as you would during the recording. If you play too quietly or too loudly, or with a different technique, it'll give the engineer an inaccurate representation of your signal, which will throw the recording out of balance. If you're a guitarist playing rock music, don't test your level with some clever country-style fingerpicking. If you're playing multiple techniques during any one song, be sure to warn the engineer to expect a change in your signal level. You'll be asked to play each style and to compensate accordingly to cover the change, or you'll be asked to record the different techniques separately or on separate tracks to determine the best signal when you track.

Once every signal is tested, your engineer will work on the band's headphone mix. When recording, musicians listen to themselves and the band through headphones. These headphones, or "cans" as they're sometimes called, have each instrument's signal sent to them, with the option of having those individual volume levels adjusted to best suit that musician. Let your engineer know any preferences. When I'm recording, I typically ask for a headphone mix that features my bass, the kick drum, and click track at a very high volume. Since I rely less on them to lock into the groove of the song, the rest of the instruments can sit back in the mix.

If you're stuck with poor-quality headphones, the mix may sound distorted. It's difficult to groove to your songs if they sound as though they're being broadcast through a cheap AM radio, but you may not have a choice. I've found that even the best studios only have one or two pairs of quality headphones, so there's a good chance you'll be stuck with a bad set. I was recently involved in a recording where my headphones were so awful my bass sounded like a distorted guitar. Unfortunately, it was all the studio could do with my particular set of cans and I had to make the best of it. I now bring my own headphones with me.

Once the band members and engineer are satisfied with their headphone mixes, your engineer will ask the band to run through a song to test that everything is working properly. Select a test song that features every instrument in the band. In this way no one will feel left out and all levels can be tested.

It's likely that, with everyone playing together, you'll need to adjust your headphone mix, because everything is going to get louder and some instruments may get drowned out in the volume. After your test, direct the engineer as to how to correct your headphone mix so you can hear what's important to you.

Ask the engineer to record the test. When you're finished performing, have it played back so you can hear how the band sounds. If your headphone mix is distorted, listen through the studio's monitors to get an accurate representation of the band's sound. If you're lucky, the test might sound good enough to be the final take. "I always make sure that I am being recorded at all times," says keyboardist Matt Rhode. "Nine times out of ten my very first take is the best."

When listening, make sure you're satisfied with the tones of the instruments and check for bleeding in the tracks. There are things your engineer can do in the mixing phase of the session to possibly correct or alter tones and bleeding, but it's always best to get tone right in the tracking phase so you aren't stuck in a position of having to accept bad tone. If you're not satisfied, discuss your concern with the engineer so he or she can work out a solution before recording begins. Don't wait for several takes to bring up your issue. This just wastes everyone's time on recordings that are going to be unusable.

Tracking Your Demo

Once you're ready to track, your engineer will press "Record" and give you a nod. Play your songs just the way you've rehearsed them. Concentrate on playing your best and having fun. I believe that when you record, you capture not only your abilities as a musician, but also your mind set. If you're having a good time, you'll hear it each time you listen to the song. I've played on many recordings, and on each track I can hear what I was feeling at the time. I believe listeners, on some level, can hear this too. Consequently, I make it a point to be in a positive frame of mind when I record. I don't want to have to listen to myself in a bad mood, and I certainly don't want anyone else to hear it either.

Everyone makes mistakes, and if you, or one of your bandmates, make one while tracking, don't stop playing unless the song totally falls apart. If one member comes to a halt, it can throw the band off, and there will be more mistakes to correct when the song has ended! If you can't correct mistakes later, keep playing anyway. What seems like a horrible error at the time may turn out to be inaudible or no big deal.

After performing each song, play it back to determine whether it sounds good enough to use on your final demo. Every member of the band should focus on his or her own instrument. If there's a problem, it needs to be addressed and corrected by punching in or by having the band record another take.

When listening, also pay particular attention to how the whole song feels. Individual mistakes may prove insignificant when compared to the overall feel of the tune. If what you've recorded matches the band's vision of the song, then move on to the next tune. If it doesn't, try recording it again. Sometimes it takes a few takes before a song really gels.

Mixing Your Demo

When all the songs have been tracked move on to the next phase: mixing. *Mixing is transferring recorded audio from a multiple-track format to a stereo format.* In layman's terms, it's combining all your tracks into two tracks (left and right signals), which can then be mastered to a CD or converted to an audio file that's playable through a standard CD or MP3 player. During the transfer, or *mixdown*, tracks can be manipulated to alter the sound. You can add effects like reverb and chorus, adjust the equalization to accentuate certain frequencies, and increase, or decrease, volume. If you recorded with just one mic, there will be no tracks to mix since you've recorded directly to stereo.

What defines a good mix is subjective. Still, there are standards you can use to judge your efforts. For instance, each instrument must be distinctive yet blend with the other instruments to create a pleasing sound. Bad mixes can also sound lop-sided, with vocals and cymbals crowded together in the same frequency, or on the same side of the left and right stereo spectrum instead of being balanced evenly.

Although it takes a skilled engineer to create a great-sounding mix, anyone with some knowledge of recording can mix a functional demo that represents the band and that won't turn off listeners. It just won't blow anyone away. If you're mixing the demo yourself and are unsure of what you're doing, you'll have to feel your way through the process. Fortunately, you know how the songs are supposed to sound so you can navigate through the basics like setting volume, panning, and creating simple effects to match the sound you've heard in rehearsals and gigs.

Mixing is a delicate balance of adjusting volume, equalization, panning, and effects. Any of these items can impact the sound of the track and the entire mix. Because of this, mixing is a constant process of making adjustments, listening back, and making more adjustments.

There are many ways to begin a mixdown, but my preference is to start by setting each instrument's volume in relation to the others instruments so that all can be heard. Start with each track's volume set at the same level, just below the point where it peaks in volume (if you have colored level indicators, this is just below where the signal turns red) and play the song. As it's playing, adjust levels. For example, if you're mixing a four-piece band and have two tracks of drums, and one of bass, guitar, and vocals, respectively, be sure the drum tracks are set as high a volume as possible without peaking. Then, bring the bass level down to match the drums. If the level of the bass isn't loud enough to compete with the drums at their highest point without peaking, move the drum levels down to match the bass. Once you have the bass and drums set, work in the guitar track so you can hear all three instruments. Finally, add the vocals. If you can hear every instrument and no track is peaking, you can move on to panning. If you're mixing a band with additional instrumentation, you can use this same approach and add the other tracks until you find their balance. Once the volumes are set, future changes in panning, equalization, and effects can throw them off balance again, so you'll need to readjust them during the process.

Panning is spreading the audio of a track throughout the stereo spectrum. For example, if you pan a track hard left, you'll only hear it out of the left speaker. If you pan a track in the center, you'll hear it equally out of both speakers. If you pan between hard left and center, you'll hear roughly 75 percent of the track through the left speaker and the remaining 25 percent through the right.

When panning your tracks, start with every track panned to the center. Using the above example of two tracks of drums, and one each of bass, guitars, and vocals, begin with the drums. Since there are two tracks, pan them on opposite sides, hard left and hard right. This will put them in stereo, which is an excellent way to pan instruments that have been recorded on multiple tracks. Since the other instruments have been recorded on one track each, you may keep them in panned center, or move them to different sides, or partial sides, of the mix. Experiment until your instruments sound balanced in the mix. Peter Slankster says, "Try to find a place for each instrument in the stereo spectrum and keep them all balanced (that is, don't pan two guitar tracks left)." Be aware that when you're done panning the tracks, you may find the volumes are no longer working in relation to each other. Instruments, like the drums, that have been panned off-center may become quieter. Readjust your volumes and move on to equalizing your tracks.

For your purposes, *equalizing*, or EQ'ing, is when you accentuate or diminish certain frequencies on the track by raising or lowering their specific volume. This is done to create a more appealing sound that also has separation. For example, if you have a vocal track that's sonically competing with a cymbal that's making a "clanging" sound, you may want to accentuate the vocal's high to midrange frequencies by selecting a frequency between 2 and 4 kilohertz, and by boosting its volume.

EQ'ing can be difficult if you aren't an experienced engineer. If you aren't sure which frequencies to adjust, use the process of elimination on each track by selecting frequencies and then raising or lowering their volumes to see if the change appeals to you. When in doubt, leave everything flat and let the natural EQ of the instruments suffice.

The final step in mixing is to add effects to your songs. The most common effects used are reverb and compression. *Reverb* is a common effect for vocals, drums, and guitar. It can make instruments sound like they were being recorded in a concert hall, small club, or even a bathroom. It can also add space and depth to your mix. In layman's terms, reverb moves audio from the front of your mix to the back. If you discover that too many instruments and frequencies occupy the same space, reverb can help separate them.

Compression is the process in which audio's dynamic range is affected. You can use it to balance audio by lessening the impact of high and low volume swells in the track. For example, if you've recorded a vocal track that gets overly quiet or loud, you can use compression to even out the volume. You can give audio more attack (sound more aggressive, even distorted) as well, a common tool to make drums sound loud and exciting. As with EQ, if you aren't sure how to use these effects, either let the natural sounds of the track suffice, or go through the process of elimination by trying different reverb and compression settings until you find one that improves the sound of the song.

As with panning, making changes to your equalizer and adding effects can affect the volume levels of your tracks. While adjusting a track's EQ, you may find the volume gets louder or softer. Or, the EQ may not sound as good as it did before you set the reverb on a track. As you make adjustments in your mix, you need to constantly revisit your tracks to gauge whether they meet your vision for the song. This is called "building the mix."

When mixing songs, set egos aside. If you, or one of your bandmates, insists that your instrument be excessively loud in the mix, it'll throw the song out of balance. I once did a demo with a band whose drummer was never satisfied with the volume level of his drums. Exasperated, the band and the engineer finally asked him to give us an example of the level he wanted. After he raised the fader to an almost comically high level, we could barely hear any of the other instruments. The song turned into a drum solo, which didn't cut it with the band.

Remember to stay true to your music and don't let your bias toward your own instrument affect the mix. If you're a guitarist in a pop band, being too loud will drown out the vocals, which give most pop music its appeal. If you're a bassist in a Latin band, demanding that your instrument be predominantly featured will bury the clave and other percussion sounds that are necessary in the Latin groove. Everyone in the band wants to be happy with his or her instrument's sound (and this will happen if there's a good mix where every instrument is clearly audible), but this can't happen at the expense of the demo. Once you're satisfied with the way a song sounds, you've completed its first rough mix. Repeat the process until you've finished mixing every song.

If you're recording in a studio, the engineer will run the mixing session. This means your role won't be as hands-on as if you were mixing your own demo. With the engineer in charge, the band's job is to listen to the mixed songs and offer direction to assist the engineer in capturing your vision.

By this point in the recording process, the engineer knows your band well and should be able to build the mix in a manner that accurately represents your band without much input. If you're working with an engineer who didn't track your band, give him or her your ideas on how the songs should sound. You may choose to be intentionally vague in your descriptions to gain a fresh perspective on the songs. An unbiased engineer may have an idea you really like. "My producer and I selected a mixing engineer and just gave him basic song information like if we wanted a particular instrument to be prominent, or come in at a certain part of the song," says singer/songwriter Erica Canales. "In the end, for the most part, we were really happy with his ideas."

Trust your engineer to do the job and take a break from the studio to rest your ears. You'll need them when he or she is ready to add effects or set EQ. "There are many aspects of a mix, like setting the attack time on a compressor, that probably won't make a meaningful sonic difference to the band," says Peter Slankster. "I often ask the musicians to come into the studio toward the end of the mixing session. That way I can deal with all of the things that go into a proper mix and the artist can come in with fresh ears when the mix is 90 percent complete. This is when the artist opinion counts most. The artist can ask for more reverb, brighter guitar, or louder bass."

Once the band, or the engineer, has mixed every song, burn a test CD of the mixes. At this point in the process, you'll probably be exhausted from listening to your songs dozens, if not hundreds, of times. After this assault on your senses, you may have lost any objectivity, or worse, allowed significant errors to go unnoticed. Once you allow some time to pass before listening to the music again, you'll regain your objectivity and be able to hear elements you'd like to correct or change.

When you're ready to listen to your test CD, have a pen and paper ready to take notes. Write down everything you feel needs to be addressed. Be especially attuned to your first impressions. After repeated listenings, you may forget your concerns, or just not hear them anymore. This does not necessarily mean the problems aren't still there.

Before you play your demo, make it clear that band members should keep their opinions to themselves until you've all finished listening to the mixes. If a band member talks about what he or she is hearing in the mix it can influence other members of the band. For example, if one member thinks the vocal track is too loud and raises that view, everyone in the band might start thinking it, too, before they've had a chance to independently form an opinion. Each band member can raise any concerns he or she might have after the songs have played through.

Once you've finished your first listen, speak with your bandmates about what you've heard. Discuss each song, going over every concern. If the drums were too tinny sounding, or the vocals weren't loud enough in the mix, talk about it. Whatever concerns you have are worth discussing.

After listening to your test recording, play the CD of the artist you wanted to emulate in the recording studio and compare the sound to your mixes. This process is called "A/B'ing" your audio because you are comparing audio A (your demo) to audio B (the artist whose recording you want to emulate). Check that your mix is in the same ballpark as the A/B CD. Are the guitars similarly aggressive? Does the bass have the same low-end thump you were seeking? Are the vocals at the same volume level compared to the other instruments? When you've finished A/B'ing the other recording, take notes on what you'd like to change, if anything, and discuss them with your engineer.

Now listen to both your test CD and the A/B CD through other sound systems. Every system is inherently different, so the music is likely to sound a little different as well. Listen on common, everyday systems like car stereos and iPods. This is where the majority of your listeners will hear your music, not on expensive systems that few people can afford. Make sure you can still hear every instrument and that no frequency disappears. If your mixes sound good on a cheap system, you know they'll sound great on an expensive system. This doesn't necessarily work in reverse because elaborate sound systems with sub-woofers and tweeters and every bell and whistle are built to make music sound wonderful. Cheap systems are not. Essentially, you want to be sure that the people who'll listen to your demo will hear a similar-sounding result. If the mixes sound very different, your engineer will need to tweak them so they aren't so sensitive through a variety of systems.

When you've finished listening to your CD and your A/B CD, and have played them both through different sound systems, review your notes to determine whether you're still hearing the things that bothered you before. If so, have another discussion with the band before making a new set of notes for the engineer. Your notes should include everything you'd like changed in your mixes as well as how they sounded through different systems. When you've completed your review and have your notes ready, set up a return visit to the studio and discuss proposed changes with your engineer. If not all members in your band agree on certain issues, write down the different comments and let the engineer, who should be neutral, weigh in on the discussion. It will have been awhile since your engineer has heard the mixes and he or she will likely have fresh opinions on elements that might need to be changed, too. Once the changes are made, you're ready to master your recording.

Mastering Your Demo

Mastering is the final stage of the recording process. Technically, mastering is the process of preparing and transferring mixed audio to a store device, like a CD or audio file. This device, or file, is then called the "master" since it holds the final version of an audio recording. A simple way to understand mastering is to think of it as mixing your mix. Instead of adding volume and effects to individual tracks, you add them to your mixed song. This is also the stage where the band decides what order to list its songs and how much time to place between songs. When this is done, you'll have a final product that will be used to create more copies of your recording.

If the band has a large budget, you may be able to afford to master your demo in a professional mastering studio. If you can, seek out mastering studios the same way you did recording studios—through print ads, the Internet, and word of mouth. Mastering is expensive, typically starting around $250 per hour.

It's rare for bands recording demos to professionally master though. After all, the demo's purpose is to land gigs and create a buzz among fans, not to sell as a full-length album. In most cases, bands recording their own demos master their recording by simply ordering their songs, deciding how much space to place between them, and burning them to a CD.

If you're recording in a studio, your recording engineer will work with the band to order your songs and place space between them. The engineer may also be able to add some effects, such as compression and equalization, to the final mix to give it a little extra volume and sparkle. If any changes have been made to the sound of the final mix in the mastering process, you'll need to review them the same way you reviewed your mixes. Listen to your mastered songs a day or two later through different systems and A/B to CDs in your genre.

When you're finished, go back to the studio and make any necessary changes. Your engineer will then burn you a final copy of your demo. This is the version you will duplicate for distribution to fans and bookers. Your next step is to dress up your demo with artwork and information, as well as to create marketing materials that promote the band.

CHAPTER 7

CREATING YOUR BAND'S PROMOTIONAL MATERIALS

Bands that are ready to perform have got to be able to create their own promotional materials. The materials should ideally feature eye-catching photos and artwork, but they must certainly provide information about the group and their music. These materials are then shared with bookers, special-event planners, and fans in order to distinguish the band from other local bands, land gigs, and increase their fan base.

There are several types of promotional materials that bands can create to market themselves. The most common are a demo package, a press kit, and a Web site.

CREATING YOUR DEMO PACKAGE

Once your band has recorded a demo, you've got to create a package for it. An effective package draws in potential listeners. It compels them to open the jewel case, read the liner notes, and look at the photos. This package can be a powerful promotional tool, because it's an opportunity to impress everyone who receives your demo. If it does impress, it can lead to bookings and interest in the band. If it doesn't, it can detract from the music and it will be harder to impress listeners.

The first step in creating a demo package is to compile basic information about the band and its music. You then need to take or contract for a band photo and, if you can, create or acquire artwork you'd like to include. The process ends by getting your package duplicated, after which you're ready to distribute the finished product to bookers and fans.

Compiling Information for the Package

Creating a demo package begins by compiling the information you want to have in it. The minimum you should include is the band's name, song titles, and contact information. This information will either appear on the surface of the CD itself or on inserts that fit into the CD's jewel case. It can also be used in your press kit and your Web site. Here is Funky Minnow's basic information:

Band Name:	Funky Minnow
Songs:	Funky Like a Fish
	Dollar Signs Tell All
	Your Love Is Like a Big Mac
	(It Always Makes Me Sick)
	When the Lights Go Down
Contact:	www.funkyminnow.com

Other considerations include adding the names of your band members, your recording, your engineer(s), and the studio where the band recorded, as well as acknowledgments and song lyrics. If you want to incorporate this additional information, you'll most likely have to use a jewel case with inserts to hold it all. Here's more information from Funky Minnow:

Funky Minnow is:	Tracy Spading—drums
	Drew Consanti—guitar/vocals
	Reggie L.—piano/vocals
	Moe—bass
Name of the Recording:	funky like a fish
Recorded at:	Buzzer Studios, Boulder, CO
By:	Vic Lighter

Acknowledgments: Funky Minnow would like to thank all the fish in our pond for believing in our band! Also, special thanks to Tracy's mom, Jane, for making this recording possible.

Taking or Contracting for a Band Photo

You're going to need at least one band photo for your demo package. The photo generally appears on the cover of the CD, or on the insert. Every band needs a photo because bookers, event planners, and fans want to see who's performing the music. Photos can also say a lot about the band. If a booker sees a picture of five young musicians wearing ripped clothing and sporting dyed hair and multiple body piercings, he or she will probably assume you're an alternative rock band. If there's movement in the photo, perhaps members of the group climbing a chain-link fence or hanging from rafters, the booker may conclude your band plays energetic music that will get an audience moving.

To avoid misleading bookers, event planners, and fans, the image your photograph(s) or artwork presents should match the band and its music. If you're in a band that plays classic R&B, using a photo of the group waiting in line at a copy center to photocopy their butts wouldn't match your sound, and a booker for a sophisticated jazz club would more than likely think your band is a poor match for the venue. The same photo would, however, complement a raw-sounding punk band whose attitude is to defy convention and authority. A booker of a punk or rock club wouldn't hesitate to hire the band in this photo.

There are, of course, bands that try to trick viewers by posing as if they play a different style of music. A hip-hop band might pose as rockers. A nationally recognized band might be able to get away with this because they're well known, and fans and bookers will understand that the group is poking fun at themselves and the two stereotypes. But if you're in a relatively unknown band, you risk being misunderstood, which will not advance your musical career.

Look at other band photos and even photographer's images that you like and determine if you'd like to model them. This can help you flush out ideas. "I love the photography of Katerina Jebb," says Erica Canales. "I ended up taking a bunch of pictures using my MacBook's iSight with her photos in mind. They are very mysterious, and shot up-close."

The clothing you and your bandmates wear is integral to the photo as well. Wear clothing that's true to your musical style, but that is simple and features solid colors that translate well on camera. Heavily striped clothes or clothing with complex graphics can be distracting to viewers who need to focus on the band, not on an Escher painting T-shirt. A photo faux pas would be a plaid shirt, leopard-print pants, and checkered sneakers, which might make a booker think he or she's on the verge of hiring the Ringling Bros. instead of a band.

The location of your photo shoot is important too. Unless you plan on using a tight close-up of the band members' faces, the location will define your shot as much as your clothing. The best backgrounds relate to the band and its genre. If you're trying to project an urban image, you might consider incorporating gritty elements like the dirty brick walls in an alley behind an industrial complex, or a dirty, dilapidated building. If you're going for a hipster setting, you may want to shoot in a posh nightclub or position the band next to a luxury car. When all else fails and you just cannot find, or settle on, an appropriate setting, use a neutral backdrop such as a black or white wall, in which case the band's pose and clothing will become the sole focus of the photo.

When considering locations, it's best to avoid clichés. Shots that include landmarks like the Golden Gate Bridge or the Chicago skyline lack the creativity of a more interesting setting like a funky storefront. They're also more obtrusive than plain backgrounds and can be distracting to viewers. Worse yet, a photo in front of a tourist landmark looks more like a snapshot from a family vacation than a band promotion.

When the band members know what they're going to wear and where they want the photo to be shot, consider both the poses and the overall photo composition.

Posture and body language can convey the essence of the band. While, as mentioned earlier, movement can signal that you're a high-energy group, if you're stationary and straight-faced it can suggest that your band is more serious. Keep in mind, too, that if the members of your band are posed but one person is distinguished in some way, either because he or she is the only one standing on a platform or is front and center while the others are in the background, that one member will be viewed as the band's vocalist or front-person. If you want band members to be perceived as equals, no individual should be the focal point of the shot. If one member is a lot shorter, or taller, than the others, move them forward or backward to compensate for the height differential.

Once you've worked out the details of the shoot, you've got two choices for a photographer. You can ask a friend to photograph you for free, or you can hire a professional. You'll most likely be using your band photo for quite some time, so you've got to be satisfied with the results. If you ask a friend to take your photo and the result is poor quality, it'll end up costing you because it won't be the credible professional image that bookers, event planners, and fans are used to seeing. If you do decide to use a friend, make sure he or she has some photography experience.

A professional photographer can be found through the Internet or the Yellow Pages, or through referrals or photography schools in your community. Photography rates range between $75 and $250 a session. If you use a professional, make it clear that you want the negatives or digital files from the shoot. Many photographers want to keep the negatives because they can then charge for reproductions, which may be priced at $25 a print. If you need twenty glossy photos for your press kit, this will get pretty costly.

The photographer you select has to have some understanding of the band. He or she will need to know what kind of music you play and how many members there are in the group. In addition, it's a good idea to discuss with the photographer any ideas you and your bandmates may have regarding where you'd like to shoot, what you'd like to wear, and what poses you feel might be effective.

This may help the photographer shape his or her own ideas concerning locations for the photo shoot, as well as how to frame the shot. Listen to these suggestions. The photographer is a professional and will have ideas on how to get you a photo that will meet your expectations.

On the day of your shoot, dress appropriately and meet at the location prepared to work. A photo shoot can take anywhere from a few minutes to all day, so be patient. It will take as long as it takes. And try to have a good time, even if your face or pose is intended to depict you as a member of a serious group.

Once all your planned shots have been taken, improvise. Try some different poses and see what happens. You never know what can come out of straying from your plan. You may end up with a shot that really captures the spirit of the band.

Place the band's name and contact information in the top or bottom margin of the photo. This information absolutely must be included because, if the photo appears in your press kit, it's likely bookers and special-event planners will remove it while listening to the demo. Once the photo is out of the package it can end up anywhere, and, without some way of connecting it with your band, it may simply be discarded.

Once the shoot is complete and you've got the digital images or negatives, you can use them in your press kit and on your Web site as well as in your demo package.

Creating or Acquiring Artwork

If you decide to use artwork in your demo package (and possibly in your press kit and on your Web site), determine if you can create the art or if you will need to acquire it.

If you want to create your own art, you need to have at least one bandmate who is artistically inclined. The rest of the band members can offer their input on the basic parameters of the work. For instance, "We'd like a painting of a cherub wearing a cowboy hat swimming in an inflatable kiddie pool," or "We'd like to take a photo of a traffic jam on Bundy and Olympic Boulevard."

If the art must be acquired, you'll either have to use an existing piece or commission someone to create something for you. If you find an existing piece of art that you'd like to use, you'll need to get permission to use it. It's also possible the art is copyrighted. A *copyright* protects artists from having their art used against their wishes and without payment. To use copyrighted material, you've got to obtain permission from the copyright owner (typically the artist, but it can be another party if the copyright was sold). Once you've found the rights holder, explain that you're in a band that wants to use the art for a demo package. If consent is granted, which may involve a fee for use, be sure to get written permission either with an informal e-mail or a short authorization letter such as the following:

> By signing this document, _____ authorizes the band Jazz by Numbers to use the artwork entitled "Low Lit Magic" on the cover of the band's demo CD. Jazz by Numbers will pay the sum of $200 for this use.

A former band of mine felt a connection to the artwork of Jay Lynch's Wacky Packages by Topps. We agreed that Lynch's work, with its edgy humor, epitomized the band. Our drummer contacted the artist, who agreed to grant permission to use his art on our cover. We also worked out an agreement with him to design the artwork we used on the CD itself. For his work, he received a small fee and credit in the liner notes of our CD booklet.

Do not use copyrighted art without permission. You run the risk of being sued by the artist. In addition, think about how you'd feel if someone used one of your songs without permission. As a fellow artist, you should treat the work of others with respect.

A good way to find affordable artists is to visit art schools in your area and post a note on a bulletin board or on the school's Internet message board. Here's an example:

> Metal band Sword of Damocles is seeking to commission an original painting for the cover of our demo and home page of our Web site. Call Marc at (818) 555-5555 for more information.

In one of my groups, we decided to appeal to students at the Art Institute in San Francisco for artwork. One student answered our bulletin-board ad and painted an inspired piece in oil, which we used on the cover of our CD. If you can't afford to purchase art from an artist, offer to pay a lesser fee to cover their materials (canvas, paint, brushes, paper, clay, etc.), or let them know you plan to circulate your demo and Web site all over town. The possibility of exposure may make creating your art worth their time.

Once you have your art, make sure it can be uploaded as a digital file. This will be necessary for you to reproduce the image using a computer printer. Some artwork and graphic design images are already digitized, so you won't have to convert them into digital files. If you've chosen a painting or drawing, you'll either have to scan it at a very high resolution or have a digital photograph taken of it. If you have a scanner, you can do this yourself. Otherwise, inquire at photography stores and copy centers in your area.

Designing the Demo Package

Now that you've compiled your key information, had the band photo taken, and decided whether to include artwork, you're ready to design your demo package. This begins by determining whether you'll be placing these materials on the surface of your CD or whether they'll appear in the jewel case inserts.

If you decide to use the CD itself, you've got two options. You can either write it with a permanent marker, or you can print CD labels and affix them to the discs. Using a marker isn't a good way to distinguish your band (in a positive way). It looks amateurish and will lead bookers and special-event planners to believe that your band isn't very serious about landing gigs. If at all possible, print CD labels. You'll need a computer and software to design your information, photos, and artwork. This software is available free (either as a data CD or a download) with the purchase of CD labels.

If you want to package your demo in a jewel case, you can use inserts to organize your material. An *insert* is the paper that fits inside the CD jewel case.

It's described by the number of panels it contains. Each panel matches the height and width dimensions of the jewel case, so it fits snugly. A two-panel insert is one piece of paper, front and back. If the insert unfolds once, it becomes a four-panel insert. If it unfolds three times, it's a six-panel insert, and so on.

Your band, for example, might opt for a four-panel insert with the band's key information printed on the front and back panels (the interior panels might include information about where the band recorded and the people they would like to thank for their help).

The back insert on a jewel case is called a *tray card* (because it sits underneath the tray that holds the CD). The tray card is typically one-sided and can only be viewed on the outside of the jewel case. Some, however, can be two-sided provided the tray that holds the CD is transparent and frees up viewing of the opposite side. The last element of a jewel case is the spine, which usually features a band's name and the name of the recording.

Duplicating the Package

Once you've designed your demo package, you'll need to have copies made. There are a couple of options: doing it yourself or professional duplication. Before you decide, keep in mind that you'll probably be passing out demos like candy on Halloween. Everyone from bookers and assistant bookers to friends and friends of friends will want one. To accommodate them, you'll need a minimum of two hundred copies.

If you intend to duplicate the promotional package on your own, buy as many of the materials as possible in bulk. Large companies like Office Depot and Staples offer low prices, especially if you order a sizable quantity. You'll need recordable CDs, jewel cases or CD sleeves, CD-shaped stickers to place over the disc, and insert paper if you're using a jewel case. As with CD labels, jewel-case inserts will come with software to help you with the design. While printing out your inserts and labels, find a computer with a CD burner and start making copies of the disk itself.

Professional duplication is expensive, but if you're making hundreds of copies it can save you time and, perhaps, money. Duplicating CDs takes a lot of time, since each demo and insert must be created individually. You can spend twenty minutes or more creating one copy. Still, self-producing a run of twenty CDs can be completed over a weekend without much trouble. Self-producing two hundred CDs, on the other hand, can take weeks.

The cost of professionally duplicating CDs evens out as the number of discs increases. For example, if you order five hundred copies from a professional company, the cost will run you roughly $1,000, which is virtually identical to the cost of producing them yourself. To create your own discs, you'll need to purchase the following items:

Item	Cost ($)
500 Recordable CDs	$199.80
500 CD labels	$204.75
500 jewel cases	$188.58
500 CD inserts (2-panel + tray card)	$174.50
CD label applicator	$8.99
Toner (10 cartridges)	$164.90
Total	**$941.52**

(not including tax and shipping)

Note: *Figures are based on pricing from the retailer Staples (2007).*

This cost doesn't include other benefits to having a professionally produced product, such as shrink-wrapping and a UPC symbol (a bar code that identifies your CD).

If you do decide to duplicate your demo professionally, seek out service providers in the same way you sought out musicians, bands, and studios—in local music publications, print ads on bulletin boards, and on the Internet. Two reputable services in the industry are Oasis and Diskmakers. They can be found online at www.oasiscd.com and www.diskmakers.com. I've used them both with great results.

Any professional service will need two things from you: a digital file of the design of your artwork and your final mastered audio recording. Each duplicator has specific requirements, so when negotiating your order, discuss exactly what is expected.

CREATING YOUR PRESS KIT

To create your band's press kit and Web site, which will be covered later in this chapter, you'll be able to use much of the information you created for your demo package. You'll also need to include additional items like a band bio and press clippings.

Writing a Band Bio

A band *biography*, or *bio*, is the story of a group and its members. At minimum, it must include the name and genre of the band and provide a sense of its current status. If you want to expand on it, you can add background information on the band members and highlight positive news that distinguishes your group from competitors—such as being the opening act for a well-known act, or performing live on the radio.

A bio comes in two forms: short and long. A short-form bio is concise, typically one to three paragraphs. Its directness is preferred by bookers and special-event planners, who only want essential information. A long-form bio provides the same information but adds interesting facts and anecdotes about the band. Both short- and long-form bios should be written, because you'll need both for different promotional packages. The short form will fit on a page in your press kit, and the long form is ideal for your Web site, where there's more room available.

Here is Funky Minnow's short-form bio:

> *Funky Minnow brings da' funk from the old school world of Parliament and Graham Central Station. Funky Minnow features the rock solid foundation of drummer Tracy, the tickled keys and vocals of Reggie, the wah-wah love of Drew on guitar and vocals, and the slip-slidin' groove of Moe on bass.*

A two-year staple of the Boulder scene, Funky Minnow is always gigging and bringing new minnows to their pond.

Funky Minnow's bio begins with their band name and quickly lets the reader know that they're a funk band in the vein of well-known acts Parliament and Graham Central Station. It also names the members of the band and their respective instruments, using funky adjectives that fit their genre, and concludes with their current status as a two-year-old Boulder, Colorado, band that gigs frequently while attracting new fans.

A long-form bio contains multiple paragraphs and tells more about the band's history. A long form usually reads more like a story than a short form but still contains basic information. However, it has a more creative bent and can provide a more intimate level of detail for bookers, special-event planners, and fans who want as much information as possible. If your band hasn't been together long enough to accumulate the history for a long-form bio, use what information you can and develop your bio over time.

Here's a sample long-form bio from Cage9:

Swimming in the categories of such like minds as Foo Fighters, Cave In, and A Perfect Circle, Cage9 takes the format for a spin that leaves listeners wondering, "Why the f**k haven't I heard this before?"

Cage9 is comprised of Republic of Panama transplants Evan Rodaniche and Gustavo Aued on guitar/vocals and bass, South Bay native Jesse Beltz on guitar, and Gordon Heckaman on drums. The band chose the moniker "Cage9" after a trip to Europe, joining the German word for "no" with "cage" to epitomize the group's no-limits approach toward creating music. The band's dynamic thrives on their cultural mix. Evan grew up speaking mostly English in the ten-by-fifty-mile strip of land known as the Canal Zone, while Gustavo grew up a few miles away in the heart of Panama City. Now living and jamming together in a rented downtown LA/Echo Park apartment, the two founding members of Cage9 relate verbally in a rough mix of English and Spanish slang but musically they deftly maneuver from the subtle pop grooves to staccato, melodic overdrive.

Cage9 recently performed on G4's Attack of the Show, whose other guests included Milla Jovovich, Jim Rose from the Jim Rose Circus, and Triumph, the Insult Comic Dog. The band has gigged with Seether, Amy Lee of Evanescence, Buckcherry, Smile Empty Soul, Cheap Trick, Adema, Depswa, Authority Zero, Spineshank, Cro-mags, James Iha, Big City Rock, and Opiate for the Masses, touring from Europe to the East Coast to Central America. Often seen sitting in on guitar with Powerman 5000, Evan's relationship with that band landed Cage9 the opening slot on PM5K's upcoming East Coast tour.

Recently signed with LA's Long Live Crime Records as well as BMG Music Publishing, the quartet can be heard in the trailer for the Dukes of Hazzard movie performing the first rawked-out version of Waylon Jennings' "Good Ol' Boys," as well as on FX's popular cop drama, The Shield, on ESPN/Japan, and Stephen J. Cannell's new thriller, Demon Hunter. The track "Breaking Me Down" from Cage9's new album, El Motivo, is featured in the movie American Pie: Band Camp. The band was mentioned in Billboard magazine as well as in Rolling Stone (Latin America), where Cage9's last EP received a cool 3.5-star review. El Motivo was just released nationwide in Japan in January thru BM3/ Triple Vision Entertainment.

Cage9's newly unveiled opus, El Motivo, is now available in both English and Spanish versions nationwide. The album includes "Hearts and Stars," which has received repeated spins on LA's World Famous Rock Station KROQ and has already been the #2 most requested song on Panama's top rock radio program. Of "Hollywood Car Crash," USA Today says "the initial impact could cause whiplash, but this Panamanian rock band makes great use of subtlety, too, like the layered guitars and the falsetto that kicks in just when you expect a scream." "My Doppelganger" also received Single of the Week status along with a great album review at Popbang Radio.

"We've been seeing these guys' stencils ALL OVER the streets of Los Angeles ... these guys are definitely in it to win it," says Streetwise.com. Recognized by many notable locals, such as Dino Cazares, as one of the "hardest working bands in town," this band is the real deal. Kludge *magazine says "Cage9's work model is one that should be taken by many other bands. They have steadily cultivated a fan base based on tremendous hard work and dedication, not only to bringing new people to shows, but also to refining their songs, constantly growing and evolving."*

This long-form bio is an entertaining read, while offering interesting and impressive information. Cage9's singer/guitarist Evan Rodaniche says, "The bio has grown a lot because we've been together for so long. Every year I grab some of the cooler stuff that has happened to us and add in a few sentences. I start with the most interesting stuff that I know will grab people's attention. Things like opening for bigger bands, being played on the radio are good. Then I go with the backup stuff like a famous person saying something cool about the band or how we spray paint our name on the street."

Getting Press

Press refers to reviews and quotes about the band. It adds objectivity to your promotional materials, because they're opinions about the group and its music from outside sources such as a music publication or a Web site, or someone of note in the music industry. Press can be an impressive component of your promotional materials, especially if the source is well known. If a radio DJ from a popular station in your area says, "These guys put on the greatest live show I've ever seen. They're outrageous, entertaining, and will keep you dancing until dawn," you've got press that gives instant credibility to your band.

Not every band has press to use in its promotional materials. After all, if you're a new group that no one has heard much about, it's unlikely anyone will be writing or talking about you. If you don't have any press, don't wait for it before completing your promotional materials. You can add it later.

The easiest way to get press is to already have a personal connection with someone in the music media. If you, or someone in your band, knows local radio station DJs, a writer for a local music publication, or a blogger for a popular music blog, ask him or her to listen to your band and, if they like what they hear, provide you with a quote or a review. If you don't have any media contacts, start cultivating them. You'll need to find music publications that do band reviews, as well as find notable industry insiders willing to provide you with a quote.

Begin your search with local music publications and Web sites. If they do music reviews, identify the writers by their bylines, and call or e-mail them to find out how your band can get reviewed. If they're willing to listen to your band, mail them your demo package (and press kit) or direct them to your Web site. You can also invite them to see a show and write a review. Be sure to learn approximately how long they'll need to review your music before you can expect to see something. This way you won't agonize over every issue of a publication or updated Web site searching for your review.

Here's a sample review for fictitious metal band Sword of Damocles:

> Sword of Damocles' new demo Battle of Empires *is a vicious blend of intense vocals and gritty guitars. This San Antonio–based foursome is poised to make an immediate impact on the local metal scene with potent metal anthems like "Catapult" and "Wings a' Fire." The band also showcases their versatility on the demo's title track, "Battle of Empires," with solid melodic hooks and a catchy chorus. Watch out, San Antonio, Sword of Damocles will be hanging over your head soon.*
>
> — *Jonathan Sully*

Music reviews are unpredictable, because you can't control what the writer thinks or says about your music. If the review isn't favorable, you don't want to include it in your promotional materials. However, if there are just certain elements of the review you don't like, your band will have to decide whether to use it in its entirety or simply use select quotes. In the Sword of Damocles review, the reviewer says that one of the band's songs has "solid melodic hooks and a catchy chorus." If the band disagrees with such a pop music connotation, they may choose to quote only the first sentence of the review, which matches their own view of their music.

Quotes supporting your band don't have to be obtained solely from written reviews. If someone says something positive about the band, and you feel the quote is credible, use it in your promotional materials. If, for instance, members of Funky Minnow know a producer for a local television show, they can ask her to listen to their music and tell them what she thinks. If she says, "Your music makes me want to shake my booty all night," then Funky Minnow's quote is the following:

> *Funky Minnow's music makes me want to shake my booty all night!*
> — *Pam Spencer*, Boulder Rocks!

To find credible, and quotable, sources, have your band members take inventory of all their contacts and friends. If there are only six degrees of separation between any person and Kevin Bacon, surely people you know must be one degree away from a good source for an endorsement. When you find them, ask them to listen to your music. If they agree, make sure they're willing to go on record with their quote.

Assembling Your Press Kit

Although digitization has led to an increasingly paperless world, there's still demand for good, old-fashioned hard copy. Web sites play an important role in marketing a band, but you'll need a marketing piece just the same that club bookers, booking agencies, and special-event planners can hold, file, and physically hand to their boss or client to review. These printed materials are called a *press kit* because they're for distribution to the press, as well as to people in the music industry who need more than the basic information in your demo package (and if your band plans on seeking special-event gigs, you'll need press kits for these potential clients as well). Your press kit should contain your demo, bio, photo, and possibly press. It can be expensive to produce, so you'll want to give copies only to people who can get you gigs. Fans can access the information on your Web site.

To assemble your press kit, you'll need to make copies of your text-only items like your bio and press, and for this you should avoid using generic copy paper and use high-quality heavyweight brochure paper or a thicker card stock, since the print will stand out more and the material won't rip as easily. The standard photo size for a press kit is 8 × 10 inches and has a glossy finish, not a standard matte. If you have a photo printer, you can print the copies. Otherwise, you should find a store like FedEx Kinko's or Staples, or a photo lab that can mass produce good quality copies.

When considering the assembly of your materials in your kit, or even what kind of envelope to use (if you're mailing copies), understand that people in the industry receive thousands of press kits a year. It's important to create something that "pops." Otherwise, it may be dismissed before it's even opened.

While studying at Tulane University, I was an associate editor for the *Tulane Hullabaloo*, the weekly college newspaper. The staff and I received hundreds of press kits every month from bands and labels seeking write-ups. Because it was difficult to sort through—and impossible to listen to—that much material, the staff picked through the press kits that they thought would contain interesting music. Those that made an immediate visual impression were reviewed. The others, often in plain manila envelopes, were tossed. I've been on the sending end of hundreds of press kits as well, so I hate to think about all of those unheard bands, but there was no possible way to review that much information and listen to that much music.

There are many ways to get a press kit noticed. You might consider using a colored envelope to house it. I've mailed many kits in neon yellow envelopes. It wasn't exactly a representative color for the band, but every booker I spoke with remembered our kit arriving in the mail and knew where to find it on his or her desk. You can also use a cool action photo or a vibrant design on the cover that really catches the eye.

When assembling your kit, make sure the completed unit is in one piece. Kits that contain these items loosely floating in an envelope will inevitably become separated or lost as soon as the envelope is opened. Don't use paperclips, either, because once your items are unclipped, they'll scatter, and whoever is reviewing the kit will lose your information. Press kits may be bound with wire, string, or staples, or any other secure method.

BUILDING YOUR WEB SITE

A band Web site is an electronic version of a press kit, with two key advantages: It can be updated quickly and it can contain more information such as additional audio files, video, and concert photos. A band can incorporate fluid information like band news and upcoming gig dates and locations, as well as new audio and videos that haven't been released yet. A frequently updated site lets visitors know there's "always something going on" with the band, and this can keep them coming back to learn the latest developments. "The key to a Web site is change, although maintain some consistent thread, like a logo or other defining element," says Los Angeles–based singer/songwriter Toddy Walters. "Keep changing the look and feel of your site and people will stay interested and keep coming back."

There's nothing more disappointing than a Web site with information that's months (or years!) old. This can kill fan interest quickly and definitively. Fans will think the band is either stagnant, lazy, or has disbanded. "Our goal is to keep people coming back to the site, checking it out, listening to new music," says Cage9's Evan Rodaniche. "You want people getting excited about it. You have to come across in a way that appeals to people."

Your site can be one page or multiple pages, as long as it contains essential information such as audio, video, photos, bio, news, and a way to contact your band.

Free services such as MySpace and PureVolume can host audio, video, photos, a bio, news updates, and even a blog on one page. These sites also allow users to link to "friends," which can increase traffic to your page. Your band should set up a free page in a community-based online world, even if you plan on building your own Web site. To set up a page on www.myspace.com or www.purevolume.com, you just need to register and fill out the templates with your band's information. There are no fees.

If you want to set up a Web site independent of sites like myspace.com, there are other free options. Yahoo! and Tripod allow users to set up sites that use a limited amount of disk space for free, with additional space available for a small fee. The drawback to some of these free sites is they may not have much (or any) room to host audio. "Your Web site doesn't have to be an expensive one," says singer/ songwriter Buzz Meade. "I've maintained a free Yahoo! site for years, and it's just as good as the high-priced ones."

The first step to launching your own Web site is securing a *domain name*, a name that identifies a site on the Internet, usually followed by .com, .net, or .org. Domain names are affordable, usually costing around $12 a year, and can be purchased through sites like joker.com and godaddy.com. If you're lucky, you can purchase a domain name that's the exact name of your band, like funkyminnow.com. Having your identical band name plus "dot com" helps people easily navigate to your site.

If the domain name you want to use is taken, you may have to modify your preference. Try adding an extra word on the end of your name. For example, if funkyminnow.com is taken, the band might try funkyminnowrocks.com or funkyminnowmusic.com. I know members of a California unit called That 80's Band who discovered that a band with the same name had registered the domain name that80sband.com, so they chose the name that-80s-band.com. Because all that separates these two groups is a pair of hyphens, it led to confusion for fans interested in the band. Personally, it prevented me from seeing my friends play live, because the page highlighting upcoming gigs had no record of the show I wanted to see.

If you plan on building a multiple-page site, you've got to create a *site plan*, which is a map that outlines a Web site through its various links. If, for instance, the band Funky Minnow wanted a multiple-page site, their map would begin with the home page that would, in turn, link to other pages within the Web site. Here's an example of Funky Minnow's site map:

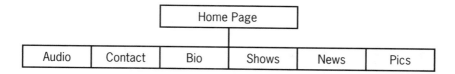

Once you've set up your site plan, you'll need to import your information into software like Microsoft's Front Page or Hot Dog that allows users to build and manage their Web sites. Your first step in doing this is to create your *home page*, which, in the case of Funky Minnow, is the page that opens when a user keys www.funkyminnow.com into the browser.

Your home page is the first thing visitors to your site will see, so it should make an impression. It should be clearly identifiable as belonging to your band. You can do this by including your band photo, or artwork, as well as news about upcoming shows, and even audio or video.

Your remaining Web pages should maintain a similar look and feel to your home page so visitors don't wonder whether they've been redirected to a different site. To create them, use your home page as a template and make the necessary changes.

Now that you've created your promotional materials, you're ready to show them to bookers and special-event planners to get gigs.

CHAPTER 8

FINDING GIGS FOR YOUR BAND

You've spent countless hours honing your musical chops, you've found compatible musicians, and your band has practiced and prepared its promotional materials. You're almost ready to play. But first you've got to determine how much your band needs to charge and then contact bookers and special-event planners to line up gigs for you.

DECIDING HOW MUCH TO CHARGE FOR PERFORMING

Before beginning your search for gigs by contacting *bookers*, people who typically work for venues that frequently hire bands, and *special-event planners*, people who hire bands to play one-time gigs like holiday parties and weddings, you need to decide how much money your band requires to perform. You do this by first understanding how bands are paid, and then by establishing your band's fixed costs so that you know what it will take to show a profit. You and your bandmates also should discuss whether some gigs are worth playing for less money, or for free.

Understanding How Bands Are Paid

Bands are generally paid in one of three ways: a flat-rate agreement, a percentage agreement, or a "pay-to-play" agreement. A *flat-rate agreement* is a guaranteed fee earned for a performance. Flat rates are often used for special events where the host is likely to be covering all the expenses, including the music, the catering, and the venue rental. An agreement as to the price to be paid is reached before the show by written contract or by verbal agreement.

The terms of the agreement address the length of time the band is to play, along with the gig's start and end times. Terms may be very specific as to the clothes that must be worn and the songs that must be performed. For example, clients usually require bands to wear tuxedos or suits at weddings and often request that "What a Wonderful World" be the first dance song. If the band fails to live up to the agreement, they may forfeit their pay.

The advantage of a flat rate is that it covers a band's costs and guarantees the amount of money that will be paid, which hopefully includes a healthy profit. Guaranteed pay is crucial for touring bands that must earn money to pay for food, lodging, and gas when they're on the road. It's also imperative for nontouring bands that have expenses like paid members and rented music equipment and can't afford to take gigs that could leave them paying for these expenses out of their own pockets.

The disadvantage of a flat rate is that it can interfere with your ability to maximize your profit potential. Let's suppose your band has the choice of playing for 100 percent of the admission price (or *the door*, as it's sometimes called) or for a flat rate of $200. Now let's say you decide to take the flat rate. If the performance draws one hundred people, each paying $5, the take at the door is $500. But the club only has to pay your band $200, which is $300 less than you would have earned had you taken the percentage deal. Of course, if your band isn't sure they can draw enough fans to generate a sum equal to the flat rate, you're probably better off accepting the guarantee.

The second method by which bands are paid is a *percentage-rate agreement*, whereby they earn either some, or all, of the venue's revenue at the door, the bar, or a combination of the two. Percentage agreements are primarily used in clubs, where there is a cover charge for patrons to enter the facility as well as a charge for alcohol. Special events are typically held for a person or an organization, and guests may be admitted free of charge and the drinks may be free.

When a band gets a percentage of the door, it is paid based on the number of customers paying to see the show. Some venues offer 100 percent of the door, others less. When other bands are playing on the same bill, they split the proceeds, possibly with the venue as well. Not all bands on the same bill get an equal percentage, however. Popular bands and headlining bands may receive more of the take based on their drawing power.

If a band is to receive a percentage rate of the bar, the band's pay depends on alcohol sales, usually during the duration of the performance (a venue will rarely agree to pay a band a cut of the bar for the entire evening). After the gig, the club will print out cash register receipts that are time-stamped exactly when the band began and ended playing. Then, they'll calculate the band's percentage of the total. The standard percentage is 10 percent.

Since there's relatively no risk in offering a band a cut of the money they bring through the door, clubs prefer percentage agreements to flat-rate agreements. If the band doesn't draw a large crowd, the club pays the band less, as opposed to a fixed-rate agreement, which may result in the club owner having to pay more than the club earned that evening.

There is one potential problem when you are paid a percentage rate: the club's honesty. I've worked in many clubs where I've suspected they lied about how much money was collected at the door or the bar, given the notable difference between the money we were paid and the number of people in the venue. Clubs know that it's difficult to prove they're shorting the band. Bands really have no recourse other than to stop playing the club, and this typically doesn't amount to much of a threat because there are ten other bands dying to play there.

FINDING GIGS FOR YOUR BAND •

Your only hope of countering a dishonest club is for you, or a trusted friend, to keep a close eye on the number of patrons that enter. If you can estimate the number of audience members, you can roughly calculate the total take. Since you, or your friend, might not be able to watch the door every second of the night, and you might not be aware of what people are getting in free because they're on the guest list, it's not a perfect solution, but at least the club will be aware that you're paying attention. If they then try to cheat you, you can confront them with numbers and ask for an explanation.

The disadvantage to being paid a percentage of the bar is that alcohol transactions are done primarily in cash. Unlike using a credit card, cash transactions can be completed without a record. The bartender can simply open the register and insert the money without inputting the amount, so the transactions aren't recorded. If this happens, bands have no way of knowing if they're being cheated. I used to play a percentage-of-the-bar gig in the French Quarter of New Orleans. Even though the bar printed out time-stamped receipts from the register for my band, it never seemed to jibe with the number of people holding drinks. Plus, unlike counting people in the audience, it's impossible to estimate bar sales, because drink costs vary, and there may be multiple active bars and bartenders working during your set.

The third payment option for bands is called a *pay-to-play agreement*. Bands purchase the tickets to the show and sell them to their fans. In essence, they pay the club for the privilege of playing the venue. A band that sells tickets for a marked-up price can make a profit. A band loses money when they can't recoup what they've spent on tickets. Clubs like this method of payment because it guarantees that all tickets will be sold in advance, but it's a horror show for bands that must spend hundreds (or thousands) of dollars on tickets.

Pay-to-play can strain the relationship between bands and their fans. Fans want to support their favorite groups, but if they are hounded to buy tickets, they can feel used and stop supporting the band. Fortunately, pay-to-play has fallen out of favor with clubs. Many bands couldn't afford to play these gigs, leaving clubs unable to find groups to perform in their venues.

Once you've determined a payment agreement, you need to ensure you'll actually be paid for the gig. There are two standard methods bands and clubs or special events use to come to terms on payment: a verbal agreement or a written contract. Most clubs use verbal agreements and will likely balk at signing a contract, because club gigs don't typically pay enough money to merit the club owner hiring an attorney to review a written agreement (they may make an exception for touring bands, however, since they are dependent on earning a minimum amount of money to cover costs). If a band tries to force the club to use a contract by threatening not to play, the club will most likely just hire a different band willing to play the show on a handshake or verbal agreement. Incidentally, it's in the club's interest to pay bands the agreed-upon fee. If it doesn't, word will get out, and bands may refuse to play there in the future.

Contracts are almost always used for special events. These shows typically involve a larger sum of money than a club gig and are worth covering with a legal document. The following sample contract is a good template for your band to use for both club gigs and special events. If you're planning on playing many gigs that require contracts, consult a lawyer first to fine-tune your agreement to suit your needs. You may consider adding sections about wardrobe, the PA system, and payment options. Here's a sample contract for a special event to be played by fictitious band Groove Mission for a company called Acme Environmental Products:

Musical Services Agreement

This contract is for the services of Groove Mission (herein called "Artist") and Acme Environmental Products (herein called "Purchaser") for the engagement described below and is made this 20th day of July 2008, between the under-signed Artist and Purchaser.

1. Venue: The Sheraton Hotel, Pomona, CA—the Regal Ballroom
2. Date(s) of Performance: August 24, 2008
3. Times: Load-in: 5 PM Sound Check: 7 PM Start: 8 PM
4. Number and Length of Sets: Four 45-minute sets with 20-minute breaks after each set
5. Agreed-to Compensation:
   a. Musical Services: $3,500.00
   b. Lodging: None Required
   c. Meals: Dinner will be provided for the band
   d. Other: _____
   e. Total Compensation: $3,500 plus dinner
6. Payment to be made by check no later than: August 3, 2008
7. Artist's obligations under this contract are null and void if unable to perform due to accidents, riots, strikes, epidemics, or any other Act of God that could endanger the health or safety of the Artist.
8. In the event Purchaser fails to fulfill its obligation provided herein, Purchaser will be liable to Artist in addition to the compensation provided herein.
9. In the event Artist fails to fulfill its obligation provided herein, Artist will be liable to Purchaser for the amount set in 5e. / Total Compensation.
10. Either party may cancel this agreement without obligation to other if notice is received twenty-one (21) days in advance of show.

Debbie Goodsen	John McNown
Acme Environmental Products	Groove Mission
Purchaser	Artist

Note that John, the band's leader, has typed in all of the pertinent information about the gig and the client into his contract template. This includes: the names of the band and client; the date the agreement was signed; the name of the venue; the date of the performance; the load-in, sound check, and gig start times; the number of sets and their duration (including breaks); and the compensation and method of payment for the gig, as well as a date by which the payment must be received.

The last four provisions of the contract protect both the band and the client. Clause 7 protects the group if they are unable to perform due to an unforeseen tragedy such as an accident involving a band member, the outbreak of war, or an Act of God like an earthquake. Clause 8 gives the band the right to sue Acme Environmental Products for an amount greater than the $3,500 total compensation if Acme fails to honor the contract, perhaps by not paying the band in full. Clause 9 protects Acme in that it allows them to get their money back (by agreeing to this contract, Acme is agreeing to pay for the gig in advance) if Groove Mission fails to honor the contract, perhaps because the band leaves after only playing three sets instead of the agreed-to four. Clause 10 gives either party the right to cancel the agreement if one informs the other at least twenty-one days prior to the engagement.

You'll need to modify this contract depending on how you've agreed to be paid. This sample is for a flat-rate agreement. If you want to change it to a percentage-rate agreement or a pay-to-play agreement, you'd simply alter Clause 5. Also, Groove Mission's contract requires clients to pay in advance. This is not uncommon for special-event bands, but club bands will not be able to demand this. If you're playing a club, expect to get paid after the gig.

Determining Your Band's Overhead and Profit

Once you understand the different methods by which bands are compensated, you need to determine your *overhead*—the expenses your band will incur to perform—and how much profit you'd like to make. *Profit* is the amount of money that remains once you've subtracted your overhead from the payment you received for a gig. Establishing your band's overhead will help you determine if you should accept a gig. If it doesn't pay enough to cover your overhead, and enable you to make a profit, it's probably not worth playing.

Some bands have no overhead and no real desire for profit—at least early in their careers. Their goal is to get gigs, win over fans, and build on their successes so they might make money in the future. They play for whatever they can earn, and if that number falls below their expenses for the gig, they chalk up the loss to the cost of being in a band. Other bands have higher expenses and must be able to cover those costs with gig revenue, or else they risk going into debt or being unable to pay the members. These bands typically ask for flat rates at gigs to guarantee they won't lose money, but they may also accept a percentage rate and pay-to-play agreement if they feel confident they will earn enough money to meet their needs.

Overhead is unique to every band and show, because every group and gig is different. A ten-piece band playing a gig two hundred miles from home will incur considerably more overhead in transportation costs, food and lodging, and band-member pay than a trio playing a gig five miles from their rehearsal space.

To calculate your band's overhead, take all expenses into consideration, both fixed and variable. *Fixed expenses* are set, like the cost of renting a drum set for every gig or paying band members. *Variable expenses* change depending on the circumstances of the gig. Both transportation and gas costs are variable because you have to travel different distances to the venues where you perform. Other variable expenses include lodging, equipment rental, and fees. Fees include any monies due to people or organizations, such as booking agencies and management companies that may have had a hand in landing the gig for the band.

To illustrate how a band calculates overhead, let's use two fictitious groups as examples. The first is club band See Jack Fall, a newly formed trio whose members are unpaid. See Jack Fall wants to play a gig at a local club called the Nightbreak. Here's the band's projected overhead:

See Jack Fall June 8th Gig at Nightbreak	
Item	**Overhead Cost**
Labor for three-piece band	
• Jack	$ 0
• Kenny	$ 0
• Jim	$ 0
Total Labor Cost	$ 0
Transportation (gas)	$10
Lodging	$ 0
Meals	$ 0
Equipment Rental	$ 0
Fees	$ 0
Total Overhead	**$10**

As you can see, See Jack Fall's sole expense for this gig is for transportation. Because the overhead is so low, the band is able to take gigs that pay little, or even nothing, without going into debt. When the band speaks with the booker at the Nightbreak, money won't be an issue.

The other band, Groove Mission, is a ten-piece special-event band based in San Francisco and led by bandleader and guitarist John McNown. Here is John's projected overhead for a gig he's considering at Half Moon Bay, thirty miles from the band's base.

Groove Mission October 23rd Gig at Ritz Carlton, Half Moon Bay	
Item	**Overhead Cost**
Labor for 10-piece band ($200 per piece)	
• Male Vocalist	$ 200
• Female Vocalist	$ 200
• Drummer	$ 200
• Bassist	$ 200
• Guitarist	$ 200
• Keyboardist	$ 200
• Tenor Saxophone	$ 200
• Alto Saxophone	$ 200
• Trombone	$ 200
• Trumpet	$ 200
Total Labor Cost	$ 2,000
Transportation Rental + full tank of gas	$ 120
PA Rental	$ 500
Fee	$ 200
Total Overhead	**$2,820**

Groove Mission's projected overhead is considerable, primarily due to labor expenses. John can't even consider gigs that pay less than $2,820 because doing so would mean he'd have to go into debt to pay his band (including his own $200 fee as a member of the group). For this particular gig, John also needs to rent a powerful PA system ($500) because the band is playing a room larger than what his usual equipment can handle. He also needs to rent a large vehicle to haul the equipment to the gig ($120), increasing his overhead by $620. Fortunately, the gig is only thirty miles from the band's base, so he doesn't need to factor lodging into his overhead. However, since he landed the date through an agency he must add a $200 booking fee.

Once you know your overhead, you can determine how much profit you may be able to make. Although every band is happy to make as much as possible, clubs and special-event planners can only afford to pay so much. Thus, you need to settle on a fee that won't scare them away. To figure this amount, you need to know the going rate for bands like yours in your area.

Every music market is unique. Live music, like most other commodities, tends to cost more in large cities like Los Angeles and New York City than it does in smaller cities like Bend, Oregon, and Tampa, Florida. While booking a special-event band in Los Angeles costs approximately $6,000, a similar band in Tampa may cost just $2,000. The bands may play the same music, but they perform in different markets and consequently the cost of hiring them is dramatically different.

Bands in different genres also command different rates, despite performing in the same area. A punk band that plays one forty-five-minute set at a club may earn up to $100, depending on its popularity. At the same time, a jazz band may earn up to $400 for a similar night's work. It's difficult to boost your price because there are likely numerous bands of a similar style in your scene. If one band won't accept a certain price, the club or special-event planner will find another one that will.

To get a better sense of the pricing in your market, talk to bands and musicians to find out what they're earning. This will provide a good starting point to determining how much you can ask for a gig. Don't be afraid or embarrassed to set your price on the high side. If you're worth it, you'll find clubs and clients that are willing to pay. "My not-so-humble motto is, 'Be the best and charge the most,'" says Cincinnati-based singer/songwriter Steve Sparks. "If you think you're worth $100, guess what? You're right. If you think you're worth $400—same thing. It's the self-fulfilling prophecy."

Groove Mission's John McNown has set his fee based on the market in his hometown of San Francisco, where the average rate for special-event bands is $5,000. This gives John a profit of $2,180 ($5,000 fee – $2,820 overhead = $2,180 profit)—not bad for a night's work. Because he has a solid profit margin,

John can also consider bringing his price down to accommodate clients that can't afford a $5,000 band, if he feels the gig is worth playing.

If clubs or clients don't want to pay your asking price, there are a couple of approaches you can try to persuade them. You can suggest that you have another offer for the same date at your requested fee, which may pique their interest when they hear the band is popular and in-demand. Playing hardball can be risky, though, and you may lose the gig altogether. Usually the worse that happens is the client will still not agree to your asking price and you're left to consider reducing your profit margin or losing the gig. A second approach is simply to offer to play a longer set, or more sets, for the fee you've proposed.

The biggest factor in deciding whether to accept a lower profit margin is whether the band can land another gig for the same date. If, for example, John from Groove Mission can find another job at his asking price, he should take it. If he can't, then he may have to consider lowering his profit margin on the Half Moon Bay date. It's usually better to accept less money and play a gig than to stay home and make no money at all. Plus, if the members of his band miss an opportunity to make money and don't feel they're working often enough, they may leave for another group. "Remember the old adage about 'a bird in the hand,'" says bandleader Doug Waitman. "Sometimes it's more important just to get that date on the calendar. As an agent, a manager, and a bandleader, my first priority is to find work for my band members."

Playing for Free

Musicians usually don't want to play for free. Bands work hard to get ready to gig and that effort, as well as the entertainment they provide, deserves to be compensated. Still, there are situations where performing for free should be considered.

One such situation is when a band simply plays for the sheer pleasure of it. Band members play for fun for the same reason they picked up their instruments in the first place—because they enjoyed it, not because someone hired them.

Just-for-fun gigs typically take place at parties and other low-key events. Because the gigs are informal, a band playing them can relax and enjoy performing without having to worry about keeping an eye on the door person to make sure he or she is not skimming money, or about being able to draw fifty people to the gig to impress the booker. The only expectation at a free gig being played for fun is to have a good time.

There are three other reasons for bands to play for free: to audition for a gig, to get exposure for the band, and to gain experience.

A band may need to play for free if it is new to the scene. It can understandably be difficult (though by no means impossible) to break into playing clubs when those clubs need to generate revenue by booking acts they know will draw patrons. Thus, if your band is an unknown commodity, you may be asked to audition to see what kind of crowd you can draw.

If your band is asked to audition, you will perform for free and the slot will probably be during a slower time for business, such as a Monday night. The club will not risk booking an unknown on a busy night like Friday or Saturday. On popular nights like these, the club will probably have a good crowd regardless of who's performing—people tend to go out on weekends—but they need a band to make it a great crowd. Clubs also need to attract people on off-nights, like Mondays. Clubs take advantage of unproven bands by insisting they fill the venue if they want to play there on a better night. When the band succeeds in packing the venue, the club makes more money than it typically would. If the band fails, the club doesn't do any worse than expected. The club manager, the owner, or the staff will then decide if the band is a good fit. If the audition goes well, the club may offer a paid gig at a future date.

A band may also play for free for exposure. Any show where you can potentially pick up a significant number of fans should be considered a high-exposure gig. Winning over new fans is tremendously important to a band because, if people like your music and begin to follow your group, they add to your draw, enabling you to play better clubs on the best nights. For bands struggling to make it, this is worth more than money, as long as the people you'll be performing for have the potential to become regular fans of your band. If you're in a country band, playing a free gig for a local rock radio station may not generate new fans, but if your band has the opportunity to play on the same bill as a more popular band of the same genre, you can significantly increase your fan base.

Some gigs that seem like a great opportunity to gain exposure don't end up that way. And, unfortunately, there isn't any way to know if the audience will take notice, or even show up, until you play the gig. Singer/songwriter Toddy Walters says of a free gig she played on the popular Third Street Promenade in Santa Monica, California, "I thought the show would be good exposure, but I think because I was competing with a lot of activities on the street, very few people stopped to listen."

Finally, a band may play for free to gain experience. Beginning bands that haven't performed live need to play a few shows in order to become comfortable with playing in front of an audience. Even seasoned bands can gain experience from doing certain shows. I was once in an alternative rock band that had a chance to open up for the legendary rock band Blue Oyster Cult. We had absolutely nothing in common with BOC and there was no chance we could attract any of their fans, but it was a chance to play on a massive stage in front of hundreds of people. BOC fans were politely indifferent to our performance, but it was a great opportunity for my band to gain a valuable, and memorable, experience.

GETTING GIGS

Once your band understands how to determine overhead and profit and decides how much to charge per performance, you're ready to get gigs. Your first step is to prepare to contact bookers and special-event planners. Then you call or e-mail them in hopes of landing a show.

Preparing to Contact Bookers and Special-Event Planners

In Chapter 1, you evaluated your music scene to determine what kinds of bands are gigging where. In doing so, you identified numerous clubs and venues where you could possibly play, as well as booking agencies and special-event planners who could help you get gigs. Now it's time for you to prepare to contact these individuals.

You need three key attributes to assist you in booking shows: persistence, drive, and organization. Bookers and event planners can be difficult to reach, and even more difficult to convince to book your band. If you can stay focused on your goal of landing gigs and keep from becoming discouraged, you have a chance. Toddy Walters says, "Having the drive to book your band is important because once you start gigging—and you're a good, professional performer—you'll move up the ladder quickly and start playing better times and better venues."

It's important to be organized. You'll be contacting a lot of people, so you'll need to be able to keep your information straight. The most effective way to do this is to document every communication on a *contact sheet*, which is a form you can create to hold all pertinent contact information like names, phone numbers, and e-mail addresses. Much of the information you'll include on these sheets will be available in local music and entertainment publications, in the Yellow Pages, or on Web sites.

It's also important to keep track of all communication between your band and the booker or event planner on your contact sheet so you don't forget important details like the hours a club booker is available, or the sound check time for a gig. When, for instance, you're told the time your band is supposed to load in, this information can be added to the contact sheet and read something like this: "Spoke to Jaime at the Music Spot. He told me the band should load in at 6:30 PM." You can then follow up on your contact sheet with your action, which in this case is "I'll pass this information to the rest of the band at rehearsal tonight."

Here's a sample contact sheet for fictitious Club Comet in Los Angeles:

Club Comet

Address:	**7000 Hollywood Avenue**
	Hollywood, CA 90028
Phone:	**(323) 555-5125—Info. Line**
Booking #:	**(323) 555-1673—Booking Line**
Web site:	**www.clubcomet.com**
E-mail:	**info@clubcomet.com**

4/14: Called the booking line. The recording said the club is booking national, local, and tribute acts. Press packages should be sent to the address of the club. For further information, we need to call the information line. Will discuss this tonight at rehearsal and see if we want to move forward with trying to book this venue.

Once you've created a contact sheet, your next step is to prepare what you're going to say to the booker or planner by writing a brief overview of your band and addressing any concerns the person interested in booking the band may have. The individual you speak with will want to know the name of your band, the kind of music it plays, and other general information like how long the band has been together and how many times the band has gigged.

Since bookers deal with hundreds of bands, they tend to have a developed sense for detecting inexperience and fraud—some call it booker's intuition. This sense leads to three concerns that, if they come true, can lead to a booker losing his or her job. The first concern is booking a band that won't show. If you come across as flaky or unreliable, the booker will not hire you. For example, you're not going to land the gig if your response to a general question like "Tell me about your band" is, "Well, we're pretty good ... I don't know, I guess it's because we practice a bit on the weekends—except for last weekend because Bernie went fishing. Anyway, what was I saying?..."

This is especially true of special-event gigs with corporate clients. Bandleader Paul McDonald says, "These are businesspeople. They expect things to be done in a professional manner. That's what they are used to dealing with. The way to get these gigs is to approach it like a business and be professional."

You can address this concern by telling the booker about past gigs you've played. This will help to establish your band's credentials and, by extension, your reliability. If you have no experience, then you'll need to convince the booker that you have no intention of tarnishing your band's reputation by missing your first show.

The second concern is that the band will be awful and will drive people out of the club or event. The only way to put this concern to rest is to offer to send a press kit that includes your demo, or to direct bookers to the audio portion of your Web site.

The last concern is that the band won't attract an audience. To address this issue with a booker, tell him or her how many people typically come to your shows. Most small clubs will be happy with a band drawing thirty people, because if they book three bands on the same bill, and they all bring thirty people, that's at least ninety people paying a cover charge, eating, and drinking. If you've never, or rarely, gigged, and you have no real history of drawing a crowd, you'll have to convince the booker that you understand the importance of bringing a crowd and that you can deliver.

Be honest when discussing your band's ability to draw a crowd. If you exaggerate, you could end up being banned from ever playing the club again. I once played an unfortunate gig in New Orleans on a Tuesday night, an unusual night for this particular venue to be open. It was usually closed due to lack of interest in live music so early in the week. Unbeknownst to me, my bandmate who booked the show promised the booker that we would bring sixty people to the club if they opened for us. They did, and paid a club manager, a doorman, a bartender, a sound engineer, and the cost of electricity for the lively crowd they expected.

The crowd of sixty never materialized. Instead, the number of employees outnumbered our draw fifteen to one. The owner entered the club about a third of the way into our set, took one look at the crowd, approached the stage, and drew his index finger across his throat. The power was immediately cut and we were treated to a profanity-laced tirade that left us speechless. We were also barred from ever playing the club again.

Once you understand what bookers need to know, you can prepare what you're going to say to them. Here's how See Jack Fall would provide information about themselves:

> "We're a three-piece pop rock band, featuring vocals, guitar, bass, and drums. Our sound has been compared to Weezer and Bowling for Soup. We're a new group, but our members have been playing in different bands in the area for the last two years and always have had good draws."

By disclosing that the band is a new project, yet features members with experience in the scene, See Jack Fall bandleader Jack Fallinski is letting the booker know that despite their newness, they can draw like a veteran act.

Here's how Groove Mission would address the same subjects:

> "Groove Mission is a ten-piece band that covers music from the Swing era of the 1940s to current radio hits. We take pride in both our professionalism and our ability to lead a party. We've been performing and entertaining clients for more than five years in the San Francisco Bay Area and throughout the region."

It's always best to select one person in your band to do the talking. If you're the bandleader, this should be you. If you're in a democratic band, it should be someone who is articulate and organized. Booking gigs is a detailed process, and having just one person handling the booking process prevents confusion and overlapping tasks.

Contacting Bookers and Planners, and Landing Gigs

There are two ways to contact bookers and planners to get gigs: by e-mail and by phone. Do not simply stop by. Both bookers and planners are busy people and don't appreciate musicians appearing unexpectedly in their offices. "I prefer to find clubs that hire my style of music and then call," says singer/songwriter Steve Sparks. "I've never been a fan of just showing up to meet the manager. I figure I can call twenty-five places in the time it took to visit one."

E-mail communication is becoming more popular for business purposes. It's especially convenient for bookers and bands that already have a relationship, and simply need to confirm the date and time of gigs. But if your band is trying to book a show at a club for the first time, e-mail is not the best approach; it provides the booker more of an opportunity to blow you off; whereas, it's impossible to avoid communications when both parties are on the phone. E-mail can also be a slow method of communicating. For the person who doesn't check e-mail regularly, there may be a time lag of several days. I recommend using the phone. Once you've reached the booker you can immediately have a productive interaction that addresses each other's questions quickly and without ambiguity or confusion.

If you can't get a booker on the phone, leave a message. The rule of thumb is to only leave one message per day he or she is taking calls (i.e., during office hours). So if a booker works Monday and Wednesday, you can leave two messages per week, one on each day. You can keep calling to try to get through, but just don't leave additional messages. If you leave multiple messages per day, you're going to come across as high-maintenance and rude, and you may not get a callback.

Your first step when attempting to contact bookers and planners by phone is to introduce yourself to whomever answers and to ask to speak with the person in charge of booking. "Find the person who is directly responsible for booking the bands," says bandleader Paul McDonald. "If you get stuck dealing with a receptionist or bartender who's not the decision maker, your message or press kit will likely end up in the trash can."

When Jack from See Jack Fall calls a club for the first time he begins by saying, "Hi. My name is Jack, and I'm with the band See Jack Fall. We're interesting in playing the Nightbreak. I'd like to speak with the person who books your club." If he's calling a booking agency he might say, "Hi. My name is Jack, and I'm with the band See Jack Fall. We're interested in working with you to provide live musical entertainment for special events. Could you please direct me to the person who books the bands?"

At this point, if you aren't fortunate enough to get the booker on the first try, you'll be directed to the right person. Be sure to ask for his or her name and contact information, as well as a good time to call for future reference (and don't forget to add this to your contact sheet).

Here's an example of a telephone conversation between See Jack Fall and Club Boomerang:

Club Boomerang:	*Hello? Club Boomerang.*
Jack Fallinski:	*Hello. My name is Jack Fallinski. I'm with the band See Jack Fall. We're interested in playing your club. Could you please direct me to whoever handles your booking?*
CB:	*Sure. That's Scott. He's not in right now, and he has pretty random office hours. I think he'll be in tomorrow afternoon.*
JF:	*That's great. What's the best way to contact him? And what's his last name?*
CB:	*You should call him at this same number. He has an office here. His last name is Patterson.*
JF:	*Perfect. I'll do that. Does he have an e-mail address you could share?*

CB:	Yes. It's spatterson@boommusicclub.com. He prefers the phone, though.
JF:	Great. Thanks for your help. What's your name?
CB:	I'm Jennifer. I'm one of the bartenders here.
JF:	Thanks, Jennifer. I'll call Scott tomorrow afternoon. Take care.
CB:	You, too. Bye.

Jack immediately begins his band's contact sheet for Club Boomerang. It is as follows:

Club Boomerang

Address:	**101 First Street, Big City, CA 55555**
Phone:	**(310) 555-5555**
Web site:	**boommusicclub.com**
Booker:	**Scott Patterson (spatterson@boommusicclub.com)**

9/21: Made contact with club and spoke with a bartender named Jennifer. She said Scott Patterson is the booker; he's reachable at the club, but his hours are irregular.

Jack calls back the next day, and Scott answers the phone.

Jack Fallinski:	Hi, Scott. My name is Jack Fallinski. I'm with the band See Jack Fall. I called yesterday and spoke with Jennifer. She recommended I talk with you about the possibility of my band playing a show at Club Boomerang.
Scott P.:	Yeah, I book the club. Tell me about your group.
JF:	We're a three-piece pop rock band, featuring vocals, guitar, bass, and drums. Our sound has been compared to Weezer and Bowling for Soup. We're a new

SP: group, but our members have been playing in different bands for the last two years.

SP: What groups were your members in before?

JF: I was the singer of Armchair Warrior, and our drummer and bassist were in Hydra 7.

SP: I haven't heard of either band. Where did you play?

JF: Armchair Warrior played a lot of private parties. We also played a lot at Mephisto's and the Night Break. Hydra 7 played those clubs too.

SP: Well, I usually book new bands here on Sunday afternoons. If they work out, then we move them to weekday gigs and finally weekends. We rely on our musical acts to bring a crowd. If you want a chance at a weekday or weekend gig, you'll need to draw.

JF: That's not a problem. We have a fan base from our previous bands, and they're really excited to hear us play.

SP: That's cool. You'll need to send me your demo. If the band's music fits with the club and our clientele, I'll book you for a Sunday show.

Call me in a couple of weeks, and I'll let you know what's up.

JF: Great. I really appreciate your time and consideration. You can actually hear our demo online at www.seejackfall.com. Check it out. Can I call you in two weeks?

SP: Sure. Sounds good.

JF: Thanks again for your time. Bye.

Jack updates the band's log as soon as he finishes the call.

9/22: I called Scott. He told me that a show was a possibility if he likes the band. New bands are intro'd on Sundays. I directed him to our Web site and will call back in two weeks to see if he'll book us.

At the end of the phone call, Jack found out that it would be okay to follow up with Scott in a couple of weeks. It's always a good idea to ask when is a good time to follow up with a phone call or e-mail. If you don't, you'll be waiting for the booker to get in touch with you, and that might never happen.

Here's an example communication between Groove Mission and the fictitious Riverbend Resort and Country Club, which hosts weddings:

Riverbend:	*Good morning, Riverbend Resort and Country Club. How may I direct your call this morning?*
John:	*Hello, my name is John McNown. I would like to speak with your event planner please.*
RB:	*One moment. I'll connect you.*
Trish Browning:	*Hello, this is Trish.*
JM:	*Hello, Trish. My name is John McNown. I lead a special-event band called Groove Mission. We're a ten-piece band that covers hits from every style of music. I'd like to send you our package in hopes that you might refer us to some of your clients in need of a great party band for their events.*
Trish:	*I would be happy to accept your package. I will say, however, that the majority of our clients use their own planners and hire bands independent of the Riverbend. We do offer referrals, but it's the exception rather than the norm.*
JM:	*I understand.*
Trish:	*Please send us multiple press kits and we'll share the information with our clients. If they're interested in your group, I'll have them contact you directly. Do you have our address?*
JM:	*Yes. And thank you very much. What's your last name, Trish?*
Trish:	*It's Browning.*

JM:	Great. Is it okay if I call you back in a month to check in and see if our package has generated any interest?
TB:	Sure, feel free.
JM:	I appreciate your help and your time.

John updates his contact sheet when he finishes the call.

Riverbend Resort and Country Club

Address:	**15200 Riverbend Lane**
	Anytown, California 94000
Phone:	**(408) 555-5555**
E-mail:	**information@riverbend.com**
Contact:	**Trish Browning**

6/29: Spoke with Riverbend event planner. Her name is Trish Browning. Trish will accept our package and pass along our materials to any interested clients. Trish said it was okay to call her back in a month to check on things in the future.

Mail packages to Trish <u>tomorrow!</u>

John then mails the packages and adds the following:

6/30: Mailed five packages to Trish today. Will follow up with her next week.

Two weeks pass, and it's time for Jack of See Jack Fall to call Scott, Club Boomerang's booker, again. Jack finds his contact sheet for the club and reviews his notes. He sees that Scott should have reviewed the demo by now. Jack now needs to find out if Scott liked it and if he's ready to book See Jack Fall for a Sunday afternoon show.

| Club Boomerang: | Boomerang. Scott here. |
| Jack Fallinski: | Hello, Scott. It's Jack Fallinski from See Jack Fall. We spoke two weeks ago about the possibility of my band |

	playing a show at Club Boomerang. You were going to check out our demo.
SP:	Right. I did listen to it. Let's set something up. Let me grab the calendar and see what we have for you.
JF:	You mentioned when we spoke before that you might have a Sunday afternoon show for us.
SP:	Right. How does November 6 at 3 PM work for you?
JF:	I'm pretty sure that date will be perfect for us. Is it okay if I run it by the band and get back to you tomorrow?
SP:	Okay. I'll hold the spot for now, but please get back to me soon. I need to get this booked.
JF:	I'll call you back tomorrow. Thanks.
SP:	Talk to you then.

Jack updates the log.

Success! Jack's band has just landed a gig at the Club Boomerang. The two final steps to solidifying the show date are to confirm it with the other members of the band and work out the show details with the booker. After Jack calls his bandmates, who are all available for that date and excited to do the show, he calls Scott back to work out the final details.

SP:	Club Boomerang, Scott speaking.
JF:	Hey, Scott, It's Jack from See Jack Fall.
SP:	Hey, Jack. Are we in business?
JF:	Yes! We're really looking forward to November 6th. I know it's going to be a great show.
SP:	I'll write you down in the calendar in pen. Sunday, November 6.
JF:	So what time should we be at the club?
SP:	I'm glad you asked. Get a pen and write this down so there's no confusion. Load-in time is 1 PM. There are four bands on the bill, and they'll be loading in at the

	same time. Just bring your gear in and put it along the sidewall until your sound check, which is set for 2 PM, when the sound guy, Carl, arrives.
JF:	*Got it.*
SP:	*The set is forty-five minutes. Since you're the first band playing, you'll be the only band sound checking. Carl just does the first band on the bill and then the rest of the groups do a quick signal check before they begin their shows. So you definitely have the premier spot. The catch is that as the first band you'll need to have your people here on time.*
JF:	*No problem. Like I said before, this is our first show and there are a lot of people who have been waiting to see us play. We don't want to disappoint them or you. I'm confident we'll have a good, lively crowd.*
SP:	*We use Sunday shows to gauge how bands play and draw. If you do well, we can talk about setting up another show at a better time.*
JF:	*We'd like that. Thanks.*
SP:	*Let's see … Also, Sunday gigs are a $2 cover charge to the audience, and bands do not get paid. How many people in your band?*
JF:	*Three.*
SP:	*You'll get three guest list spots and three drink tickets for half-priced drinks at the bar. I usually work on Sunday afternoons, so there's a good chance I'll see you at the show.*
JF:	*Sounds fine. It'll be nice to put a face to the voice. Let me repeat the information back to you so we're clear. Load-in is at 1 PM. Sound check is at 2 PM. And the gig is at 3 PM. The set is forty-five minutes long, and the cover is $2. We aren't getting paid, and we get three guest list spots and three half-priced drink tickets.*

	If we have a good draw, we can book again on a better date. Is all this accurate?
SP:	Yes, that's all correct.
JF:	Thanks for everything, Scott. I'm looking forward to meeting you in person and having a great show.
SP:	I'll talk to you soon.
JF:	Bye.

Jack updates the log. The latest entry reads:

10/14: Called Scott. Told him we accept the gig. The details are as follows:

Load-in:	1 PM—put gear on sidewall until sound check begins with sound guy Carl.
Sound Check:	2 PM—we are the only band sound checking.
Gig Time:	3 PM
Compensation:	Band is not getting paid.
Cover Charge:	$2
Set:	Set is forty-five minutes.
Other:	Band gets three guest list spots and three half-priced drink tickets. There are four bands on the bill. We are the first band playing. If we have a good gig with a good crowd, we can book here again at a better time.

Meanwhile, John and his band Groove Mission are awaiting gig news from the Riverbend Resort and Country Club. John contacted Trish a week after mailing the packages and a month has passed. John decides to call Trish again to see whether anyone has shown an interest in booking the band.

JM:	Hello, Trish. This is John from the band Groove Mission. We spoke a month ago and you invited me to send you

	some packages from my band in hopes that we might get some referral work.
TB:	Sure, John. I remember you.
JM:	Great. Have we had any leads on gigs?
TB:	As a matter of fact, you have. I've given three of your packages away to clients planning events here at Riverbend. I'm not sure if these clients have made any decisions on bands. Groove Mission was on a list of five or six groups.
JM:	Thank you so much for referring us. We really appreciate it.
TB:	No problem. I listened to your demo CD. You guys are really good. I'm sure you'll be booked here very soon.
JM:	Thanks. Is it okay if I send you three more packages to replace the ones you handed out?
TB:	Sure. I'd appreciate it. And feel free to contact me again to see how things are going.
JM:	Great. Take care.

John hangs up and updates the log.

Three weeks later, John gets a call from a prospective client:

John M.:	Hello?
Maggie Burke:	Hello. My name is Maggie Burke. The Riverbend Resort gave me a CD from the band Groove Mission ...?
JM:	Great! My name is John McNown. I'm the leader of the group. How can I help you?
MB:	My fiancé and I are planning our wedding at Riverbend, and we love your CD. We're hoping Groove Mission can play our wedding.
JM:	I sincerely hope we can. What's the date?

MB:	December 20.
JM:	Let me check our calendar … We're free that day.
MB:	Wonderful. How do we take it from here?
JM:	Let me start by telling you a little about the band and see if you have any questions. We are a ten-piece group that features both male and female lead vocals, drums, bass, guitar, keyboards, and a four-piece horn section. We also provide our own PA system. As you heard on our demo CD, we cover music from the 1940s to today. Our song list includes two hundred tunes, and we encourage our clients to select the songs they'd like to hear at their events. This is your wedding, so we want you to have what you want!
MB:	How much do you charge?
JM:	For a four-hour event, we charge $5,000.
MB:	That's a lot more than what a DJ quoted me earlier this week.
JM:	I imagine it is. Obviously a live band can't compete with a DJ when it comes to pricing. But a DJ can't compete with a live band for the entertainment value that's added to the event. A live band can bring a lot more energy and excitement to an event, and it can be more interactive with your guests.
MB:	I need to talk with my fiancé about the price. It's more than we have budgeted.
JM:	I understand completely. Before you go, though, let me tell you a little more about the services we can provide. If you'd like, our bandleader can MC the reception and direct traffic with regards to getting guests and members of the wedding party in their places, introducing the wedding party, toasts, cake cutting, and so forth. The band will be impeccably dressed

in tuxedos or any semiformal attire you request. We also can handle musical necessities other than the reception, like the ceremony music and cocktail hour if you choose to have them. We're here to work with you to make your wedding reception the most memorable event of your life.

MB: *Okay. Thanks for explaining that to me. I'm still going to talk with my fiancé. Can I call you back next week?*

JM: *Sure. Can you give me your number, address, and e-mail for my records?*

MB: *Yes. It's (408) 555-1111 and Maggie@burke.com. My address is 421 Bogart Road, Anytown, US 88888.*

JM: *Great. I look forward to hearing from you, and thanks so much for considering Groove Mission for your reception. I really hope we can do it. It sounds like it'll be an enjoyable affair.*

Because John now has a potential client, he can create a new log that corresponds to Maggie Burke's wedding.

Maggie Burke December 20 Wedding Reception

Address:	**421 Bogart Road**
	Anytown, CA 88888
Phone:	**(408) 555-1111**
E-mail:	**Maggie@burke.com**
Venue:	**Riverbend Resort and Country Club**

10/14: Spoke with potential client Maggie Burke today. She's having her wedding reception at the Riverbend on December 20, and is interested in booking the band. Trish at the resort referred her and Maggie needs to talk with her fiancé about us. They may not be able to afford the $5,000 fee, though. I took down her information, and she said she'd call in a week to discuss it further.

Because Maggie is hesitant to pay $5,000 for a live band, John now needs to review his overhead cost and his profit margin to see if he can work with Maggie on the price. After reviewing his costs, John decides he can reduce the price by $500. John calls Maggie:

JM:	*Hello, this is John McNown from the band Groove Mission. Is Maggie available?*
MB:	*This is Maggie. Hello, John.*
JM:	*I hope you don't mind my contacting you. Our calendar is starting to fill up and I wanted to check back with you while Groove Mission is still available.*
MB:	*My fiancé is still concerned about the pricing. He says $5,000 is too much to pay for a band.*
JM:	*Maggie, I understand completely. Listen. We really want to play your wedding. I think we'd be a great fit with you and your guests. What if I drop the price to $4,500 for a five-hour event? That's $500 less than our standard fee, plus you'll get a free hour of music.*
MB:	*Hmmm … that does sound like a good deal. Hang on a second … [background] Honey! [murmuring] Okay! You've got yourself a deal.*

Now that Maggie has accepted the initial terms of the deal, John moves forward to confirm the details of the gig, which include the date, time, location, venue contact, contract, and any incidentals like food for the band, song requests, order of events within the reception—cake cutting, bouquet toss, etc.:

JM:	*Fantastic. Now let's go over the details of the event. First, the date is Saturday, December 20?*
MB:	*That's correct.*

JM:	At the Riverbend Resort, 15200 Riverbend Lane in Anytown?
MB:	Yes.
JM:	Is your contact Trish Browning?
MB:	Yes! She's great.
JM:	Oh, I agree. What time does the reception begin?
MB:	7 PM.
JM:	Great. Just to let you know, we arrive at least two hours in advance of our start time to set up our equipment. We'll coordinate with Trish on the setup in the room, and loading and unloading. You don't need to worry about that. I'm going to e-mail you a contract. We require that our clients sign the agreement before we commit to the date. As professionals, we need a contract in place to protect us, and I'm sure you'll find peace of mind in having us locked in as well. Let me know if you have any questions when you receive it. I have your e-mail address, and I'll e-mail the contract to you today. If you could sign it and fax it back to me, we can get started with the fun particulars of the event, like picking songs!
MB:	Okay. I'll expect it and will get back to you if I have any questions.
JM:	Perfect. I look forward to working with you, Maggie. This is going to be fun.

John updates his log and begins preparing a contract. Using the template from earlier in this chapter, here's Groove Mission's contract for the Maggie Burke wedding:

Musical Services Agreement

This contract is for the services of Groove Mission (herein called "Artist") and Maggie Burke (herein called "Purchaser") for the engagement described below and is made this 17th day of October 2008, between the undersigned Artist and Purchaser.

1. Venue: Riverbend Resort and Country Club at 15200 Riverbend Lane, Anytown, CA 94000
2. Dates of Performance: Saturday, December 20, 2008
3. Times:
   Load-in: 5 PM Sound Check: 6:30 PM Start: 7 PM
4. Number and Length of Sets: Five forty-five-minute sets. Set 1: 7:00–7:45 PM, Set 2: 8:15–9:00 PM, Set 3: 9:15–10:00 PM, Set 4: 10:15–11:00 PM, Set 5: 11:15 PM–12 midnight. (All Set Times to Be Confirmed with Purchaser.)
5. Agreed-to Compensation:
   a. Musical Services: $4,500
   b. Meals: To Be Determined
   c. Total Compensation: $4,500 plus dinner
6. Payment to be made by check no later than: November 30, 2008.
7. Artist's obligations under this contract are null and void if unable to perform due to accidents, riots, strikes, epidemics, or any other Act of God that could endanger the health of safety of the Artist.
8. In the event Purchaser fails to fulfill its obligation provided herein, Purchaser will be liable to Artist in addition to the compensation provided herein.
9. In the event Artist fails to fulfill its obligation provided herein, Artist will be liable to Purchaser for the amount set in 5c, Total Compensation.
10. Either party may cancel this agreement without obligation to other if notice is received twenty-one (21) days in advance of show.

Maggie Burke	John McNown
Maggie Burke Wedding	Groove Mission
Purchaser	Artist

One week after e-mailing the contract, Maggie calls John:

MB: *Hello, John, it's Maggie. I'd like to ask you a few questions about the contract.*

JM: *Good to hear from you, Maggie. How can I help you?*

MB: *Going in order down the contract, first, what is "to be determined" under the meal heading?*

JM: *I'm glad you asked. As you know, you're hosting a five-hour reception. The band will actually be there a minimum of seven hours, since we arrive early for setup. And after the gig concludes, we're there for about another hour packing up our equipment. That's an eight-hour commitment. It's not a requirement of ours, but we do ask, if possible, if our client can feed the group during one of our allotted breaks during the night. Again, we don't require this, nor do we ask for the same food that you're serving. We're happy with sandwiches or hamburgers, but providing food for the group makes for a happy, well-fed band that has the energy to bring the house down with the performance.*

MB: *That sounds fair to me. How will I know what to feed the band?*

JM: *I recommend you ask the wedding coordinator, Trish, what she usually does. I'll bring it up with her as well if that's okay with you.*

MB: *That's fine. We'll be sure to feed you. I'm glad this came up. I'm clueless about this stuff. Next on the list is the method of payment. You say you need a check for the total amount by November 30?*

JM: *Yes, we ask to be paid twenty-one days in advance of our performance. There was a time when we simply asked to be paid upon arrival at the show, but, unfortunately, after a bad experience, we've changed*

	our policy. We've also found this works better for the client. You'll be so busy at your reception, and you aren't going to want to chase us down with a check. We stand by our agreement to provide you with great live music, so don't worry about us running off and not showing up. If we did that we'd never be able to work at the Riverbend again, and that's not in our best interest.
MB:	*Okay. I understand. One more thing. You mentioned the possibility you could MC our reception. Could you tell me a little more about that?*
JM:	*Absolutely. When we MC a reception, we act as the voice of your reception. We'll introduce you and your wedding party when you come out for your first dance. We'll also announce important events within the reception like your cake cutting and bouquet toss. We provide this service free of charge. Are you interested in us MC'ing the reception?*
MB:	*Yes, I am. I've been working out these details with Trish. Will you be able to coordinate with her so we're all on the same page?*
JM:	*No problem.*
MB:	*Great. Well, that's all I have. I'm going to sign this and fax it to you.*
JM:	*Perfect. Maggie, we have some time before your event. Let's plan on talking in the next couple of weeks about the schedule for the evening and what songs you want to hear. Can I call you in two weeks?*
MB:	*Yes. That's great. That will give me a chance to get everything straight with Trish.*
JM:	*If you have any questions, feel free to give me a call or send me an e-mail anytime. Bye now.*
MB:	*Bye.*

John again updates his log.

Moving forward a few weeks, John has received a signed contact from Maggie. At this point, the wedding is a few of weeks away, and the final step before the actual gig is to confirm any details that relate to the event. This activity isn't necessary for club gigs, but at a special event when the band is the MC (master of ceremonies), it's essential.

Details vary depending on the event. Activities during a special event, such as a corporate holiday party, may include speeches, award presentations, visual presentations, and raffles. Typical wedding details include the introduction of the wedding party, the first dance, the father/daughter and mother/son dances, toasts, cake cutting, bouquet and garter toss, money dance, etc. These activities occur at certain junctions in the affair and the band must factor them into the evening's schedule by taking strategic breaks during these times, playing particular requested music, and providing a microphone for a toast.

Bandleader Ted Heath says, "Most of the gigs I do are casuals and corporate parties. I contact the client a few days in advance to solidify what they expect from the group musically and otherwise. I like to detail the timeline on what they want to happen throughout the night."

When John receives the contract from Maggie he gives her a call to discuss these details.

MB:	*Hello?*
JM:	*Hello, Maggie. It's John from Groove Mission. I received the signed contract...thank you...and I wanted to check in with you to go over the details of your event. We should discuss what music you want to hear and how your wedding is going to flow.*
MB:	*Great! You have good timing. I just finished getting all of this together. Let me read to you what we have. We'd like the reception to begin at 7 PM. At approximately 7:20 PM my husband, Josh, and I would like to be introduced by the band as Mr. and Mrs. Donner as*

we come into the hall. This should be followed by our first dance. Do you know the song "I Melt" by Rascal Flatts? I know it's not on your list of songs.

JM: No, we don't know that one. But it's our policy to learn one special-request song per gig to satisfy our clients.

MB: Wow! That's wonderful. I'm glad you do that, because I don't want to have to dance to the music from the CD! If it's okay, we'd like to do a second dance. The second dance will feature the entire wedding party.

JM: Of course that's okay. What song do you want for it?

MB: We'd like "I Finally Found Someone" by Barbra Streisand and Bryan Adams.

JM: No problem. I imagine dinner is probably coming up soon after the dance.

MB: Right. Dinner is at 7:50 PM, but before that, we'd like some time for toasts from the best man and my father. During this time the caterer is going to start serving the salads.

JM: How about this? After the second dance, we'll play an upbeat dance number to get everyone on the floor and in the mood to party. Then we'll take a short break while the toasts begin and come back on stage at 7:50 PM to play dinner music while the meals are being served.

MB: That will work fine.

JM: Once everyone has been served dinner, typically that's when the band eats. This is so you and your guests have live music to listen to after your meal. While your guests and the band are eating, we'll play a CD of dinner music through the PA system. If this works for you, that puts the live music returning at 9 PM.

MB: That's fine. After dinner, we'd like to begin the dancing with a father/daughter dance. I'd like the song to be

	the Louis Armstrong tune, "What a Wonderful World." After that, just do whatever it takes to keep the dance floor jumping.
JM:	*That's what we do. Is there anything else we need to be aware of? Do you have any other scheduled events that are taking place?*
MB:	*Yes. We want to cut the cake at some point after dinner.*
JM:	*What if we schedule the cake cutting for our next break around 10 PM?*
MB:	*That should work. Is there anything else we need to work out?*
JM:	*Just let us know what songs you want to hear.*
MB:	*I really like your repertoire. If you could mix a fair amount of contemporary with 1980s music, we'll be happy. We have no specific requests.*
JM:	*We know how to keep a party going. And we'll play appropriate dance music through the sound system when we're on our breaks so people can still dance.* *During your wedding, we'll work directly with Trish at the Riverbend to make sure everything is on track. We don't want you to worry about a thing. Your reception will be spectacular.*
MB:	*Thanks for all of your help, John. I'm going to get that check off to you tomorrow. If I have any more questions, I'll contact you. I'm confident you guys will be great. I can't wait for my wedding day!*

When the conversation ends, John updates his log and includes all of the key gig information. He then gets to work on creating his set list. Once John receives the check for payment from Maggie, Groove Mission is set to do the gig!

Now that your band has booked a show, you need to promote it.

CHAPTER 9

PROMOTING YOUR GIGS

A band must be able to draw a crowd to flourish in the local club scene. Once the band has proven itself, it will be viewed as a moneymaker and will get booked on weekends and other popular nights. This can lead to an increasing fan base and landing better gigs. A band that can't draw a crowd will be relegated to performing on slow nights, often for free. This lack of interest from music fans is discouraging and can lead to a band becoming frustrated and breaking up.

To get people to shows, a band needs to promote its gigs. This is done by creating materials that are circulated to both existing fans and potential new fans so that everyone knows when and where the band will be performing.

CREATING YOUR PROMOTIONAL MATERIALS

The first step in creating promotional materials for an upcoming gig is to gather all pertinent information. You can then design and reproduce flyers and posters, as well as write any press releases and personal e-mails you want to distribute.

Organizing Your Information

Pertinent information should include when, where, and sometimes even why your band is performing. Then denote the name and address of the venue, the date and time of the gig, and the price of admission. You may also include age restrictions (many clubs only admit people twenty-one years of age or older), the sponsor (if there is one, such as a radio station or a nonprofit raising awareness for an environmental cause, for example), or the show's purpose, such as a CD Release Party.

Here's an example of gig information for fictitious rock band Three Bone:

- Venue: The Roxy Theatre
- Address: 9009 West Sunset Blvd., West Hollywood, California
- Date: January 12
- Time: 10 PM
- Admission Price: $10
- Additional Information: EP Release Party, Benefit for the H.E.A.R. Foundation— The Roxy Theatre is a 21+ venue

Creating Flyers, Posters, and Press Releases

Once you've got the information together, you're ready to create flyers, posters, press releases, and any other materials that might be useful in promoting your gig.

Flyers are advertisements that are either printed or created as digital images. If printed and distributed by hand, they typically range in size from the standard copy paper dimensions of 8.5 × 11 inches to a quarter of that (2.125 × 2.75 inches). If the flyers are digital and distributed via the Internet, they can be any size, though it's best if the files are small enough to be e-mailed and opened with a minimum amount of time needed to access them. Flyers may also be used as paid advertisements when reprinted in newspapers, music publications, and online.

To create flyers using a computer, you'll need access to software like Microsoft Word or Photoshop. To create them without a computer, you'll need access to a photocopier.

You can select virtually any image or graphic you want for your flyers. Most bands tend to use group shots, either those taken during a photo shoot or in performance. Jamie Douglass, of the Los Angeles–based band, The Distants, says, "We've done multiple photo shoots over the years, plus we have pictures taken during our shows. We'll use these as well, and any other random images we like, and splice them into flyers and posters."

There are any number of kinds of images you might consider. For instance, you may want to stage a photo shoot specifically for the purpose of promoting a gig. If your band is playing a gig on Halloween, you may want to take a picture of you and your bandmates in costume, or to use a spooky, graphic image like a cockroach on a steel operating table. If, on the other hand, you're playing a gig to release a new demo recording, you might use your cover art.

If designing your flyers on a computer, you'll either need digital images or a scanner to convert your photos and art to a digital format. If designing by hand, you'll need to create your masters on sheets of paper, adding images that you can physically arrange on a sheet, and then photocopy them to create your final flyers.

It's always best to produce more flyers than you think you'll need. Better to have a few dozen left over than to run short. Unless you have access to free paper, toner, and a printer through a friend, family member, or place of business, printing enough copies to distribute by hand can be expensive. However, it will cost you less money if you reproduce them professionally at a copy center like FedEx Kinko's, Staples, or Office Depot.

Printing flyers at a copy center allows you to take advantage of the store's ability to purchase supplies in bulk to minimize its own expenses—as well as to achieve a better-looking result. A copy center will charge approximately $0.08 per 8.5 × 11–inch black-and-white page. Color copies cost approximately $0.16 per 8.5 × 11–inch page. So if you layout one flyer on one standard 8.5 × 11–inch page, your total cost for printing two hundred color flyers is $32. This is probably cheaper than printing your own color flyers since you'd have to buy your own toner, which can cost anywhere from $25 to $75. Plus, you don't have to worry about the wear and tear on your printer, which adds additional expense.

Posters are essentially large flyers. The difference is that they're neither distributed by hand nor by e-mail, and they're much larger and often printed on sturdier paper stock. Small posters are usually 11 × 17 inches or 18 × 24 inches, while large ones may be 60 × 72 inches.

Posters are created in the same manners as flyers, but because of their size, you can't print them out on an ordinary home printer. If you create a poster using your computer, you'll need to save the image of your poster to disc and take it to a copy center to reproduce it. If you're creating a poster by hand, your master will have to be as large a size as you plan to use, and you'll need to photocopy it using a correspondingly large machine.

Posters are more expensive than flyers and can cost hundreds of dollars to produce. Unless your band is flush with cash, it doesn't make financial sense to create a new poster to promote every gig. Instead, you can create a generic poster featuring a band photo or other graphic, and underneath the image leave a large white space where you can add new information for each gig.

Press releases are written communications aimed at media outlets. They should be no more than one-and-a-half pages in length and set up in a specific format (see the example on the following page). When bands issue releases for upcoming gigs, they do so in hopes that the media will pass the information on to their readers, listeners, or viewers. Press releases for shows typically result in a mention in the calendar section of a publication or on television and radio as an event worth catching. They can, however, become the basis for feature stories or music reviews if the release sparks interest or if it's a slow news day.

Press releases contain the same promotional information as flyers and posters, but with more detail about the band itself, similar to what's included in a short-form bio. This information is necessary so that whoever is writing about the show, or mentioning it over the radio or on television, can add some commentary on the band. A radio DJ who receives a press release for your upcoming show will most likely want to mention more than just the name of your band and the time, date, and location of the performance. To sell the story as news, he or she may say, "Rock band Three Bone is coming to the Roxy Theatre tomorrow night! These guys hail from my hometown of Irvine, California, and have been really been shaking up the L.A. rock scene. Check 'em out!"

Here's a sample press release for Three Bone's upcoming gig.

For Immediate Release

THREE BONE
Contact: Todd Buckwoldt
(310) 555-1010

Rock Band Three Bone to Play EP Release Party at the Roxy Theatre

Los Angeles *(October 12, 2008)—Monster Rock band Three Bone will perform songs from the band's upcoming recording,* Never Go Quietly, *at a CD Release Party Thursday, October 23, beginning at 10 PM at the Roxy Theatre.*

The CD's title track currently is being played on KROQ and is available at all Southern California record stores that support local music.

Three Bone is a dynamic rock trio featuring singer/songwriter Todd Buckwoldt on guitar and vocals. Buckwoldt was named "Songwriter of the Year" in Mosh Pit *magazine for his debut solo effort* Fate Kills.

Three Bone has impressed audiences throughout Southern California with its blend of intense melodies and blistering rhythms. The band currently is working on the video for the song "Never Go Quietly."

The Roxy Theatre is located at 9009 West Sunset Blvd. in West Hollywood. The cover charge for the CD Release Party is $10. Proceeds from the show will go to H.E.A.R. to benefit musicians with hearing loss.

For more information, go to www.threebone.com.

DISTRIBUTING YOUR PROMOTIONAL MATERIALS

Once your flyers, posters, and press releases are ready to go, all that's needed is for you to distribute them. This can be done by both personal contact and by mass marketing.

Distributing Your Materials by Personal Contact

Contacting people personally is the most effective means of promoting a show. When someone receives a flyer that's been either hand-delivered or e-mailed to them by a member of the band, they feel they're more than just another warm body to fill out an audience. Someone receiving such personal attention will be more likely to attend a show than if they were given a flyer on the street or saw a poster on a signpost. Bandleader Julie Zielinski agrees, "The best way to market a show is by word of mouth and by e-mailing your personal contact list."

It's neither easy nor fun to have to work the phones and write e-mails asking your fans to support your band. A lot of musicians understandably feel that they're providing top-notch entertainment and that this should be enough to draw people to their gigs. Unfortunately, for new or less popular bands this just isn't the case. Fans have many options as to what they can do in their spare time with their discretionary income, and it's just as easy to hang out at a bar with friends, to see a movie, or to go out to dinner as it is to go to a club. Without that personal touch, many fans may simply skip the gig.

Personal communications are effective in bringing people to shows because it's more difficult to say no when you're contacted directly. It's human nature to want to please people, so it's hard to turn down a band member handing you a flyer and saying, "Mark, will you come to our gig at the Blue Board?" It's a lot easier to ignore a bulk e-mail that reads, "Attention Fans: Come check out our gig at the Blue Board tomorrow night!"

Flyers sent to fans in the form of an e-mail attachment can be as effective as those that are hand-delivered, as long as the text you write in the body of the e-mail is personalized. If fans reading your e-mail feel like they're being spammed, they may never get to the attached flyer. When e-mailing flyers, be sure to use the fan's name and, if possible, mention something unique to them in the body of your message. Here's an example for Three Bone:

To: gwen@gwendalyn.com

From: Todd@threebone.com

Hey Gwen!

I want to let you know that my band is playing the Viper Room June 10 at 10 PM. There is a $5 cover charge and it's a 21+ show (so your sister won't be able to come, bummer!). As you can imagine, playing the Viper Room is a huge deal for us. I really hope you can make it. Check out our attached flyer!

Let me know if you can come. It would be great to see you there!

Todd

This e-mail works because Todd gives Gwen all of the information she needs about the show as well as personalizes the message with his comment about Gwen's sister. When Gwen reads this note, she'll know she's not considered a faceless fan. In addition, including a sentence about the importance of the show at a great venue like the Viper Room lets Gwen know that the band should be at its best that night.

Another advantage of personally distributing your promotional materials is that, by asking people whether they'll be able to attend your gig, you'll be able to estimate how big your draw might be. This can contribute to your peace of mind, especially if you're playing a club that insists on bands bringing in a certain number of paying customers. It can also serve as a warning sign if you realize you aren't making the club's quota. Then you'll know to double your promotional efforts prior to the gig.

Distributing Your Materials by Mass Marketing

Bands promote their shows en masse for two reasons: Their fan base is too large to contact everyone personally, and they want to reach potential new fans. To mass market to your existing fan base, you can either mail or e-mail your flyers. To promote to potential fans, you need to hand distribute flyers or hang posters where they congregate. You may also attempt to get media coverage by sending out press releases and by advertising your gigs in print, online, and in broadcast mediums.

Bands with large fan bases create a database called a *mailing list* that contains the contact information of everyone interested in following the band. They are then able to refer to their mailing list whenever they are ready to mail or e-mail flyers to promote their shows.

A mailing list begins its life as a record of friends and family a band thinks would be interested in coming to its shows. Additions are then made to this list whenever the band meets someone interested in its music. This often happens immediately after a gig. After only a few shows, a band may have a mailing list with a hundred or more names, and the ability to continue to grow the list after each performance.

To create a mailing list that can be circulated at a gig, prepare a few sheets of paper with the band's name and "Mailing List" at the top of each page. The sheets should be attached to a clipboard with a pen, and the pen should be attached to the clipboard so that no one walks off with it.

Here is a sample of Three Bone's mailing list:

Three Bone Mailing List		
Name	E-mail	Mailing Address
Johnny White	jwhite@email.com	101 East Lane Street Mytown, CA 90040
Hershel Jones	hbaby@email.com	203 Viane Ave #2 Mytown, CA 90040
Martha Elanas	melanas@email.com	10100 Calcutta St., Apt A, Mytown, CA 90040

Once you have fans' addresses, you can e-mail or mail them flyers for your show. E-mailing is the easiest and most cost-effective means of distributing flyers, since it doesn't require spending money on printing or buying postage. (Remember, just because e-mail is the ideal choice today doesn't mean it will be tomorrow. Keep an ear open for new technologies that can help you communicate with your fans.)

Mailing flyers to your fans is expensive. However, since it's not something you'll do often, it will make an impression when you do. If you're promoting a big show, you might send flyers or even printed invitations to stress the significance of the gig. To mail flyers, write the name and address of the recipient on the opposite side of where the gig information is printed. Here's an example:

THREE BONE P.O. BOX 000 Los Angeles, CA 00000	Postage Here
	Johnny White 101 E. Lane Street Mytown, CA 90040

To promote your gig to potential fans, you need to know where to find people who'll enjoy your music. This means going to clubs that host bands with a similar style to yours, or going to music stores and listening for musicians jamming on songs from your band's genre. Unfortunately, that's the easy part. Once you've handed them a flyer, or they've seen your poster or press release, it's still a difficult proposition to get them to the show, because they aren't likely to risk their time on a band they don't know.

Evan Rodaniche of Cage9 has a creative method of attracting new fans. "Our secret weapon is to hit the lines of clubs with a portable CD player and try to strike up a conversation with people we meet. Then we let them listen to the music. On a good night we can get twenty e-mail addresses after two or three hours. You have to find people who look like your crowd. Sometimes we'll even sell or give away CDs to people in the lines, but getting their e-mail is the most important thing. You can't give away something like a CD or sticker without getting anything back. If you don't get their contact information, it's a wasted CD, because 95 percent of the time you'll never hear from them again. Then you need to follow up. Write an e-mail saying nice to meet you and all that. Assuming they like the CD, you can make some fans."

Once you've personally promoted your show to potential fans, you're ready to target people you haven't met with posters, press releases, and advertising. This won't be as effective as personally communicating with people, but your cool design or appealing content may pique the interest of a music fan and draw him or her to the gig.

Promotional materials also serve another purpose. Because their exposure can be widespread, people may notice and remember you, provided your publicity is catchy or you have a memorable band name. Over time, this can help your group gain credibility and awareness. When people are asked about your band they may say, "I've never seen them live but I've definitely heard of them," and be willing to spend the time to check out a show.

To decide where to hang posters, go to high-traffic areas where music fans congregate and affix them to bulletin boards, walls, and anything else people will notice. (Don't place them anywhere that doesn't allow advertising, like a light pole or a wall with a sign that says, "Post No Bills." Doing so is illegal, and you may be fined. Check local ordinances before posting.) You'll most likely find posters from other bands in the same locations. Should you find that there is so many of them that there's no room left for yours, the general rule of thumb is that you may tear down another poster if it's for a show that's already occurred. If all posters are current, either move to another location or find the most often repeated poster and tear it down or place yours over it. You may be risking bad karma (and a poster war with another band), but remember that bands don't own the locations where they hang posters and shouldn't feel they can monopolize the entire area just because they got there first.

To determine where to mail, fax, or e-mail press releases, identify every media source you normally use to get information about local music. These will include daily and weekly area newspapers, local music publications, commercial and college radio stations, and community television stations. Once you've identified these sources, contact them and ask to whose attention you should send your news. If you're lucky, you may even develop a relationship with these contacts, which may be helpful in garnering future coverage. A good source to identify all possible media outlets in your area is the *Bacon's Media Guide*, which should be available in the reference area of larger library locations.

Another approach to promoting your shows is advertising, which includes broadcast, online, and print. Broadcast advertising, including television and radio, is typically too expensive for bands to purchase, so unless you know of a small station which charges an affordable fee, you'll need to just consider online and print ads. To find the best place to purchase an ad, check out sites and publications that are popular in your area. Call or e-mail advertising managers, and if they're receptive to your ad and the price is affordable, send them a copy of your flyer. Keep in mind that you may have to resize it to fit into the ad space you can afford.

You may also consider certain online networking Web sites like www.myspace. com, www.garageband.com, and www.craigslist.com that feature pages devoted to gig promotion. These pages usually are free to users. However, these appear on huge sites that serve national and international users, and it's hard to distinguish your band in a crowd of acts from all over the world.

If you can't use advertising because it's too expensive and not available for free in your area, it's possible that the venue you're playing will advertise the gig. It's pretty common for venues to have agreements with music publications and Web sites to post calendar listings. This won't highlight your band more than any other band playing the venue, but it will put your band's name in print or online.

Now that you've promoted your gig, you're ready to complete your final preparations for the show.

CHAPTER 10

PREPARING FOR YOUR GIG

Gigging is a highly competitive business. There are always plenty of bands competing for bookings at comparatively few venues. Given the opportunity to show what they can do, bands need to impress bookers and potential special-event clients with both their performance and their professionalism. Bands increase their chances of landing more gigs when they distinguish themselves.

The best way to guarantee a great gig is to prepare for every aspect of the performance. Successful bands leave nothing to chance. They organize every detail of their shows to ensure they'll arrive at the gig on time, with all the necessary equipment, and play their songs in the order they rehearsed to entertain their audience.

A band's performance is representative of its preparation. If the band effectively organizes and rehearses, its show is likely to run smoothly, and the band will be able to overcome any unexpected obstacles that may arise. Without sufficient preparation, a performance can be shaky, and incidents like breaking a string or playing the wrong part can derail a show. The stakes are high. Fans, bookers, and event planners are unlikely to forget a poor performance, and even one bad show can be damaging to a band's career.

To prepare for a gig, a band needs to arrange the order and rehearse the songs it plans to perform. Then, on the day of the performance, band members should follow a preshow routine that gives them confidence that they are ready, willing, and able to play to the best of their abilities.

PREPARING YOUR SONGS FOR THE GIG

Once a gig is booked, you and your band need to prepare your songs. Your first step is to create a set list. Your next step is to rehearse your show.

Creating Your Set List

A *set* is the period of time that a band performs. Its duration may vary, but it's usually about forty-five minutes. Depending on the club, you may be asked to play one or more sets. Clubs that book bands that play original music typically expect them to perform one forty-five-minute set. They'll usually book three or four bands on the same night, and assign each a specific performance time. Other clubs (and special-event planners) will hire one band to perform multiple sets and be the sole entertainment. The duration of the gig is established during negotiations with the booker or event planner.

A *set list* is the catalog of songs a band will play during a gig. Bands create set lists to establish the songs they plan to perform and the order in which they'll perform them. Before you can create a set list, you need to know how long you're expected to play. You then want to order your songs to make the greatest possible impact on your audience, which I'll address later in the chapter.

To be sure your set list contains the right number of songs for the set's duration, time the songs you want to play and calculate the total minutes. If each song is approximately four minutes (the length of a typical rock, pop, blues, or country song), you can theoretically play eleven songs in a forty-five-minute set. However, this does not include variables that can either add or subtract time. For instance, you'll probably talk to the audience at certain points in the show to introduce the songs or invite people to sign up for your mailing list. Band members may also need to re-tune their instruments. Actions like these add up and need to be factored into how many songs you can reasonably expect to be able to play.

There's another variable that can affect the length of your set, but this one is harder to calculate in advance. Given the excitement of playing in front of an audience, you may find that your band will perform the songs quicker than you've anticipated. When the adrenaline starts pumping, mid-tempo songs can quickly become up-tempo songs, causing you to finish your set ahead of schedule, perhaps leaving room for one more number. At one of my first live performances, my band played a cover of the Police hit, "Message in a Bottle." The drummer was so excited he counted off the song about twenty beats a minute too fast. The arpeggios the guitar was supposed to play had to be converted to chords—the guitarist couldn't pick the strings at the new tempo. As a result, we cruised through a four-and-a-half minute song in less than three minutes!

To accommodate unforeseen delays, or a fast set, allow a five-minute cushion. Instead of planning to play eleven four-minute songs in forty-five minutes, plan on playing ten songs. If there's time remaining, you can play that eleventh song as an encore, or leave the stage—provided you aren't under contract to play until a specific time. Most clubs won't care, or notice, if you end a few minutes early.

Be careful not to exceed your allotted time, though. Running long can have a domino effect on the entire evening and lead to negative repercussions. If you're playing a club with multiple bands on the bill, every band that plays after one that runs over will most likely have to cut songs from its set list to make up the time. Clubs operate under strict guidelines that dictate how late they can feature live music and stay open to the public, and club managers will not risk being shut down so that a band can play all of its songs or play a few extra songs to accommodate the crowd. In addition, most special events, whether weddings, corporate events, or holiday parties, have tight schedules and won't want to postpone activities like a cake cutting or a raffle so your band can play a bit longer. Doing so can result in your losing other potential bookings or referrals to any of their colleagues.

If you insist on playing beyond your scheduled time at a club gig, you risk being shut down by the venue and facing the wrath of other bands and their fans. I've seen club managers cut the power to the stage, or turn off the stage lights, to get bands to stop playing. I've seen other bands and their fans leap onstage and shut down amps in the middle of a song. Sadly, I've witnessed this from both the audience and the stage. I learned the lesson firsthand, but you shouldn't have to!

Once you've established how many songs you can play in your allotted time, you're ready to create a set list. This means determining which songs work best at which times. All songs have certain attributes that lend themselves to particular placement in a set. They may be exciting, mellow, or danceable, and there will be a right time in your performance for each. The goal is to arrange your songs in an order that captures, and sustains, your audience's attention.

Most bands try to grab an audience's attention by kicking off their sets with a song they're confident will win them over. This is particularly important for bands new to a venue, because they'll only have the first thirty seconds or so to get the crowd to take notice. Failure to do so may mean losing them to the bar, the pool table, or any number of other diversions.

Consider your audience when picking your first song. You want to give them what they'll want to hear. If you're playing a gig where the crowd expects to dance, play your best dance song first. Special-event bands typically open wedding gigs with proven favorites like "We Are Family," "In the Mood," or "Brown-Eyed Girl." These are standards guaranteed to draw everyone onto the dance floor. If you're playing a jazz club where the audience wants to hear impressive musicianship, play a song that features your best chops. If the venue books bands playing popular music, play your catchiest tune so the crowd will want to sing along.

Once you've selected your first song, skip to the end of the set list and choose your final number. It should be similar in style to your opener, because you want to leave the audience with the same feeling you evoked at the start. Many bands save the best song for last to end the show on a high note. This only works if you're sure the audience will stick around long enough to hear it. There's no point holding back a killer song if you may be playing it for an empty room.

After you've identified your closing song, fill in the rest of the slots in your set list. Think of the middle songs as mini-sets and structure them in groups of two and three that work well together. Then tie the mini-sets to each other using the same logic. For example, a mini-set might consist of a trio of songs that feature a mid-tempo tune first, a ballad next, and an up-tempo closer to round it out, or two mid-tempo numbers that sound good when played back to back. These two mini-sets may work well together, because the series of three songs ends with an upbeat song that sets up the two mid-tempo tunes that follow.

Once you've completed your set list, select an additional song to play as an encore. Again, it should be similar in style to your opening and closing songs because it will be used to close the gig. For instance, a special-event band might end its show with an energetic disco song and then encore with a classic like "Shout." Both of these songs will have an enthusiastic crowd on their feet.

After you've determined your set list, you may want to add some written notes to it that will serve as reminders for band members to, for instance, tune guitars, banter with the audience, or play a song at a certain tempo. Notes can be invaluable when a member of the band forgets something in the excitement of the gig.

Here's a sample set list for a 1980s tribute band playing one forty-five-minute set:

1. Walking on Sunshine
2. Obsession
3. Come on Eileen
   Audience Banter—"Hello, Cleveland! It's great to be here! We're That 80s Band, and we're going to take you back in time to that magical decade!"
4. I Melt with You
5. True
   Bass Reminder—don't rush the intro.

6. Turning Japanese
7. Jesse's Girl
8. Tainted Love
9. Total Eclipse of the Heart

    Audience Banter—get people on the mailing list, announce the next gig, and introduce the members of the band.

10. We Got the Beat
11. Million Miles Away (encore)

Notice the opening and closing numbers: Both are attention-grabbing, up-tempo songs. After the opening "Walking on Sunshine," "Obsession," and "Come on Eileen," comprise a mini-set that maintains the energy level. These songs are followed by audience banter.

The next mini-set is the mid-tempo "I Melt with You" and the ballad "True." These tunes bring down the energy from the opening mini-set, giving the audience some relief for their ears and some slow dancing for their feet. Once the ballad ends and the room is hushed, the band kicks the set back into full throttle with two high-energy songs—"Turning Japanese" and "Jesse's Girl"—before bringing the energy level down a bit with the mid-tempo "Tainted Love" and the ballad "Total Eclipse of the Heart," which features a dramatic finish guaranteed to pump up the crowd. Once the audience is again addressed, the band goes into the frenetic "We Got the Beat" to end the set. If an encore is demanded, the band can play "Million Miles Away," another up-tempo tune that, following "We Got the Beat," will bring the show to a close on a high note.

Here's another sample set list (without audience banter), this time from a cover blues/swing band's gig:

1. House Is Rocking
2. Messin' with the Kid
3. Sweet Home Chicago
4. That's All
5. Red House

6. I Can't Make You Love Me
7. Texas Flood
8. What I Say
9. Jailhouse Rock
10. Crossroads

The gig opens with the raucous Stevie Ray Vaughan song "House Is Rocking," followed by a mini-set of two other crowd pleasers, "Messin' with the Kid" and "Sweet Home Chicago," intended to get everyone on their feet. These songs are followed by the mid-tempo dance hit, "That's All," that ties into another mini-set of three quieter, slower songs—"Red House," "I Can't Make You Love Me," and "Texas Flood." These songs clear the dance floor for slow-dancers and give the audience a break from the high energy of the first few tunes. The band then kicks the set into high gear again by concluding with up-tempo favorites "What I Say," "Jailhouse Rock," and "Crossroads."

The last sample here is the set list that a special-event band plans to use for a wedding. Notice the ebb and flow of the song tempos and mood and how they create a predictable flow, which is carried through the entire event. For instance, each set taking place after dinner features a lot of energetic dance numbers intermixed with a couple of slow-dance songs. Also note the activities listed on the set list like the entrance of the bride and groom and the cake cutting.

Set #1: 7 PM to 7:35 PM

1. How Sweet It Is
2. Cruisin'
3. Let's Stay Together
4. Fly Me to the Moon
5. Girl from Ipanema

Grand Entrance of Bride and Groom
Introduce Bride and Groom, Josh and Maggie Donner
First Dance—I Melt
Second Dance—I Finally Found Someone

Third Dance—*Get This Party Started*
Band Breaks (15 minutes; toasts given)

Set #2: *7:50 PM to 8:30 PM*

1. Unforgettable
2. Don't Know Why
3. Wonderful Tonight
4. Our Love Is Here to Stay
5. What a Wonderful World
6. Crazy
7. Through the Years
8. How Do I Live
9. It Had to Be You

Band Breaks (30 minutes; dinner for band)

Set #3: *9 PM to 10 PM*

Father/Daughter Dance—*There You'll Be*
Introduce the Father of the Bride, John Burke

1. We Are Family
2. Brown-Eyed Girl
3. All I Wanna Do
4. Twist and Shout
5. Surfin' USA
6. Son of a Preacher Man
7. The Way You Look Tonight
8. You're the One That I Want
9. Johnny B. Goode
10. It's Not Unusual
11. Le Freak
12. Brick House

13. At Last
14. Respect

Band breaks (15 minutes; cake cutting)

Set #4: *10:15 PM to 11 PM*

1. Jump Jive & Wail
2. Celebration
3. Game of Love
4. Old Time Rock and Roll
5. What I Like About You
6. I Feel Good
7. Proud Mary
8. Let's Get It On
9. Rock Your Body
10. Beautiful
11. Hot in Herre

Band breaks (15 minutes)

Set #5: *11:15 PM to Midnight*

1. Hot, Hot, Hot
2. Walking on Sunshine
3. Love Shack
4. Funkytown
5. I Will Survive
6. Sweet Home Alabama
7. Hey Ya
8. We Got the Beat
9. Lady Marmalade
10. I Had the Time of My Life
11. Disco Inferno

Rehearsing Your Show

Once you've finished drafting a set list, you're ready to rehearse the show. Every band has its own approach to preparing for a gig. In some bands, members rehearse the set list individually; in others, they meet to work on the songs that aren't very tight. Most bands, however, practice their entire set list as a group, in order and without stopping. The goal is to simulate the actual gig, including making announcements to the audience. Evan Rodaniche of Cage9 says, "We run through the entire set about two or three times the week before the gig. By that point, we pretty much have it down."

Before beginning rehearsal, band members need to arrange themselves and their gear as they intend to appear onstage. They also need to discuss how they plan on handling any problems that might arise during the performance. Additionally, many bands face each other when they practice so they'll know when it's necessary to stop and discuss the songs. Obviously, this won't work on stage, because the audience wants to see the band members' faces, not their sides or backs, and, of course, a band's amps have to point toward the audience, not to the individual members of the group.

Your position onstage will most likely reflect the instrument you play. Drummers are almost always in the center-rear of the stage, because all of the other musicians onstage need to connect with the band's timekeeper. If the drummer is on the right side of the stage, there may be some players on the left side who lose the beat because they're unable to hear the drums. Bass, guitar, and keyboards are usually set up parallel to the drums to form a line behind the vocalist(s). Horns are typically placed on one side of the stage, with the singer(s) up front and center, where they can act as the front person(s).

Discussing how you'll deal with working through errors in your performance, as well as how you'll handle equipment malfunctions onstage, is important as well. During rehearsals, you might stop a song when a member makes a mistake to talk about the fix, just as you'd probably take a break if someone breaks a string or has to replace a shorted-out cable. You won't be able to stop during a show though; it's the cardinal rule of performing live.

Unless audience members are seasoned musicians themselves, they rarely notice mistakes and are usually oblivious to equipment malfunctions, provided the musicians can recover from them. However, short of a power failure or something similar that's beyond the band's control, if musicians stop mid-song, an audience will know something's wrong and will think the group is, at best, a bunch of rank amateurs, and, at worst, incompetent and not worth their time. Neither opinion bodes well for bands that want to continue to work.

There are two kinds of mistakes a musician can make during a gig: minor mistakes and train wrecks. A minor mistake is one that a musician can easily recover from—like briefly forgetting a song lyric or melody. A train wreck is a minor mistake that escalates until it threatens the entire song.

Minor mistakes occur when musicians forget their parts, play in the wrong key, or blank out on the structure of the song. These kinds of mistakes don't have a lasting impact on a band's performance; they occur and are rectified quickly. To prevent them from becoming train wrecks, you need to know how to recover. If you don't, you can end up in a musical tug-of-war, fighting with fellow band members over which direction the song will take. This can lead to a song coming to a clumsy, crashing halt.

The general rule to avoid turning a minor mistake into a train wreck is to follow the vocalist. There are two reasons for this: The singer is fronting the band and is handling the melodic nature of the performance. The audience naturally fixes its attention on the singer. No one notices when a drummer misses a beat, but everyone notices when a vocalist forgets lyrics or is out of sync with the rest of the band.

If a keyboard player begins playing the bridge section of a song too early, as long as the other instruments stay with the singer, the band can hopefully stay on track until the keyboardist finds his or her way again. If the band has no set rule to follow the vocalist, the song may dissolve, with half the band sticking with the singer and the other half playing the bridge with the keyboardist. This is what leads to a train wreck.

Also, vocalists sing melodies, while the rest of the band usually plays some form of harmony to accompany the vocal part. Consequently, singers can't easily jump between different sections of a song in an attempt to rejoin the rest of the band after making a mistake. It's far easier, and less noticeable, for the rest of the band to identify where the singer is in the song and to begin playing that part.

I once played in a band where the singer would almost always begin singing a verse section in the middle of a saxophone solo section. As a result, each time we played the song, when that section neared, the entire band had to anticipate whether she'd come in at the right time. If she did, the sax player was able to play his entire solo. If not, he'd have to skip the second half of it and move back into the verse section with the rest of the band following.

If your vocalist stops singing, it's up to the rest of the band to cover the mistake. To do so, your instrumentalists can take a solo or repeat the section until the singer is able to recover. If he or she cannot cover for the mistake, all you can do is end the song as gracefully as possible. It can be awkward, but it's still likely that the majority of the audience will have no idea what has happened.

Equipment malfunctions have the potential to have an even greater negative impact on a performance, as they can cause one or more instruments to drop out of a song. You never know when equipment malfunctions may strike, but regular maintenance of your instrument can help minimize failures. This includes frequently replacing accessories, such as strings, batteries, and cables. Nonetheless, sometimes equipment simply breaks down, and you need to be able to deal with it before it derails the song, or the gig.

The first thing to do to correct an equipment malfunction is to identify the problem quickly. This isn't always easy and it can involve going through a series of steps to isolate the problem. For example, if you're a guitarist and there's no sound coming out of your amp, you'll need to go through the logical progression of your signal chain to find the problem. You can start with your guitar to determine whether the cable is plugged in. If so, then make sure it's plugged into any effects you use. If it is, then move to your amp and check to see that it's powered up and the cable is plugged in properly. If all of this is in order, begin switching out cables to find the one that isn't working.

Certain issues can be handled quickly, such as replacing dead batteries in effects pedals, replacing shorted-out cables, and changing fuses. Addressing these issues can be done in less than a minute if you're prepared and have the proper backup equipment.

"I have a spare of everything all the time," says keyboardist Paul McDonald. "I have a bag full of extra cables, power cords, surge protectors, and more. If you get to the gig and the power cord for your keyboard fails—and you don't have a spare—you don't have a gig. It could be a one-dollar cord from Radio Shack; if you don't have it, you blow the gig."

Some repairs take longer and require backup amps and instruments for the band to continue the show without pause. Changing strings, for instance, can take a minute or more if you don't have a backup instrument. You may be able to get through a song with a broken string, but you probably won't want to move on to the next one until the problem is corrected. If you have to change a string, the time it takes to do so can equal one song. More important, during the time you're changing the string, your audience may lose interest. When the guitarist busted a string in the middle of a song at a gig I played, he didn't have a backup instrument. After finishing the song, we paused the show for two minutes so he could change the string. He did, and we continued … to half the crowd. Not thirty seconds later, he broke another string. The club was nearly empty by the time he replaced that one.

Some gear malfunctions are too big to go unnoticed. Your audience will instantly know there's a problem when an amp or public address (PA) system crashes and you lose sound. If you use an amp, you can get back up and running by sending the signal through a direct box that's connected to the PA system, though you'll probably lose some of the character and tonal elements of your sound. It may not be a perfect solution, but it can get you through the gig.

When the PA crashes, either the sound person or a band member is going to have to trouble-shoot to identify the problem. If the system has blown up, you'll have to just use your amps and possibly send vocals through an extra channel in one of the amps for the duration of the gig.

If there's a chance you can get the PA working again, you'll still have to fill time while repairing it. You can by playing solely through your amps or performing acoustically until the problem is solved. Drums don't use amps, of course (unless they're electronic), and neither do acoustic guitars, voices, or percussion equipment. I played a gig where the PA crashed, and while a band member was fixing it, the band did a percussion jam with our drummer that kept the audience dancing until the PA was restored.

When you do have an equipment malfunction, calmly address the issue. Don't create a panicky scene onstage that detracts from your performance. Once you've fixed the problem, jump back into the song.

Once the band is ready to deal with minor mistakes, train wrecks, and equipment malfunctions, practice the songs in your set list without pause. While doing this, you may choose to videotape your rehearsal. Bands do this to ensure they look like a cohesive unit and to check that everyone has an entertaining stage presence.

You don't need to throw your guitar in the air or hold your microphone upside down to have good stage presence. You simply need to convince the audience that you belong onstage. This can be done in a number of ways. Some musicians just smile and stand up straight onstage. Others jump up and down. It's up to you to find your own stage presence and sell it to an audience.

Videotaping your rehearsals, or even your live performances, can be very educational when it comes to evaluating your stage presence. Small quirks like shuffling your feet or not making eye contact become glaring when you watch them on video. I'll never forget my first experience watching myself on video. My signature move of keeping my eyes closed and feeling the music came across like I was nervous and detached. I quickly learned to keep my head up and involve myself with my bandmates and the audience.

When you're satisfied with your performance and the set, write it down on paper (either by hand or using a computer printer). If by computer, use a large-size font. Most musicians keep their set list at their feet or on top of their gear, so it needs to be readable from ten feet away. Then distribute it to band members so they can practice on their own.

PREPARING FOR THE GIG ON THE DAY OF THE SHOW

On the day of the gig, musicians should warm up in order to be in top form physically to be ready to play. Then they need to pack their gear and head to the show.

Warming Up

There are few situations one wants to enter cold. A gig certainly isn't one, so musicians need to warm up in advance on the day of the show. Some bands choose to warm up by running through the set one last time. There have been bands I've worked with that felt our second run-through of the day was always better than the first, so we'd make sure to meet at our rehearsal space and play through all of the songs on our set list prior to the gig. Other bands decide against doing this. The reason? They risk overplaying the songs and having a flat performance.

Many musicians choose to warm up on their own, running through the exercises they've learned to limber up their hands or voice. "I believe in warming up on my instrument," says vocalist and guitarist Buzz Meade. "I'll play guitar and sing for at least one hour before I leave for setup." Once musicians loosen up with some technical exercises, then they will need to practice the set list. To refresh their memories, they'll go over any details of which they're unsure—for instance, the four-bar rest after a solo section or the key change in an outro (conclusion) of a song.

It's wise to warm up before leaving for the gig because you might not have an opportunity to do so later. Once you're at the venue, you may be too concerned with details like loading in and setting up gear, or mingling with your friends, to have the twenty minutes or so that you need. You also might not be able to find a private space like a dressing room or backstage area to warm up.

Playing a gig cold is risky. Your hands may cramp early in the performance, or you might lose your voice midway through the first song. When I was with a hard rock band playing songs that featured many sixteenth-note patterns on bass, I once played cold. Not a minute into the first song, my plucking hand cramped intensely. I was barely able to fudge my way through the up-tempo songs.

Packing Your Gear

Once warmed up, you're ready to pack your gear. To prevent forgetting essential equipment at home, develop a *pack list* that contains every item you need to bring to a performance. Then simply check off each item on the list as it's packed into the car or van. Creating and using a gear list can be tedious, especially if you have a lot of equipment, but the reward is significant. It takes some of the stress out of preparing to perform.

The length of a pack list varies depending on the instrument. Vocalists, for example, might just have a microphone, a mic stand, and a bag with extra cables and batteries on their lists. Drummers use a number of items, including each tom in their drum kit, tuning keys, extra heads, stands, sticks, and more.

Here's a copy of my pack list:

- Ken Smith 5-String Bass
- Fender Jazz Bass

- Levy Double-Bass Gig Bag
- Guitar Strap × 2
- Peterson Tuner Pedal
- Keeley Compressor
- Boss Chorus Pedal
- MXR Direct Box
- 20" Instrument Cable × 3
- 6" Instrument Cable × 6
- 9-Volt Batteries × 10
- Galien Krueger 1001 RB Bass Amp
- SWR 2 × 10" Speaker × 2
- Amp Power Cable × 2
- Speaker Cable × 3
- Surge Protector × 2
- Extension Cord × 2
- Music Stand × 2
- Music Stand Light
- Music Stand Light Bulbs × 2
- Guitar Stand × 2
- Music Charts and Notes × 2
- Cart to Transport Gear

Although my list seems sizable, most of the items are small enough to fit into a medium-size sports bag (cables, pedals, etc.). I bring my bag with these smaller items, my basses, and my amp and speakers inside the venue with me. Some of the duplicate items (the music stands and charts) stay in my car. It's unlikely I'll need the duplicates, but they're within sprinting distance if I do.

Here's another example of a gear list that comes from drummer Matt McGlynn, who chooses to bring his own mics to gigs in order to better achieve his sound:

- 1 carpet
- 1 kick drum, in a road case

- 2 heavy duffle bags of pedals, hardware, sticks, charts, water bottles, etc.
- 1 drum cage with 4 toms and 11 cymbals mounted
- 2 snare drums
- 1 hi-hat stand with cymbals
- 1 throne
- 1 crate of mics and cables
- 1 drum machine
- 1 headphone amp
- 1 pair headphones
- 1 bar stool
- 2 mic stands
- 1 music stand

Getting to the Show

Once your gear is loaded into either your own vehicle or that of a friend, a family member, or a bandmate, it's time to head to the show. Before you go, make sure you have the directions, as well as the venue contact information. You'll need it in the event that something like car trouble or getting lost prevents you from making it to the gig on time, or just makes you run late.

Leave well in advance of your load-in time, especially if you're traveling a distance greater than twenty miles, or if you're unfamiliar with the location of the venue. You never know what to expect on the road, so give yourself enough time to offset hitting traffic or getting lost. Plus, if you're running late, you'll become stressed. That's not the state of mind you need prior to a gig. Drummer Matt McGlynn suggests, "Arrive an hour earlier than you can possibly imagine needing to arrive. You won't be able to focus on your performance if you didn't have time to set up, warm up, and sound check."

I once arrived at a Mardi Gras gig in New Orleans with ten minutes to spare. Because I was so late I had to haul my equipment through the crowd to get to the stage. By the time I reached the stage, I was so frazzled I plugged a speaker cable into the "Effects Send" output of my amp instead of the speaker output. It produced a deafening hum that took what felt like an eternity for me to correct, much to my dismay, as well as that of my bandmates and the perturbed club owner.

On the ride to the gig, listen to your songs to keep them top-of-mind. I keep my gig material on playlists loaded into my portable MP3 player, which I can connect to my car stereo. To practice without my instrument (I am driving after all), I sing along with my parts. By doing this I feel more self-assured and confident I can execute them. Los Angeles–based vocalist Sara Oliver also does her final preparations in the car on the way to a show. Oliver says, "I listen to the songs in the car on the way to the show. Listening and singing to the material at this point keeps it fresh in my mind before the gig."

When you arrive at the gig, you'll need to find parking. With luck, you'll have designated space reserved for you to park or unload, but if not you may find yourself parking far from the venue and carrying your gear some distance. Some venues have loading zones where you can park for a few minutes before you may get a ticket or be asked to move. If you park in a loading zone, leave a note on your dashboard that says, "Band Vehicle." This might not prevent you from getting a ticket, but it should buy you the time you need to drop your gear and rush back to move your vehicle to a parking space.

Once you've parked, you're ready to unload, set up, and play.

CHAPTER 11

PLAYING THE GIG

Gigs are the ultimate measure of a band. Bands either thrive or flounder based on their performances. Most audiences, bookers, and event clients don't know—or don't care—how hard it is to get to the point of being able to gig, and bands rarely, if ever, get any credit for having a cool graphic on their promotional flyer or creating a perfectly timed set list. It's all taken for granted. Bands are judged on their shows, period. If audiences, bookers, and even clients enjoy a gig, they might catch another performance or book the band again. If they don't like the band or have mixed emotions, they'll most likely move on to another group the next time they want to hear, or book, live music.

Because the stakes are high, gigs can be pressure filled. It's easy for musicians to get caught up in the intensity and forget the final steps in taking their band to the stage. To avoid losing focus, they need to take care of all final preparations at a club or special event. Then they're ready to play.

PREPARING TO PLAY

Once bands arrive at the venue, they're ready to complete their final preparations. The first step is to load in and set up the equipment. Then they need to conduct a sound check. Finally, they take care of any remaining details prior to relaxing before the show.

Loading In and Setting Up

Once the band is inside the venue, check in with an employee of the club or the event planner (or one of their staff) for the special event. They need to know your band has arrived so they can go about their business without having to worry that you'll be a no-show. They should also be able to tell you where to set up, stow your gear, and park.

If you can't find a contact, continue the load-in. If there still isn't a contact by the time you've finished, you've got a dilemma. On one hand, if you wait for someone to direct you, you risk wasting time that could be spent getting ready for the gig. On the other, if you set up without guidance, there's the possibility you'll set up in the wrong spot, or before your turn, and that you'll end up having to move all your gear from the stage. When faced with this situation, go ahead and place your gear onstage; just don't get too comfortable. This way, once you do make contact with the venue's representative, you'll be in position to expedite your setup since your gear will already be in place, and if you have to move, you'll be able to do so quickly with little trouble.

Setup can be chaotic. Band members will have their equipment strewn all over the stage. If the stage is small, you'll be in someone's way. Try to set up quickly; then run an equipment test to make sure everything is working and in the right position. Once you're confident your gear is functioning properly, leave the stage until you're scheduled to sound check. If you want to do some further warm-up and you play an instrument that's portable (unlike a drum kit), take it offstage. Don't stand around noodling while your bandmates are trying to set up. It only adds to the existing chaos.

Sound Checking

Once the band is set up, it's time to sound check, which is a test that bands conduct to ensure they're playing at the right volume, with the instruments properly mixed together, and without tonal irregularities—low frequencies that may be too loud or feedback from a vocal microphone.

Sound usually is run through a public address (PA) system that features powerful speakers that amplify every instrument in the band, although some bands use a PA only to power vocals and other instruments that don't have their own amps, like drums and percussion. A band's sound is checked by mixing the volumes and equalizations of all the instruments using a mixing board that's connected to the PA If the PA system includes *monitors* (speakers aimed at the musicians so they can hear themselves), the sound check is a good time to set the volumes and equalization settings for these as well.

A *sound person* conducts the sound check. If the venue owns the PA, the sound person probably works for the venue (venues will not allow bands to run their system for fear it will get damaged). If the band brings its own PA, a member of the group will have to be the designated sound person, preferably someone (like a vocalist) who can take his or her instrument or microphone into the audience area to listen to how the band sounds. If the band isn't using the PA to amplify certain instruments, then the sound person listens to the sound and instructs band members to adjust volume and tone as needed.

To get an instrument's signal to the PA system, a sound person will use either a microphone or a direct box. As with recording, certain instruments can only use either a mic or direct box. (For example, a drum kit—unless it's electronic—can only be mic'd.) Other instruments can use either means. It's up to you to know which method works best for your instrument. When I gig using an Ampeg SVT, I prefer to be mic'd, as opposed to my Gallien-Krueger rig, which sounds best going direct. If you don't have a preference, ask the sound person what works best in the venue.

Your sound person may have a strong opinion as to whether your instrument should be mic'd or taken direct. When given, it's best to accept his or her advice. There's a downside to annoying the sound person, as they can become disinterested in your sound or, worse, vindictive, and your show can suffer as a result. "Having a competent and attentive soundman is key, because a good performance can't rescue a lousy mix," says drummer Matt McGlynn.

In addition, a sound person is often a representative of the venue, and aggravating him or her can affect your chances of being booked again. If he or she doesn't like your band, you can bet the booker will hear about it. Conversely, if the sound person likes you and your band, he or she may be in the position to give you a positive recommendation. Needless to add, it pays to be friendly, polite, and accommodating.

When the sound check begins, the sound person asks each musician to play his or her instrument separately from the band. This is done to check volume and tone without other instruments impacting the sound. When it's your turn, play what's stylistically and technically representative of how you'll play during the show. This will enable the sound person to adjust your sound accurately. If you're a keyboardist using primarily organ sounds, for instance, don't sound check with a piano sound, because when it's time to play, the unexpected organ sound will throw your sound off.

If you use multiple effects and playing styles that affect your sound, be sure to tell the sound person so you can test each one. For example, if you're a guitar player using clean and distorted sounds, play each one. This will assist the sound person in either finding a workable middle ground for your sounds or agreeing to manage the levels during your performance and make adjustments as needed. If you don't mention this in advance, your suddenly altered signal may distort your sound because it's too loud for the PA, or it could become so quiet it disappears in the mix. If your instrument isn't running through the PA, you'll need to manage your own volume during all changes in your sound.

Bandleader and guitarist Paul Mitchell says, "When we're doing the sound check, I like to give the sound guy a typical A chord using the tone and amp setup that I'll use through the majority of the show. If I'm going to be using different tones—a clean tone or a lead tone—I tell the sound guy during the check, so he can adjust levels accordingly. Lastly, if the sound guy is cool, I'll ask about him adjusting the levels between my different sounds through the house system, so I don't have to do it onstage. If it's going to be a problem, I just do it myself."

When setting individual instrument levels and tones, the sound person is primarily making sure the volume doesn't peak and distort. He or she is also checking that the tone works in the room. Every venue sounds different, and an instrument's tone must be tailored to fit it. Rooms with low ceilings and a lot of windows, for example, sound more trebly than rooms with high ceilings and no glass, which have more bass. So if you're in a venue that amplifies low frequencies, your sound person will equalize some of them from your signal, since they'll naturally be replaced with the sounds from the room.

You may not agree with everything the sound person is doing, but try to trust his or her expertise. Musicians need to understand that they and the sound person may be hearing different things, because the sound onstage can be dramatically different from the sound out front. Instruments' sounds project from their amps, so what you're hearing five feet from the speaker might actually be quieter than the sound thirty feet into the audience. Instruments also project sounds in different directions, which can impact your perception of stage volume. Bass, for instance, is omnidirectional: The sound disperses from the amp and fills the room. Instruments with higher frequencies, like guitar or horn, are directional; the volume dissipates when you move to one side of the amp.

Once every instrument's signal has been checked individually, it's time for the band to play together. This allows the sound person to ensure the music sounds even and that no one instrument is overpowering the others. A full-band sound check also serves as a time for band members to listen to their monitors to make sure they're satisfied with the mix. To complete this stage of the sound check, the sound person will ask the band to perform a song as a test. Choose one that's representative of your set. If you're in a rock band playing a ten-song set of which nine songs are high-energy tunes and one is a ballad, don't play the ballad.

If the first song on your set list is representative of your set, play it during sound check. Doing so serves as a sort of test-run for the gig. If the sound check performance goes well, you and your bandmates will be able to carry this momentum into the gig by repeating the same song when you start performing. Nothing heightens a musician's excitement and anticipation for a gig like a great sound check.

After running through the test song, talk with the sound person about any changes you'd like in your monitor mix. A monitor should be able to amplify any signal that's running through the PA system, depending on what each musician wants to hear. Personally, I like to hear whatever instruments are not amplified onstage in my monitors, like vocals and sometimes keyboards (guitars and drums are usually loud enough already for me to hear them clearly). Vocalists always need to hear themselves in their monitor, so they can stay on pitch and accurately harmonize with any other vocalists.

Once you're satisfied with your monitor mix, ask the sound person what he or she thinks of the sound. Some won't offer suggestions either because they're too reserved or because they feel it will compromise the band's sound. Giving them a chance to voice their opinions may provide some good advice from an objective source.

There's another good reason to communicate with the sound person. If the sound person likes you, he or she may be receptive to managing your sound throughout the gig—rather than just setting the levels once and then heading to the bar for beers. If the sound person agrees to help you out, provide a separate set list with cues to follow. Remember that the sound person is likely to be unfamiliar with your music, so make the cues obvious and simple. For example, a cue might be, "Put extra reverb on the vocals in the third song."

If you make cues too complicated, such as, "On the first chorus have the guitar signal running in mono, then switch it to stereo and crank the volume for the second verse," it's likely the sound person won't know the verses from the choruses in your songs and won't be able to follow your direction. If the venue features a lighting system that's run by the sound person, lighting cues can be included on the set list too.

Here's an example of a set list for the sound person for a gig by fictitious original rock band Push Cart.

Push Cart Set List

1. Pill Popper (Song starts softly with clean guitar and then goes distorted for the big chorus. Please keep lights off until the crescendo and then turn them on.)
2. Purple Sun
3. Why? (This song is a ballad. Please put extra reverb on the vocals.)
4. It Ain't True (Please remember to take the extra reverb off here.)
5. Silver Devil
6. Iron Wrought
7. Red Eye (This song features a drum solo. Please turn on the strobe light.)
8. Jackson Plush
9. Tiny People, Tiny Town
10. Flick My Switch (Please cut the lights as soon as the song is over.)

When the sound check is complete, thank the sound person and promptly leave the stage.

Taking Care of Everything Else

Once the sound check is complete, any remaining details that need to be addressed should be. These details usually break down into two categories: venue items and band items.

Venue items may include submitting guest list names to the door person so that these people can either be admitted free of charge or at a reduced cost, picking up drink tickets (which enable the bearer to receive a free drink at the bar), and introducing yourself to bookers and coordinators you've previously interacted with by phone or e-mail.

Band items might include mingling with friends and fans and identifying a trusted friend to help you manage the gig. This friend has a key role. He or she will be the person in charge of circulating your mailing list in the crowd. If you have demos, stickers, or T-shirts to sell or give away, your friend will handle this too. His or her most important job, however, is to be your "ears" in the audience.

As mentioned earlier in the chapter, your band can sound different from the audience than from the stage. It's the sound person's job to ensure that you sound as good as possible, but some take this job less seriously than others. Having someone you trust in the audience to inform you about deficiencies in the sound can overcome this inattentiveness. I've done many shows where the sound person also worked the bar and wasn't able to pay attention to the band during the set—whether it was to raise the volume on a vocal or to turn down a kick drum microphone. I've also seen sound people leave the venue altogether to go outside to smoke or read once the performance began.

The simplest way to communicate with the person in the audience is to ask him or her to point to a particular instrument and motion that its volume be raised or lowered. If the bass is too loud, the friend can point to the bass player and give a thumb's down signal. The bass player can bring the volume down until your friend gives the "A-OK" hand sign.

Your friend can also try to inform the sound person about any concerns, but this may be a risky proposition. Sound people are not without ego and may balk at being told how to do their jobs. Unless the sound is a disaster and the audience is picking up on it, your friend should probably avoid interacting with the sound person.

Once the band has set up, sound checked, and addressed any other last-minute items, try to relax before your performance. Gigs can take a large amount of mental and physical energy to pull off. Relaxing before the start can help you prepare for this. "I have a better gig when my head is focused on the music, and I'm relaxed," says DU★DS drummer Will Strickland. "If I'm focused and ready from the start, I'll end up playing better, listening better, interacting with the music better, and being happy because of it."

Every musician has his or her own idea of mellowing out before a gig. One may choose to socialize with friends at the venue, while another may leave to get a bite to eat or just find a quiet place to be alone. Some venues will have what's called a *green room*, which is a room located close to the stage that's reserved for band members to hang out away from the crowd.

Vocalist Sara Oliver says, "I like to take it easy before the show and drink tea. I'll also listen to some of the songs I'll be singing and maybe sing along a bit." Vocalist Erica Canales also keeps her voice fresh by staying hydrated and says, "I use a throat-coating medicine like Halls cough drops and I stay away from smokers." Drummer Eric Hoemann says he likes to make himself available to the other band members if they want to discuss something about the gig. "I also talk with the other band members to see how they are doing and what has been going on with them personally," adds Hoemann. "I don't always get a chance to hang out with my friends in the band, and this is a good time to chat about something other than music."

Even though you're relaxing, it pays to keep an eye on the clock. You don't want to lose sight of your start time. You don't want to be so surprised when the booker or coordinator tells you to get onstage right away that, in the excitement, you forget the tempo of your first song or how many bars there are in the first solo section.

PLAYING THE GIG

When it's time to play the gig, you and your band will take to the stage and perform. After your performance, you'll follow up with the booker or event planner and load out.

Getting Ready to Play

At least ten minutes before show time, plan to meet with the person at the venue who dictates when you play (at clubs this is usually the sound person; at special events it's the event planner or client). You want to make sure you're still on schedule to perform at the agreed-upon time. If the band preceding you is running long, or the wedding party has decided to add another fifteen minutes of toasts, you won't be starting as planned. If there's been a delay, it's best to find out when you're due onstage and go back to relaxing. If all is on track, then you need to prepare to take the stage.

During this ten-minute period, be sure to use the restroom. Even if you don't have to go, go! The last thing you need onstage is to have to go with thirty minutes left in your set. Once that's done, get together with your bandmates and reaffirm that everyone has the set list and is ready to go.

When it's finally time, get onstage and turn on your equipment. Make sure your amp is working, your microphone is on, and your drums haven't shifted in any way. This shouldn't take more than thirty seconds. The sound person will then give you a nod, or possibly introduce your band to the audience. Then make eye contact with your bandmates to be certain that everyone is ready, count off the tempo of your first song, and play!

Performing

The most important thing you can do to have a great show is to have fun. An audience will feed on your energy and return it with their screams, applause, and dancing. You might struggle with technical difficulties or mistakes during the songs, but if the crowd is having a great time swaying to the music or singing along, the gig will be remembered as a success by both you and your audience. "Playing great in a vacuum sucks," says singer/songwriter Steve Sparks. "Playing lousy to a good crowd is better."

Playing for receptive crowds—no matter the size—is exhilarating. "Understand that the audience is part of the show," says guitarist Peter Smith. "Involve them as much as possible, and make them feel like they are contributing to the good time."

Bandleader Ted Heath agrees. "Get into it," Heath says. "Give it everything you have. Music works when you feel it, and the audience grooves on that sensation. When the band comes together as a group, and everyone feels the energy, you've got a great performance."

During the gig, communicate with your bandmates. This is essential if you're planning to improvise and, for instance, extend a jam. You also need to be able to communicate with other members of the band to pass on information about the set, such as adding or skipping a song or just reminding someone in the group about a key change or four-bar rest after a chorus.

This communication doesn't have to be verbal. In fact, it's tough to speak onstage. It's usually too loud to talk over the music. Many musicians become accomplished lip-readers over time, while others perfect hand signals. "A lot of communication goes on without saying a word," says Ted Heath. "You can usually convey what you want to do through visual communication. It's tricky with a big band—the one I'm in now has ten people onstage. I ask the band to keep an eye on me for hand signals or body movements to determine our course."

Common hand signals include tapping a hand on one's head to indicate going to the top of the song, waving a finger in a circular motion to indicate vamping or keeping the song going, and pretending to break a stick between two hands to signify that the band needs to take a break.

While performing, keep an eye on your bandmates. Someone may get lost in a song or miss a hand signal. If you suspect a band member is confused, or about to become confused, get their attention and help them out.

And don't forget to promote your band! It's easy to become so focused on the music that you forget to address the crowd, but if you do forget, you'll miss out on promoting yourselves. A simple shout-out to the crowd—inviting them to join your mailing list, to pick up a business card, or to check out your Web site—is the least you should do. You may also briefly introduce your favorite songs, introduce the members of the band, and thank the venue, client, and any other bands on the bill.

Singer/songwriter Buzz Meade says of pushing his band and Web site, "The best promotion I've found is a good, real live performance. And by good, I mean you played well, sounded good, and people enjoyed the music. You'd be surprised how many people go to the Web sites of bands they just heard and go on to support them."

Managing a gig is tough, but good bands find ways to do it without affecting the performance. Ted Heath says, "I have to sing, run the band, and run the sound onstage. I have to interchange those hats during the show and at the same time not let on to the audience that that's what I'm doing—they don't care about that. They just want a great performance. There are a lot of things going through my mind during the performance as I adjust monitor mixes and feedback, pay attention to clients and coordinators, and keep the party rolling. It's a challenge, but it can be done.

"During the gig, I try to keep in contact with the client or their rep and see if we are where we need to be in terms of the timeline and music. I want to make sure the client is happy with us. A lot of that goes without saying. I've been lucky to be in great bands. Any concerns clients may have had before the gig disappear once we start playing, and they realize we have it under control, which is obvious from the professionalism of the band and the quality of the music. They stop caring as much once they sense they are in good hands with the band," Heath adds.

Leaving the Gig

When you've finished your last song, thank the audience, and turn off your equipment. The gig may be over, but you'll still have work to do packing up your equipment and loading out. Only then will you be able to mingle with friends and fans and to check out with the venue.

If there aren't any bands playing after you, or any other reason why the stage must be immediately cleared, you can take your time packing up your gear. You can even skip this step in favor of hanging out with the audience. If there are bands waiting, though, you need to get your gear off the stage right away, because the next band is most likely just as eager to set up and perform as you were. If you take your time and schmooze, you may find that someone else has moved your equipment for you, and probably not gently!

When packing up, move large items like speakers and bass drums offstage before you put away small items like a music stand or an effects pedal. There's no need for you to do time-consuming tasks like putting away cables or collecting drum felts when you're taking up valuable real estate onstage. Just grab your amp or drum rack, and move it aside. Clearing large equipment frees up the stage for the next band to bring up its own large equipment without having an unnecessarily long wait.

Load-out is even more chaotic than load-in, so keep a close eye on your gear. If you allow yourself to become distracted, especially by fans that want to congratulate you on your performance, you might forget to pack some equipment. You probably won't leave large amps and guitars behind, but small items like guitar stands and cables are easy to forget. I've had to replace numerous guitar stands in my career because I'd become too involved in the distractions after the show to remember to properly pack them away.

The best thing you can do to prevent this is to use the same list you used to help you pack up your gear in your car. If you don't use it because you're in too big a hurry (or because you don't want to be seen as a Type-A bean-counting accountant), you need to at least be methodical in your packing. If you can develop a routine and execute it without distraction, it can serve you like a pack list.

"I have a simple system with my equipment," says Sara Oliver. "I know my music stand and music book go together with my mic stand. The microphone goes in its case. My in-ear monitor and other accessories go in my gig bag. I just keep track of these three pieces and double-check them before I leave the venue. This mental checklist works for me."

Once you've packed up, either set your equipment aside in a safe place, or pack it in your vehicle. Then you're ready to sign off with the venue. Your first stop should be with the sound person. Being a sound person can be a thankless job. When a band sounds great, everyone credits the band. When it doesn't, everyone blames the sound person. "After the show, if the sound guy has done a good job, do something nice for him," says guitarist David Wood. "Tell him what a good job he did, and either give him a few bucks or buy him a drink."

After you've thanked the sound person, find the booker or event coordinator. You need to speak with these people and make one last positive impression before you go. If you can't find them, find another venue or event employee like a manager, a bartender, a door person, or an event assistant with whom to talk. If you leave the gig without signing off, you miss out on an opportunity to punctuate your great performance with your desire to repeat it, possibly on a weekend night or for more money.

When you speak with these people, make it clear that you enjoyed playing the gig and that you (hopefully) met their expectations. By articulating these points you're letting everyone know you want to perform for them again. And, if you drew the right amount of people or kept the crowd rocking until closing, you want to subtly emphasize that you have held up your end of the agreement with the venue or event client.

This final parting communication will set the tone for your next phone call or e-mail, which might go something like, "Hi, this is Jack. I'm calling to see if we can book another show at your club. We played there last week and really had fun. We had a great crowd, and I know they'd love to come back to see us there on a weekend night."

Finally, if you haven't done so already, mingle with the audience. This is your opportunity to thank your fans for coming to see you perform and to interact with potential fans. A friendly "Good to see you and thanks for coming to the show" goes a long way to keeping fans connected to the group and willing to continue supporting the band. When you speak with existing fans, you have a chance to meet any friends they brought with them to see your show and to turn them into fans as well.

After you've spoken to your existing fans, mingle awhile longer, and look for people who are trying to make eye contact with you. These people probably want to say something to you but are just too shy. When you notice them, walk up to them, and say hello. If they respond in kind without any further comment, keep walking. If they say something like, "Nice show," stop, thank them for coming out, and speak with them. You might ask if they added their names to your mailing list, if they see many bands, or if they are musicians themselves. Making a connection with the more shy members of the audience will make them more comfortable and more likely to attend another of your shows.

Congratulations on playing the gig! Now you're ready to book more shows and build on your band's momentum.

CHAPTER 12

BUILDING AND MAINTAINING MOMENTUM

Bands that thrive in their local music scene share one trait: They understand the importance of building and maintaining momentum—an energy that increases when they persist in meeting their goals. It's apparent when bands have this momentum. They're relentlessly booking more shows, continually creating new material or playing new songs, and constantly adding to and updating their Web sites. Good things just seem to flow from and to them.

Bands without momentum look at these groups and wonder why they're catching all the breaks. The truth is, breaks have nothing to do with it. Bands gather momentum by building a fan base and by creating a buzz about themselves and their music. The goal is to become a visible—and hot—commodity to clubs and special-event bookers and music fans alike.

BUILDING A FAN BASE

To build a fan base, you've got be aware of the different types of fans out there and understand which can be counted on to attend shows and, perhaps, even help out with nonmusical tasks. Then you have to build relationships with them so that they feel invested in your success and will continue to support you and your music.

Understanding Your Fans

There are three types of fans: casual, core, and those with benefits. *Casual fans* are those who will occasionally come out to see you and your band perform. They're either too busy to go to clubs on a regular basis or they don't particularly like to hear live music. You can't rely on them to be at every gig, but if you have an important show, and contact them personally, chances are they'll be there.

Core fans are those who will come to the majority of your shows. Some of them simply love your music; others are family and close friends who may not even care what kind of music you play or even be concerned with whether you sound good. They'll show up because of their relationship with you or a bandmate. Core fans are often easy to spot at gigs. They're the older couple cheering on the singer or guitarist (who is a son or daughter in the band) at a death metal show, or the girl (a band member's girlfriend) who can't help but dance, even if she's the only one on the floor.

Core fans are essential. They're the ones you can count on to be in the audience, and because of this you can confidently book clubs that require a minimum number of people to show. Core fans are especially important when you're just starting to play gigs. At this stage of your musical career, they're most likely the only people who've heard of you. Core fans carry bands through their infancy, keeping them afloat until they're able to add new fans to their fan base.

Sometimes, core fans are the reason a fan base grows. When these fans bring their friends to a gig, their friends may become fans in their own right and later come to shows with some of their own friends, and so on and so on. A former band of mine had one particularly popular core fan who continually brought ten or more people to our shows. Eventually, the band got to know these people and they became core fans as well.

Core fans may need special attention from band members to keep them coming to shows. Phone calls, e-mails, and even scheduled face time are necessary for them to understand that their time and energy are not being taken for granted. You might even consider thanking, or motivating, them by putting them on your guest list, giving them free drink tickets, or reserving a table for them in the club.

Fans with Benefits (FWBs) are core fans who have become useful helpers. They're the trusted friends who can be asked to pass around your mailing list at a show, count people coming through the door, or pass out free demos. FWBs aren't usually paid, except possibly in free CDs and drink tickets from the band.

FWBs may even take on more serious nonmusical tasks for bands. Some can help out with booking, promotions, even scheduling auditions for new members. Many bands don't have time, or just feel uncomfortable, doing nonmusical tasks, especially those that call for self-promotion. It's much easier for someone outside the band to say, "Three Bone has the best live show I've ever seen," than for a member of the band to say, "We have the best live show you've ever seen."

If you have an enthusiastic FWB that you trust, try giving him or her a nonmusical task and see how well he or she performs it. If the FWB is both competent and eager, add to the workload, and see how he or she responds. You might end up with an invaluable helper.

Take it slowly, though, because you need to be careful who you allow to act on your behalf, especially if that person self-adopts the "manager" title. The title of manager implies that the individual has the power to make decisions in all areas. If this "manager" doesn't truly represent your interests, you can end up with obligations you don't want or can't uphold. I once had an FWB manager who booked my rock band to play dinner music in a fancy restaurant every Friday for a month. She assumed we'd be willing to play a completely different genre of music for a steady paycheck. We weren't, and we had to call the restaurant back to cancel.

Most of the experiences I've had with FWBs wishing to become managers have been negative. Being a manager is hard work, and when an FWB agrees to a task like booking shows, he or she may well think it's as easy as calling a booker and picking out the 10 PM time slot on a Saturday night. In reality, the FWB probably needs to call the booker a dozen times before even getting a callback, and then it's most likely to discuss playing a Monday night. When the reality of the role sets in, an FWB may fade away, leaving the band feeling betrayed and disappointed.

Earning the Support of Your Fans

Earning and maintaining the support of your fans is as important as understanding who your fans are. A band cannot afford to neglect its fans. Even core fans and FWBs can sour on a band if they feel like their support is being taken for granted.

To make and keep as many fans as possible, your band obviously needs to play well and be entertaining to watch. Just as essential, however, is developing personal relationships with your fans so that they feel appreciated and linked to your success. This begins at gigs and it doesn't take much time or effort. You just need to make yourself available after the show, make eye contact when you speak, request—and then remember—names, and ask questions. You might ask, "Are you a musician?" or "What bands are you listening to now?" These are questions that let fans know you're interested in them and aren't self-centered—at least outwardly!

These actions, though minor, can make a big impact. Remember, when you're onstage, the fans' attention is focused on you. Furthermore, you're probably the reason they, and other fans, are there in the first place. And, of course, when you're playing a big, elevated stage, you can seem even larger than life. Unless he or she is a gigging musician, the fan is most likely impressed by you, and perhaps slightly awed. When your performance ends and you exit the stage, you're a VIP and everyone will want to say hello, comment on the show, or just be near you. If you initiate conversation and are gracious in reply, you'll either flatter an existing fan or make a new one.

"It's important to be cool and keep people interested in you and the band," says bandleader Paul Mitchell. "It's your job to win these people over. Be nice to everyone so they feel invested in your band and want you to have bigger and better shows where they can come hang out and be a part of your success."

Your interaction with fans after the gig will also most likely be your last chance to make an impression before they go home. If you're gracious and humble, fans will leave the club thinking about what a good time they had at your gig and how they want to check out your next one. If you're rude or obnoxious, they may leave thinking about your inflated ego and how they need to skip your next show.

CREATING A BUZZ

Part of building momentum for your band is creating a *buzz*, or heightened level of interest. When bands have a buzz, fans want to go to their shows; bookers and event planners want to hire them, and other musicians want to join them. To create buzz, you've got to have a good reputation. You've also got to be friendly with other bands in your scene. And finally, you've got to work hard and stay positive.

Understanding the Importance of Your Reputation

Bands earn their reputations through their actions, particularly at gigs. Good reputations are earned by being punctual, acting friendly, drawing a large crowd, and, at certain kinds of gigs, packing the dance floor. If you do these things long enough, bookers, event planners, other bands, and music fans will take notice, and you'll be rewarded with more gigs, better gigs, and higher pay. Bad reputations are also earned—by regularly showing up late, failing to draw a crowd, and being rude, and if you persist in this behavior long enough, you'll neither be able to get gigs nor fans.

Remember: It takes time to develop a good reputation, but only one show to earn a bad one. Good news takes longer to travel, because bookers and event planners will wait for it to be repeated to ensure you aren't a "one-hit wonder." Bad news, like blowing off a sound check or train-wrecking the bride and groom's first dance, spreads quickly. Bookers and event planners won't want to risk booking a group that might repeat a blunder.

When you have a good reputation, your promotional efforts become more effective because people who've heard of your band won't need much convincing to come to the show. As drummer Jaime Douglas puts it, "Promotion, combined with a solid reputation, has a cumulative effect and all the flyers, posters, and press releases really start to mean something. When people haven't heard about your band, they usually won't pay attention. But when you have the rep to back it up, everything can come together."

Reputations can outlast the life of a band. If you were previously part of a band with a good reputation, you can draw on it when negotiating with bookers and event planners. You can simply name-drop your old band's name and capitalize on its reputation. You also can take advantage of contacts you developed in previous bands by informing them of your new band, and then trying to pick up where you left off in terms of bookings and fan support. For example, if your previous band was playing weekend nights at clubs, you can let a booker know that you've proven you can be trusted to draw a large crowd and keep them drinking and dancing. If your previous band had a bad reputation, you obviously want to steer clear of mentioning your prior affiliation.

Recognizing Why It's Important to Be Friendly with Other Bands

Music can be competitive, especially for bands fighting for the same gigs and venues. Nonetheless, developing and maintaining good relationships with other bands is a great way to further your band's career and to maintain your buzz.

There are two reasons for this. First, members of other bands can become part of your band's fan base. Every beginning club band has an intimate understanding of how difficult it is to draw the kind of crowds venues require. Because of this, many bands do favors for each other by attending each other's shows. And when another band does come to your gig, they may bring friends, who might then become regular fans of your band.

"Starting out, the majority of your fans will be members of other bands, provided they like your music," says Cage9's Evan Rodaniche. "It's hard to get another band's fans to become your fans unless you really play with them a lot. If you do, they may gravitate toward your band."

The second reason to befriend other bands is referrals, either for spots on their booking or for gigs they can't accept. Many club bookers need to fill out a booking with three or four bands. If they don't have enough, they'll ask bands they've already booked to recommend other groups. Also, special-event planners who can't lock down their favorite band may ask them to recommend a group, since most planners don't book bands for a living and won't know many, if any, other bands in their area.

If your group is friendly with a booked band that can't meet its commitment, you may get the call to play the gig. Bands making recommendations need to take this very seriously. The band, or bands, they refer will reflect on them. If the recommended band doesn't draw or doesn't show, the booker will blame the band that provided the referral. Bands select other bands with good reputations to ensure they aren't left taking the heat for another band's faults.

Another good reason to be friendly with other bands is that bands do break up. If yours does, you'll need to find a new band or new band members. The more bands you know, the larger your pool of candidates. You never know which band or musician you may be gigging with next, so be cool and you won't burn a bridge before you need to cross it.

Working Hard and Staying Positive

Gigging bands work hard. To outsiders, it may seem like an invisible hand is guiding the band to more shows, larger audiences, and better press, but in reality this good fortune is a product of a band's effort.

Without putting forth effort, bands are unable to distinguish themselves from their competitors. If you don't invest the hours in writing and recording songs, taking cool pictures for your Web site, handing out flyers at a popular club, and other activities discussed in this book, you'll never earn the opportunity to be noticed. Sitting idle and waiting for MTV to break down the door to your rehearsal space is futile. It just doesn't happen that way.

Once your band generates a buzz, you've got to work to keep it alive. This can be difficult, especially when your band enters a lull when you're away from gigging, because you are busy writing new songs or recording a new demo.

To keep the buzz alive, you need to fuel the perception that your band is continuing onward and upward, even if it's on hiatus, or having a rough time booking shows, or hashing out internal conflicts. To maintain your buzz, you have to keep up a constant communication highlighting the positive things going on with your band. This is easier to do when you're gigging and can send out e-mail blasts about the next series of gigs. But even when you're not gigging, you can still communicate with fans, bookers, and event planners, keeping them up-to-date on your progress in the studio or on the release of the newest recording, so that you remain in their thoughts.

Each member of your band has got to stay on message and present a united front to maintain buzz. If your singer is saying the band can't wait to release its latest single on your Web site, but the drummer is telling people the song sounds terrible, fans will know that there's turmoil in the group and be less anxious to attend shows. Discontent within the band needs to stay within the band. Once it's out, it can kill your buzz. Fans don't want to invest time in a group that's floundering. If you work to overcome any internal struggles that might arise, and keep them internal, you can keep the buzz going and maintain your momentum.

Stay focused and keep your message clear and positive. Then the fans will come along on the ride!

INDEX

A

Advertisements (ads), 230–231
  basic, 43
  bulletin-board, 48
  calendar listings in publications, 49
  circulating/finding, 48–54
  creating, 42–48
  determining how to respond to, 60–67
  flyers, 45–46, 48, 51
  getting a positive response from, 43–44
  information included in, 44
  networking compared to, 51–54
  poorly written, example of, 44–45
  posting on a Web site, 46–47
  print, 52
  question-and-answer (Q&A)
      session, 54–60
  responding to, 54–67
  size of, 45
  using multiple methods to advertise, 51
  Web sites as, 51
Aerosmith, 118
Amp modeler, 144
Amplifiers (amps), 143–144, 241, 244–245
Appearance, *See* Dress/appearance
Artistic passion, 9
Artwork:
  copyrighted art, 168
  creating/acquiring for demo
      package, 167–169
  Jay Lynch's Wacky Packages (Topps), 168
  uploading as a digital file, 169

Audience:
  attracting, 198
  banter, 237
  estimating number of, 185
  and length of set, 234
  mingling with, 264–265
  musicians in, 17
  at Open Mic events, 54
  and song arrangement, 235
Auditions, 54–60, 68–99
  accepting offer to audition, 67
  arriving early at, 87
  asking questions following, 92–94
  audition schedule, flexibility in, 77
  audition time, establishing, 71–72
  confirming musicians' attendance at, 80
  deciding whether to attend, 60–67
  defined, 68
  delivering cover songs to the
      musicians, 76
  dress/appearance, 86–87
  e-mail rejection, example of, 96
  equipment/gear, providing to
      musicians, 72–73
  exiting, 94–95
  fitting into the group, 87
  following up, 95–99
    with the band, 95–97
    with the musician, 97–99
  interviews, 79–80
    honesty in, 92
  introduction process, 89

learning your parts, 81–82

lifestyle differences, addressing, 93

listening to auditioning

    musicians, 88–89

load-in instructions and, 74

    protocols to, 75

location of, determining, 70

mistakes/errors during, 90

multiple, on same day, 72

parameters:

    components of, 69–70

    confirmation of, 78

    establishing, 69–78

parking conditions, 74

performing at, 87–95

preparing your band for, 69–87

preparing yourself for, 80–87

providing information about, 73–74

rehearsal space:

    explaining how to get to, 74–75

    physically preparing, 80

rejecting an offer, 64–65

rejecting auditioners, 65–67

rejection email, example of, 81

schedule, 71–72

second, 94

setting date/time of, 70, 72

songs to cover for, 76

time slot, changing, 77

transportation to, 23–24

unloading your equipment, 88

Aued, Gustavo, 173

B

Bacon's Media Guide, 230

Baffles, defined, 150

BAM (entertainment magazine), 49

Band:

    ability to draw a crowd, 198–199

    band contact, 34–35

    band fund, 131–132

    band items, taking care of, 257–258

    commitment to, 18–20

    finding, 41–67

    fitting image of, 86–87

    flat-rate agreement, 182–183

    overhead/profit, 188–193

    pay rate, 182–183

    pay-to-play agreement, 185–186

    payment arrangements, 182–186

        verbal agreements, 186

        written contracts, 186–188

    percentage-rate agreement, 183–185

    playing for free, 193–195

    rehearsals, 100–117

    song list, preparing, 117–123

    vacancies in, 56

    venues, 15–16

Band bio:

    short-form bio, 172–173

    writing, 172–175

Band photo, 164–167

    appearance/dress, 165, 167

    improvised shots, 167

    location of, 165

misleading, 164

photographer:

cost of, 166

understanding of the band, 166–167

posture/body language, 166

Bandleader-driven bands, 32–33

auditions, 79

and band duties, 35

interviews, 80

and song selection, 122

Bandmates:

chemistry among, 56–57

communicating with, during a

performance, 261

confused, 261

lifestyle differences, addressing, 93

respecting at rehearsals, 116–117

Bar, being paid a percentage of, 185

Basement, as rehearsal space, 103–104

Bay Guardian (San Francisco), 16

Beatles, The, 130

Beltz, Jesse, 173

Bleed, defined, 141

Blue Oyster Cult, 195

Bookers:

booker's intuition, 197

contacting, 196–199, 200–219

examples of musician-booker telephone

conversations, 201–219

leaving messages for, 200

Booking shows, 195–219

band overview, 197

band's ability to draw a crowd, 198–199

contact sheet, 196–197

Broadcast advertising, 230

Bulletin-board ads, 48, 104

Buzz:

creating, 270–273

keeping alive, 272–273

C

Cage9 (band), 173–175, 179, 229,
241, 271

Calendar listings, 49

Canales, Erica, 131, 158, 165, 259

Carey, Dannie, 59

Carvin (bass manufacturer), 22

Casual fans, 267

Cazares, Dino, 175

CD labels, 169

Charts, for auditions, 83–85

Cheeseballs (band), 37

Chic (band), 119

Chicago music scene, 14

Circulating ads, 48–54

Cirrus bass (Peavey), 22

Classified sections, newspapers/
publications, 48–49

Coast Music Conservatory
(Hermosa Beach, CA), 53

Contact sheet, 196–197, 201

Copyright, defined, 168

Core fans, 267–268

Cover bands, 36–38, 121–122, 123

animosity between original bands and, 38–40

auditioning for, 82

Cover songs:

rehearsing, 124

writing notes on, 83

craigslist.org, 49–51, 231

Cream, 130

D

Dan Band, The, 122

Demo package, 162–172, *See also* Demos

artwork, creating/acquiring, 167–169

band photo, 164–167

basic information included in, 163–164

benefits of, 162

compiling information for, 163–164

designing, 169–170

duplicating, 170–172

cost of, 171

service providers, 171–172

jewel case, 169–170

steps in creating, 162–163

Democratic bands, 32–34

interviews, 80

Demos:

defined, 126

practice sessions, recording, 133–134

preparing for cutting, 126–127

preproduction, 126, 135

recording the band in, 135

quality of, 126

recording, 126–161

challenge of, 126

recording options, 127–133

recording studio, 135–149

amplifiers, 143–144

analog vs. digital recordings, 142

baffles, 150

engineer, 138, 140–141, 144–145, 147, 150–151

equipment/gear, 141, 144–145

evaluating, 137

finalizing the deal with, 148

finding, 136–137

headphones mixes, 152

interviewing, 137–146

mastering, 139, 160–161

mixing, 139, 154–160

multi-tracking, 142–143

nonmusical tasks, 139

project rates, 137–139

punching in, 143

rate structure, 137–139

recording a test, 152–153

recording capabilities, 141–143

recording together vs. separately, 145–146

recreating your live sound in, 143

separation, 149

setting up at, 149–153

signal test, 151–152

studio time, 139–140

"sweet spot," finding, 149–150

touring potential studios, 146–148

tracking, 139, 145, 151, 153–154

tracking rooms, 141

Detroit music scene, 14

Disciplined musicians, 108–109

Discontent with the band, 273

Dishonest clubs, 184–185

Diskmakers (disk-duplicator service), 171

Disorganized bands, 50

Distants (band), 222

Do-it-yourself recordings, 127–128

Domain name, 180

Door, use of term, 184

Douglass, Jamie, 222, 270–271

Downtown Rehearsal
      (Los Angeles, CA), 102

Dream Theater (band), 122

Dress/appearance:

   at auditions, 86–87

   in band photo, 165, 167

Drum kit, 150

Dyna-Bass Unity Series (Peavey), 22–23

E

E-mail:

   advantages/disadvantages of, 200

   follow-up, 96–97

   rejection, example of, 96, 98–99

   responses, to ads, 60

   example of, 63

E-tabs.org, 82

Electric Lady Studios, 130

Engineers, 128–129

Ensemble classes, Coast Music
      Conservatory, 53

Equipment/gear, 20–22, 141, 144–145

   and auditions, 72–73

   malfunctions, 243–245

   packing, 247–249, 263

   securing, 106–107

   unloading, 88

Experience in the genre, mention of,
      in ads, 59

F

F Bass, 22

Fallinski, Jack, 199, 201–205

Fan base, building, 266–270

Fans:

   casual, 267

   core, 267–268

   Fans with Benefits (FWBs), 268–269

   support of, earning, 269

FedEx, 222

Fender Instruments, 21

Fills, during auditions, 91

Finding ads, 48–54

Fine Artists Entertainment, 31

Fines for infraction of rules, 115

Fixed expenses, 189

Flat-rate agreement, 182–183

   advantages/disadvantages of, 183

Flyers, 45–46, 48, 51, 221–222

   color, 222–223

   designing on a computer, 222

   e-mailing, 228

   mailing, 228

   printing, cost of, 222–223

Four-panel insert, 170

Free online classified sections, 49–50

Frehley, Ace, 82

Front Page (Microsoft), 181

Funding sources, identifying, 131

G

Gambit Weekly (New Orleans), 16

Garage, as rehearsal space, 103–104

garageband.com, 231

Genre tribute bands, 37

Gigs:

    band items, 257–258

    band's ability to draw a crowd, 198–199

    beginning on time, 259

    booking, 195–219

    contact sheet, 196–197

    delays, 259–260

    final preparations, 251–259

    final song, 235–236

    first song, 235

    gear, packing, 247–249

    getting ready to play, 259–260

    getting to the show, 249–250

    leaving, 262–265

    managing, 262

    onstage position and musical
        instrument, 241

    performing, 260–262

    playing, 251–265

    playing cold, 247

    preparing for, 232–250

    promoting, 220–231

    rehearsing the show, 241–246

    set list, creating, 233–240

    sound check, 252–257

    stage presence, 245

    venue items, 257

    warming up, 246–247

Google, 49

Group identity, 87

Guaranteed pay, 184

H

Hamilton, Tom, 118

Heath, Ted, 34, 38–40, 55, 89, 90,
    260–262

Heckaman, Gordon, 173

H.I.T. Wall Studios (San Francisco, CA),
    102–103, 129

Hives (alternative-pop band), 87

Hoemann, Eric, 31, 85, 259

Homepage, 181

Hot Dog (software), 181

Howard, Sterling, 50

Hybrid bands, 37

Hyde Street Studios
    (San Francisco, CA), 146

I

Improvised band shots, 167

Insert, jewel case, 169–170

Insightful questions, 56

Insurance, equipment, 106–107

Internet, 49–51

  search engines, 49

Interviews, 79–80

  bandleader-driven bands, 80

  honesty in, 91, 92

Iron Maidens (band), 37

J

Jay Lynch's Wacky Packages (Topps), 168

Jewel case, 169–170

  insert, defined, 169

  spine, 170

  tray card, 170

Jimi Hendrix Experience, The, 130

Just-for-fun gigs, 194

K

Kelis, 122

Ken Smith basses, 22

Kingsmen (band), 122

Kinko's, 222

Kiss (band), 82

L

LA Weekly (Los Angeles), 16

Large-size recording budget recording

  budget, 129

Las Vegas music scene, 15

Lifestyle differences, addressing, 93

Live communication, with advertisers, 60

Load-in instructions:

  and auditions, 74

  protocols to, 75

Load-out, 263

Local music scene:

  and networking, 16–18

  understanding, 13–18

Lockout studios, 101–104

  costs of renting, 103

  leasing requirements, 102

  securing your equipment, 106

  sharing, 104–105

Los Angeles music scene, 14

Lyrics, forgetting, 242

M

Mailing list, creating, 227–228

Management interest, mention of,

  in ads, 59

mapquest.com, 73

Mass marketing, distributing promotional

  materials by, 227–231

Mastering, 139, 160–161

McDonald, Paul, 50–51, 60, 83, 86, 198,

  200–201, 244

McGlynn, Matt, 26–27, 50, 248, 249, 253

Meade, Buzz, 120–121, 180, 246,

  261–262

Media contacts, 176

Metzner, David, 86

Microphones, 21–22

Midsize recording budget recording

  budget, 128–129

Misleading band photos, 164

Mistake creep, 124

Mistakes/errors:

at auditions, 90

covering, 243

discussing, 124–125

equipment/gear malfunctions, 243–245

fines for, 115

following the vocalist, 242–243

during onstage performances, 241–243

recovering from, 242

while tracking, 153–154

Mitchell, Paul, 30, 52, 73, 104, 132,
135, 269

Mixing, demos, 139, 154–160

MTD (bass manufacturer), 22

Multi-tracking, 142–143

Multiple auditions, on same day, 72

Music:

as a career, 9

dominant type in your area, 14–15

and life commitments, 19–20

priorities in, determining, 25–26

as social experience, 17

Music clubs, calendar listings, 16

Music group, succeeding in, 10

Music parts:

learning, 81–82, 85–86

writing without tablature/notations,
83–84

Music scene, organic nature of, 41

Music stores, networking in, 17–18

Musical equipment, See Equipment

Musical experience, 57

Musical Services agreement,
example of, 214, 217

Musicians:

average fee of, 35

disciplined, 108–109

finding, 41–67

hiring, 35–36

offering a spot in the band, 99

rejecting auditioners, 98

responsibilities of, 68

talking with, 17–18

musiciansconnection.com, 49, 51

MusiciansContact.com, 49–50

musicproinsurance.com, 106

myspace.com, 51, 179–180, 231

N

Nashville music scene, 14

Networking, 51–54, 65

online, 231

Open Mic events, 54

and private instructors, 53–54

New Orleans music scene, 14

"No attitude" phrase, in ads, 57

"No Flakes" phrase, in ads, 57

Nonmusical tasks:

and demo production, 139

at rehearsals, 107–108

O

Oasis (disk duplicator), 171

Office Depot, 222

Oliver, Sara, 250, 259, 263

Omnidirectional, use of term, 255

Online classified sections, 49–50

number of ads in, 51

Open Mic events, 54

Original bands, 36–37, 50

animosity between cover bands and, 38–40

Original material, writing, 118–121

Overhead, 188–193

calculating viscosity by using, 189–191

use of term, 188

Overhead Door (New Orleans, LA), 102

P

Pack list, 247–249

length of, 247

Paid players, 35–36

Parking:

for auditions, 74

and gigs, 250

Parts, forgetting, 242

Pay-to-play agreement, 185–186

Peavey (bass manufacturer), 22

Percentage-rate agreement, 183–185

advantages/disadvantages of, 184–185

Performance opportunities, preparing for, 13–18

Performances, transportation to, 23–24

Personal inventory, 27–29

Personality, 30–31, 56, 87, 89, 96, 115

Personality traits, of band members, 30–32

Photographer:

cost of, 166

understanding of the band, 166–167

Pink Floyd (band), 121

Pisco, Liz, 35

Plant (studio), 130

Playing for free, 193–195

as audition, 194

for exposure, 194–195

Playing in the wrong key, 242

Playlists, 250

Posters, 223

hanging, 230

Posture/body language, in band photo, 166

Practice, 245

habits, 19

Preaudition screening, 54–60

Preproduction demos, 126, 135

Press kit, 172–179

assembling, 177–179

band bio, writing, 172–175

binding, 179

envelope for, 178

getting press, 175–176

getting the kit noticed, 178–179

media contacts, 176

music reviews, 176–177

quotes supporting the band, 177

Press releases, 223–224

example of, 224

mailing/faxing/e-mailing, 230

Press, use of term, 175

Priorities, identifying, 26–29

personal inventory, 27

Private residence, auditions at, 75–76

Pro Tools (software), 127

Professional rehearsal studios, 101–102

Profit, 188–193

determining, 192–193

use of term, 188–189

Promotional materials:

creating, 162–181, 220–231

demo package, 162–172

distributing, 225–231

by mass marketing, 227–231

by personal contact, 225–227

flyers, 221–222

organizing information, 220–221

posters, 223

press kit, 172–179

press releases, 223–224

Web site, building, 179–181

Public address (PA) system

crashes, 244–245

Punching in, 143

Purevolume.com, 51, 179

Q

Quality equipment, 20–22

Question-and-answer (Q&A)

session, 54–60

chemistry among band members, 56–57

musical experience, 57

side projects, permissibility of, 57

student vs. working members, 57

vacancies in the band, 56

R

Record label interest, mention of, in ads, 59

Recording budget, 127–128

band fund, 131–132

creating, 130–133

defined, 130

dividing among members, 132–133

funding sources, identifying, 131

paying for projects, 131

Recording options, for demos, 127–133

Recording studio:

operating hours, 129–130

selecting for demo, 135–149

studio time, cost of, 129

Rehearsal space:

explaining how to get to, 74–75

finding, 101–107

garage/basement, 103–104

lockout studios, 101–104

physically preparing, 80

physically preparing for auditions, 80

renting by the hour, 105–106

sharing, 104–105

as unfamiliar territory, 86

Rehearsals, 100–117

agenda, creating, 109

assignment sheets, 109–112

example of, 110–112

calendar/to-do list, creating, 109

determining what needs to be

accomplished at, 107–108

maximizing, 109

nonmusical tasks, 107–108

respecting bandmates at, 116–117

rules, establishing, 115–117

schedule:

creating, 108–114

examples of, 113–114

and song list, 123–124

song list, drilling, 123–125

strategy, establishing, 100–117

timely attendance at, 115–116

transportation to, 23–24

Rejecting an offer, 64–65, 64–66

Rejection email, example of, 81

Relationships with other bands, 271–272

Relaxing before the show, 258

"Reliable gear and transportation"

phrase, in ads, 58

Renting rehearsal space, 105–106

Reputation, importance of, 270–271

Responding to ads, 60–67

Rhode, Matt, 53, 77, 86, 87, 95, 153

Riffs, during auditions, 91

Rockenbach, Jock, 53–54

Rodaniche, Evan, 173, 175, 179, 229,
241, 271

Running long, 234–235

Rush (band), 121

S

Schedule, auditions, 71–72

Search engines, 49

Second auditions, 94

Separation, use of term, 149

Set, defined, 233

Set list:

creating, 233–240

defined, 233

encore song, 236

final song, 235–236

first song, 235

length of set, calculating, 233–234

sample lists, 236–240

written notes, adding, 236

Sharing rehearsal space, 104–105

Site plan, 180–181

Slankster, Peter, 138, 140, 144–145, 147,
151, 156, 158

Small-budget recording budget, 127–128

Smith, Peter, 101, 118, 260

Smith, Robert, 91, 119

Sonar (software), 127

Song list:

drilling, 123–125

preparing, 117–123

and rehearsals, 123–124

rehearsing your material, 123–125

Song selection:

and bandleader-driven bands, 122

material written by others, 121–123

original material, writing, 118–121

Song structure, forgetting, 242

Sound Arena (California), 106

Sound check, 252–257

Sound person, 260

role of, 258

thanking, 263–264

Sparks, Steve, 192, 200, 260

Special-event bands, 15, 21, 37, 121, 235

Special-event gigs, 200–219

with corporate clients, 198

Special-event planners, contacting, 196–199

Staci Twigg band, 33

Staples, 222

Strickland, Matt, 129, 147–148

Strickland, Will, 103, 258

Strings, changing, 244

Super Diamond band, 37

T

tabcrawler.com, 82

Tablature (tab), 82–83

quality-control issues with, 82–83

tabpower.com, 82

Telephone response to ads,

example of, 63–64

That 80's Band, 180

sample set list, 236–237

Tight bands, 100

TOAST studios (San Francisco, CA), 130

Tom Petty and the Heartbreakers, 36–37

Tool (band), 122

Transportation, 23–24

Tray card, jewel case, 170

Tribute bands, 37

Two-panel insert, 170

Tyler, Bonnie, 122

U

Ultra Sound Rehearsal

(New York City), 106

Unloading your equipment, 88

Upcoming shows, mentioned in ads, 59

Uploading artwork, as a digital file, 169

V

Vacancies, in bands, 56

Van Halen, Eddie, 143

Variable expenses, 189

Varna Street Studios (Van Nuys, CA), 102

Venue advertising, 231

Venue items, taking care of, 257

Verbal agreements, as payment

arrangement, 186

Village (studio), 130

Vocal mics, 150

Vocalist, following, to resolve minor

mistakes, 242–243

Voice message, as follow-up to audition, 97

W

Waitman, Doug, 31, 121–122, 193

Walters, Toddy, 179, 195–196

Warming up, 246–247

Web site:

building, 179–181

defined, 179

domain name, 180

home page, 181

hosts for, 179–180

pages, 179

posting an ad on, 46–47, 49–51

site plan, 180–181

for tablature, 82–83

Wedding bands, 37

Wood, David, 60, 264

Written contracts:

example, 187

as payment arrangement, 186–188

Written notes, 83, 89–90

Written responses, to ads, 60

Y

Yahoo!, 49

Yahoo! Maps, 73

Z

Zielinski, Julie, 33–34, 97, 116, 225